IMAGES
of America

SOUTH OGDEN

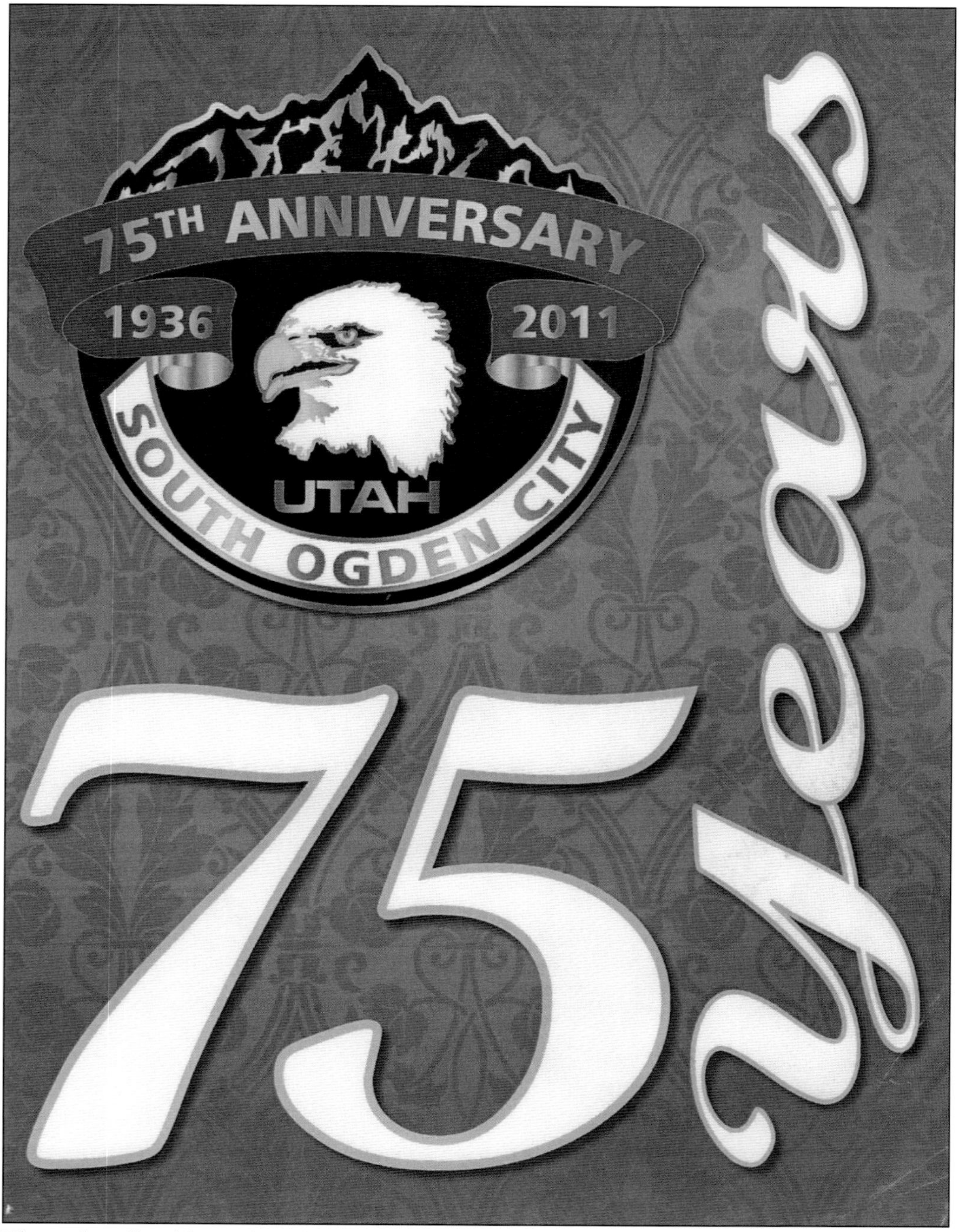

This is the official logo of South Ogden City's 75th anniversary, celebrated in 2011. The logo was designed by Symbol Arts, a local company, and stickers and posters of the logo appeared in the windows of most businesses in the city throughout 2011. (Courtesy South Ogden City.)

On the Cover: This scene is from the Independence Day parade, July 3, 1978, heading west on 40th Street between Jefferson and Adams Avenues, with the beautiful Wasatch Mountains in the background. (Courtesy South Ogden City.)

IMAGES
of America

South Ogden

Russell L. Porter

ARCADIA
PUBLISHING

ISBN 978-0-7385-8530-7

Published by Arcadia Publishing
Charleston, South Carolina

Printed in the United States of America

Library of Congress Control Number: 2011940757

For all general information, please contact Arcadia Publishing:
Telephone 843-853-2070
Fax 843-853-0044
E-mail sales@arcadiapublishing.com
For customer service and orders:
Toll-Free 1-888-313-2665

Visit us on the Internet at www.arcadiapublishing.com

To all past, present, and future residents of South Ogden.
To those who serve through election, occupation, or
most importantly, serve a neighbor in need.

Contents

FOREWORD

This new publication of our South Ogden City history is a pictorial representation of special moments in the lives of our citizens and collected for our 75th anniversary. Our first history book, *South Ogden City, Utah, History 1848–1984*, by Ida D. Draayer, was an excellent book telling of the early settlers and the creation of a new city being born in Weber County. It tells of the city's organization, of the mayors, city councils, businesses, schools, and our churches.

This new book is full of pictures collected from our citizens, showing special moments in their lives, living and serving in this great city. I would like to dedicate this book to our citizens, business owners, and all who have continued to serve each of us. Thanks to everyone who has made living in South Ogden City so wonderful; it is a special place.

I would like to give a special thanks to our past mayors who have served since the last history book was published—Lew A. Wangsgard, 1986–1989; Brent H. Frost, 1990–1993; George Goodell, 1994–2001; and George Garwood, 2002–2009.

I want to thank Councilmember Russ Porter for his dedication and hard work putting this publication together. I would like to thank each Councilmember for their service and continued support—John Bradley, Bryan Bernard, Sallee Orr, and Wayne Smith.

Serving the citizens in this great city is a pleasure.

What a special community we live in. I have lived in South Ogden for over 66 years; it is my home, a place where our children and grandchildren have been raised. Thanks to each of you for your continued service to each other.

—James F. Minster
Mayor, South Ogden City
2010–

ACKNOWLEDGMENTS

Mayor Jim Minster wanted a new South Ogden book to commemorate the city's 75th anniversary; credit him for planting the seed. The majority of photographs in this book are from scrapbooks and collections assembled at the South Ogden City offices. Credit Mae Bankhead particularly as well as Dana Pollard and Leesa Kapetanov for their efforts. Any photograph without a courtesy line comes from South Ogden City. I am also appreciative of those current and former residents who responded to the call for photographs, and Scott Sumner, the official volunteer photographer of South Ogden Days. Further thanks to those people who appear in the pictures, both named and unnamed, for being a part of this great city and its first 75 years.

Thanks also to the current city council, John Bradley, Wayne Smith, Sallee Orr, and Bryan Bernard, for their support and for letting me put my name on this project. Also, praise goes to South Ogden's special events coordinator, Christy McBride, for assistance from the very beginning to the relieving end.

A huge debt of gratitude goes to Ida D. Draayer, along with her committee of Louis A. Gladwell, Kefford M. Peek, Doren B. Boyce, Fred L. Montmorency, Chet Bruce, and Lucille Taylor, for their fine book about South Ogden City, published in 1985. The book covers the city's history from settlement, in the 1800s, to the city's 50th anniversary in 1986. Many of the dates and background information used in this book were gleaned from that work.

I also wish to thank Stacia Bannerman of Arcadia Publishing for her patience, assistance, persistence, and upbeat attitude through a process totally unfamiliar to me.

My family has continually allowed me to pursue things of importance, and this has been no different. Much love to my wife, Sherri, and children, Nicholas, Cortney, Brooklyn, and Spencer, for their support, ideas, technical assistance, and for allowing me to work while they wanted me to play. And to my parents, Mark and Barbara Porter, for moving into a house at 555 40th Street the day they married in 1961 and never moving away. I loved growing up in South Ogden . . . and I am still growing up in South Ogden!

INTRODUCTION

The area south of Ogden City, once known as Burch Creek, became an incorporated city in 1936 as the city of South Ogden. Those original 800 residents are now over 16,000, and the square miles have increased over the years as new developments were approved and additional areas annexed. Growth was a key word in the city for decades, the area even referred to as "the City of Homes." For example, between the 1940 and 1950 censuses, the population increased 167 percent. A 97 percent growth in residents occurred in the 10 years following that, much in connection with the growth of Hill Air Force Base and military arsenals in Ogden. In recent years, that growth has slowed considerably, and the South Ogden celebrating 75 years of existence is now "landlocked." Within the political boundaries is a city with diversity, older homes and newer homes, retirees and young families, businesses that have been around for decades and ones new as of this century, along with everything in between.

South Ogden enjoys a respected reputation in Northern Utah. It is known as a great place to grow up, a great place to raise a family, and a fine place to live out the retirement years. A survey conducted in 2007 found that 64 percent of residents have lived in the city for over 10 years. The same survey also discovered that 95 percent of residents feel safe in South Ogden. Residents tend not to leave by choice, only by circumstance, with many returning the first chance they get.

It is into this city that I was born, in the summer of 1969.

Growing up on the corner of 40th Street and Porter Avenue allowed City Hall Park to be my playground as well as the vacant lot of Stan Hunter's behind my house. On the grass of these open spaces I learned to play baseball, football, soccer and kick-the-can; usually with my three older brothers Thayne, Glade, and Glen Porter. More often than not, we were joined by neighbors Darren and Chad Sevy, and I hope it is not too late to apologize to Winona Robinson for disturbing her afternoon naps.

Living on 40th Street also exposed me to my first parades and fireworks shows. From the comfort of our own yard we had a front row seat to the Independence Day parades and later the June South Ogden Days parades. It is not a coincidence that the cover image I chose for this work is of a parade heading down 40th Street in front of my childhood home. As an elementary age kid, I would save up my allowance to be able to run across the street to the park on the morning of July Fourth and buy candy, compete for prizes, and knock down a random politician, fireman, or policeman in the dunk tank. When the money ran out, I would run back across the street and ask for more.

City Hall Park was where I played my first T-ball games and many a friendly tennis match. It was where, at dusk, I would go for a walk around the park with my dad, Mark T. Porter, and collect aluminum cans. Those cans made me a few dollars, money that I would generally spend on a Slurpee at the 7-Eleven above Madison Avenue, or on penny candy at Emory's Drugstore before going to a movie at the Country Club Theater. This area of the city was my world. It was half a block up 40th Street to Park View Elementary for kindergarten through third grades, then half a block down the street to Burch Creek Elementary for fourth through sixth grades. It is where I was when I got the chicken pox and where I got my first real kiss. There are a lot of photographs on the following pages of City Hall Park on 40th Street, and of the events that took place there, and I do not apologize for that.

As the city now celebrates its dodranscentennial, it is not exactly the same city of my youth. The vacant lot behind my childhood home (called the "Butterscotch Monster," by my mother, Barbara Porter) is now a duplex without grass. The 7-Eleven, Emory's Drugstore, and the Country Club Theater are no longer in business; Burch Creek Elementary School was demolished decades ago; and the junior high I attended is now a dirt field. But the more things change, the more they stay the same. I still live three blocks from where I grew up, teach at the same high school I attended, watch my children play games for South Ogden City recreation at the parks where I played, and take my family to Tony's Pizza. And even though the venue has changed, my family still sees every South Ogden Days parade, spends much more than aluminum can money in the park, and watches the fireworks after the Saturday night concert.

My decision to run for city council seemed a natural progression; for the first 19 years of life, city hall was visible outside my living room window. When people would ask how long I campaigned, I would say, "For a couple of months," though the more correct answer would be, "For 40 years." At Meet the Candidate night, I remember being asked a question to the effect of "in 20 years from now, looking back, how will you know you did a good job?" My answer was, "Because I have such great memories of growing up in this city; I still live here and want to raise my family here. If my children do the same thing, that is how I will know." Only time will tell.

The photographs in this book will include people and places long since gone as well as more recent additions and much in between. The chapters are divided into time periods from the early years of the city to the present. The logic for this organization is to allow a reader, who may have only spent time in one or two decades in the city, to focus on a section that will elicit the most memories. When all is said and done, it is really the memories of people, places, and events that mean something to us and give us our identity. For those of us who are lifelong residents, this book will serve as a collection of life around you from the earliest beginnings of your memory. In these pages we will see people we once associated with, some we are lucky enough to still see, and some we have never met. We will see schools we attended, parks we played in, businesses we frequented, politicians we voted in (or out), and parades and activities we participated in or were spectators for. Even if you do not recognize yourself in any of these pictures, you will find yourself in a South Ogden memory.

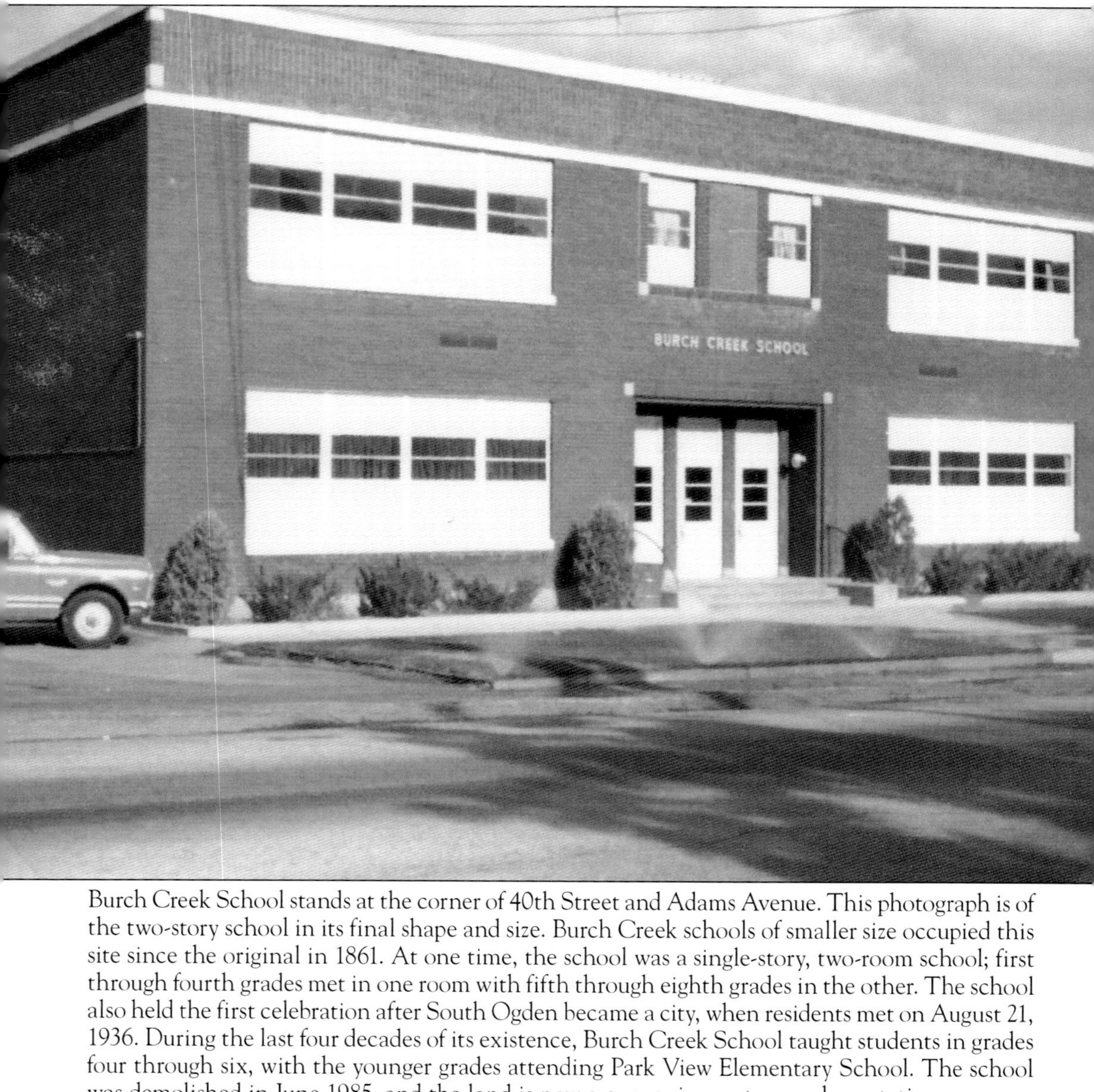

Burch Creek School stands at the corner of 40th Street and Adams Avenue. This photograph is of the two-story school in its final shape and size. Burch Creek schools of smaller size occupied this site since the original in 1861. At one time, the school was a single-story, two-room school; first through fourth grades met in one room with fifth through eighth grades in the other. The school also held the first celebration after South Ogden became a city, when residents met on August 21, 1936. During the last four decades of its existence, Burch Creek School taught students in grades four through six, with the younger grades attending Park View Elementary School. The school was demolished in June 1985, and the land is now a convenience store and gas station.

One

1930s AND 1940s

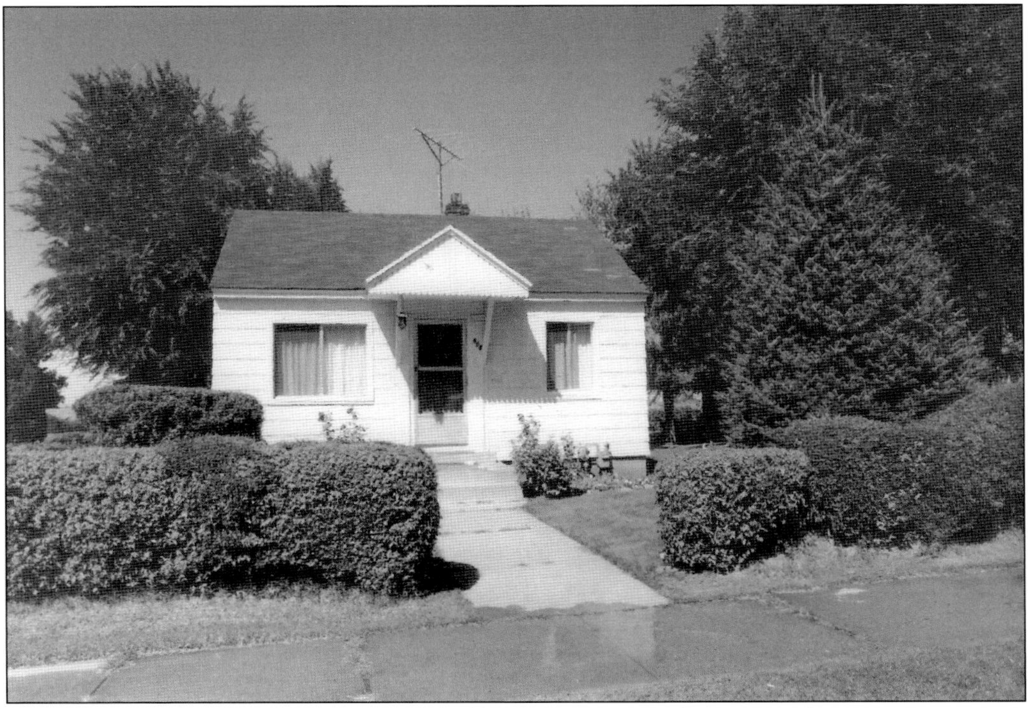

This house, at 454 37th Street, was purchased by the city in 1939 from Leo and Kate Harris to serve as the first city hall. Prior to meeting here, town meetings were held in the old Burch Creek School or a rented room of Frank Wolthius next to the Dairy Milk Bottling Plant on 37th Street.

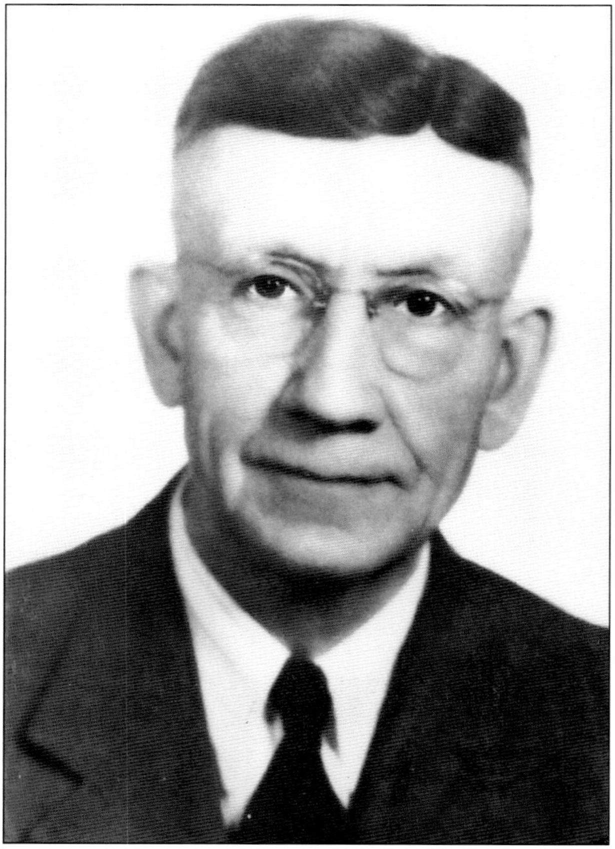

Henry Guy Child served as president of the town board before incorporation; he then became the city's first mayor, running unopposed. Child served as mayor from 1936 to 1945. An elementary school in South Ogden, built in 1966, was named in his honor.

A parade float surrounded by the city fathers, wives, and children celebrated incorporation of South Ogden City. The float has the words "Sidewalks," "Sanitary Sewer," "Pure Water System," and "Our Pioneering Days Are Over." Mayor H. Guy Child is the third man from the left in the photograph.

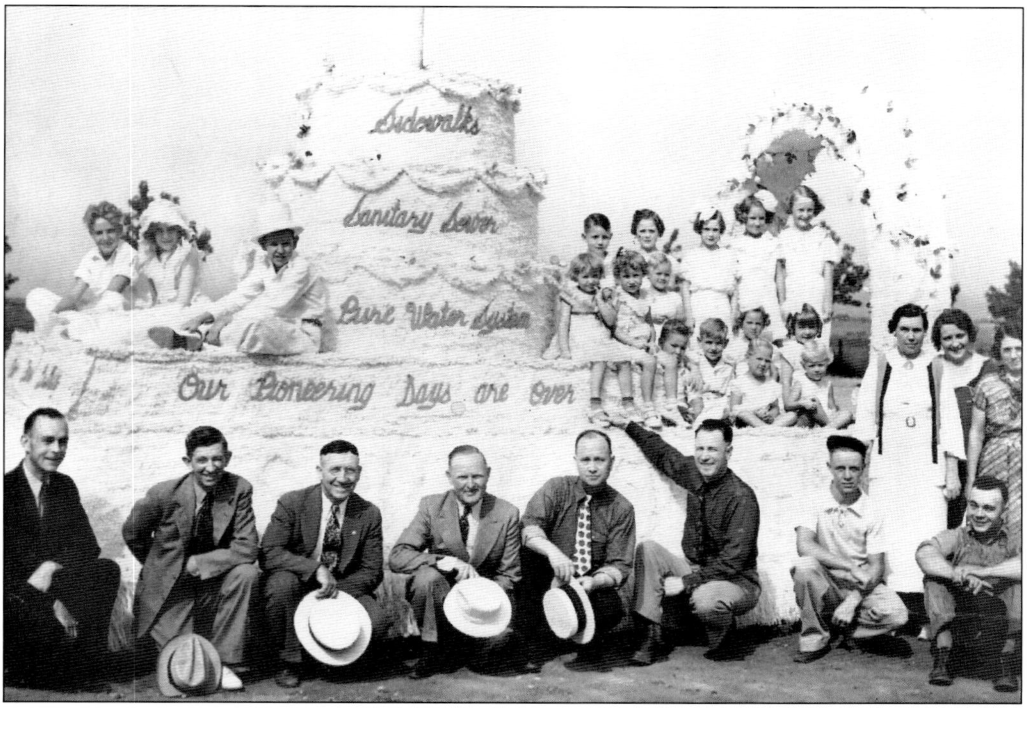

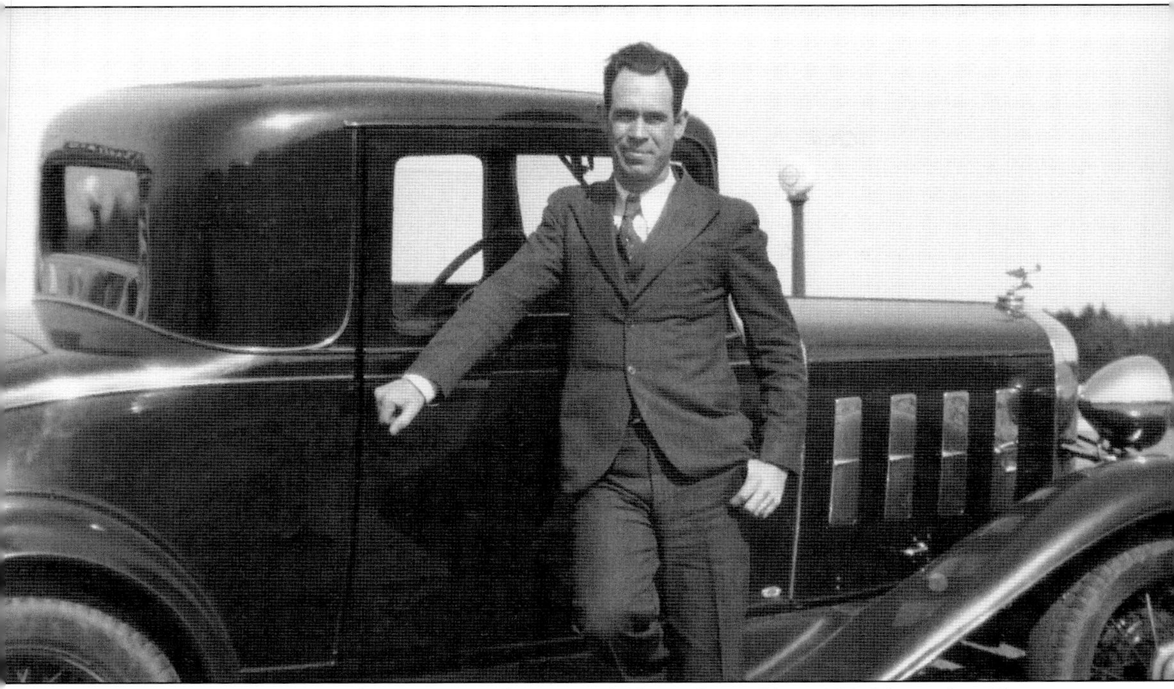

This photograph, taken in the 1930s, is of Raymond Shupe Jr. and his 1930 Chevrolet. Shupe, a building contractor, constructed over 80 homes in South Ogden between 1940 and 1960 and over 400 homes in Weber and Davis Counties during his lifetime. (Courtesy John R. Shupe.)

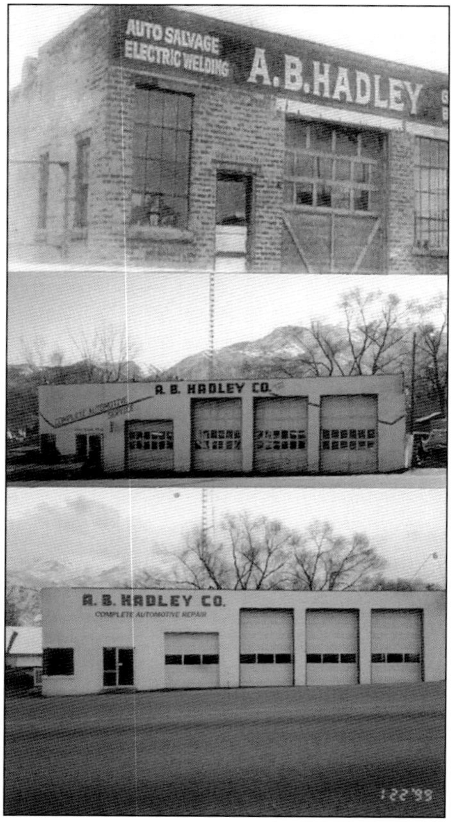

Alonzo B. and Grace Hadley opened the A.B. Hadley Garage, an automobile salvage and car and truck repair shop, on July 31, 1931, at 3640 Washington Boulevard. Through the years, the business expanded, having a gasoline pump at times. It was even a truck and car dealership from the 1950s to the 1970s, selling Federal trucks and Studebakers, and in 1978, it became an International dealership. In 1968, Boyd Hadley, son of Alonzo and Grace, took over management of the shop. Boyd, along with his son Chris, continues to work in 2011 at the A.B. Hadley Company, a complete automotive repair shop. (Courtesy Chris Hadley.)

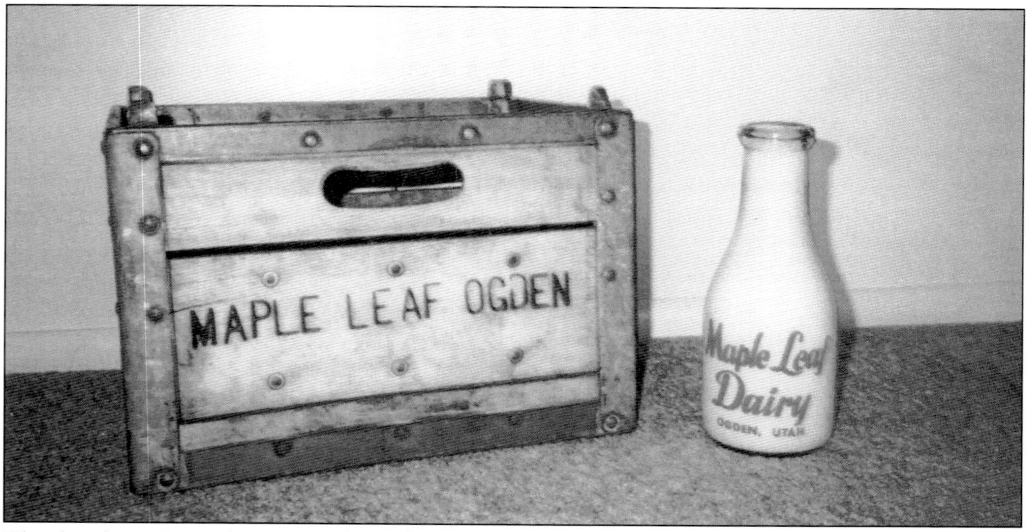

This bottle and wood crate are from the Maple Leaf Dairy. In 1945, Weston and Mabel Poulson opened one of the earliest businesses in South Ogden, the Maple Leaf Dairy. Prior to moving to South Ogden, they were involved in the dairy business in Uintah, where Mabel's father, John Combe Sr., owned a farm and cows. The Poulsons bought milk from Combe and processed and delivered it throughout Weber County, even delivering to the Civilian Conservation Corps boys working up Weber Canyon. In South Ogden, they began their milk processing plant and depot in the rear of their home at 4070 Adams Avenue. (Courtesy Elaine Clausse.)

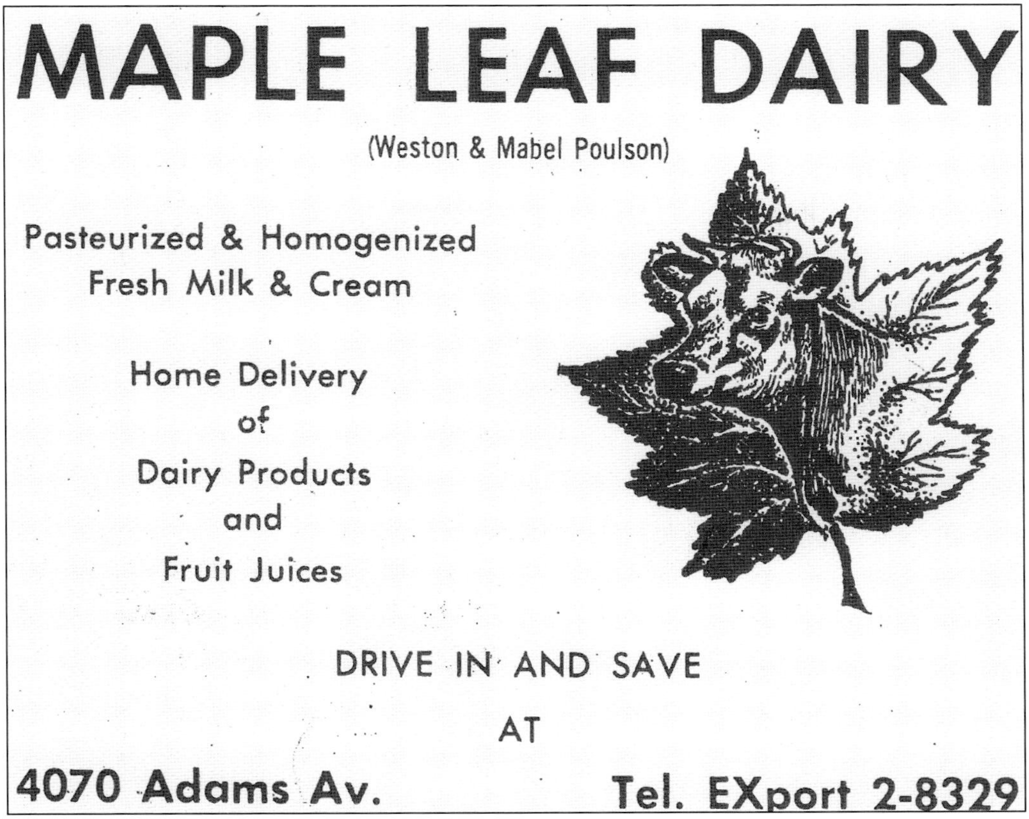

Above is an advertisement for the Maple Leaf Dairy. The latest in automatic machinery for bottle washing and pasteurizing was installed, and many awards for quality were received. The dairy closed in 1978. (Courtesy Elaine Clausse.)

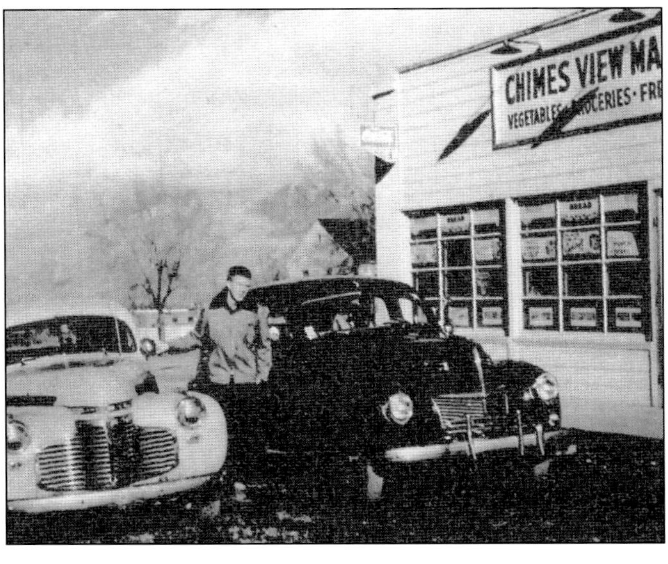

Chimes View Market, established in 1945, was owned and operated by Walt and Connie Holbrook and their son, Reed. In this 1951 photograph, Jerry Warner is pictured touching his 1941 Chevrolet coupe. The other vehicle is Reed Holbrook's 1939 Mercury. The store was at the diagonal intersection of Chimes View Drive and 39th Street. The market closed in the 1950s, and the site is now a popular day care center. (Courtesy Jean H. Mathews.)

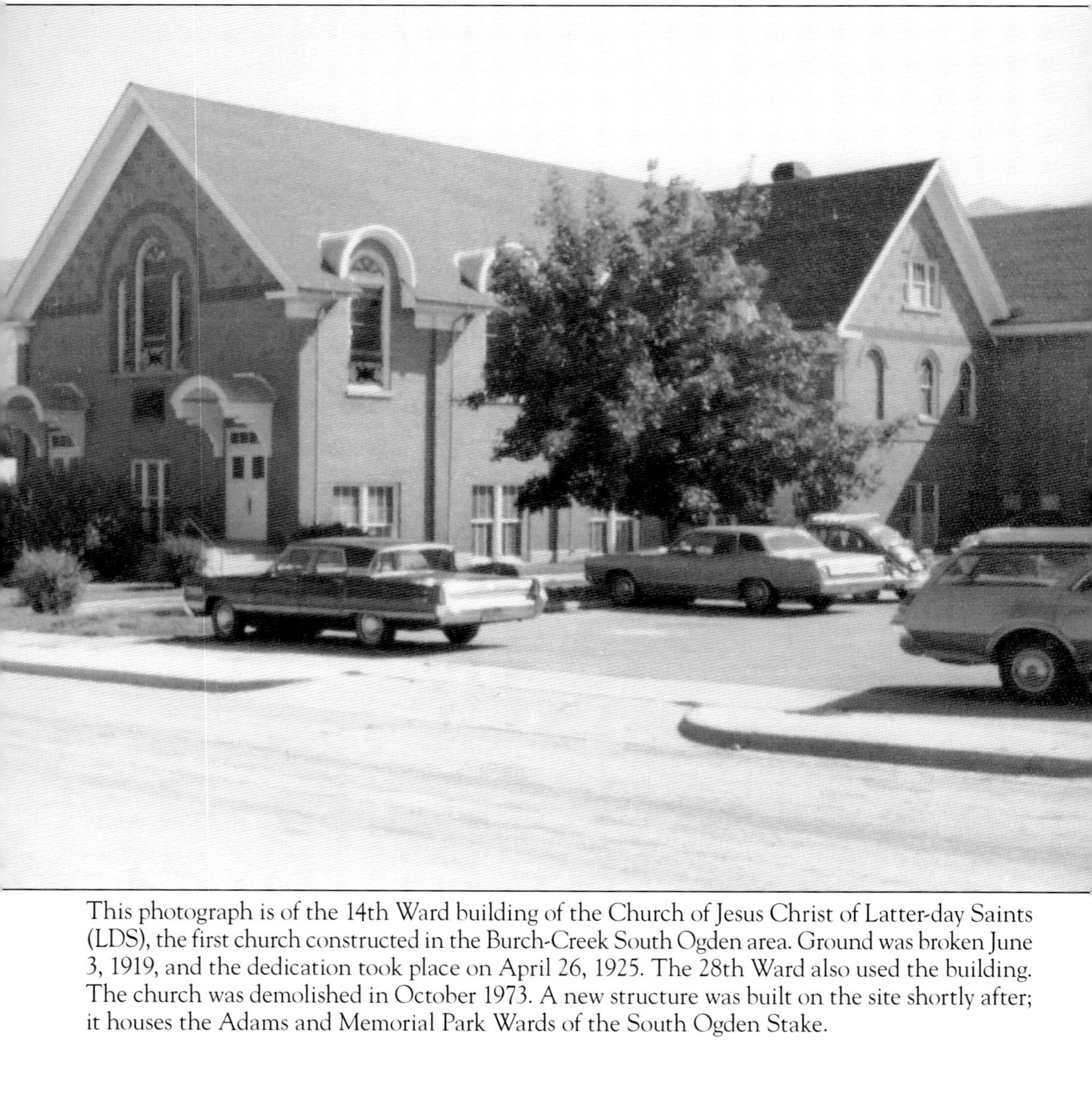

This photograph is of the 14th Ward building of the Church of Jesus Christ of Latter-day Saints (LDS), the first church constructed in the Burch-Creek South Ogden area. Ground was broken June 3, 1919, and the dedication took place on April 26, 1925. The 28th Ward also used the building. The church was demolished in October 1973. A new structure was built on the site shortly after; it houses the Adams and Memorial Park Wards of the South Ogden Stake.

Pictured is John Major Reese, the second mayor of South Ogden. Reese served from 1946 to 1949 after serving as a councilman for four years. He was also a principal for 36 years at various schools in the Weber School District, including principal at Burch Creek and Park View Elementary Schools.

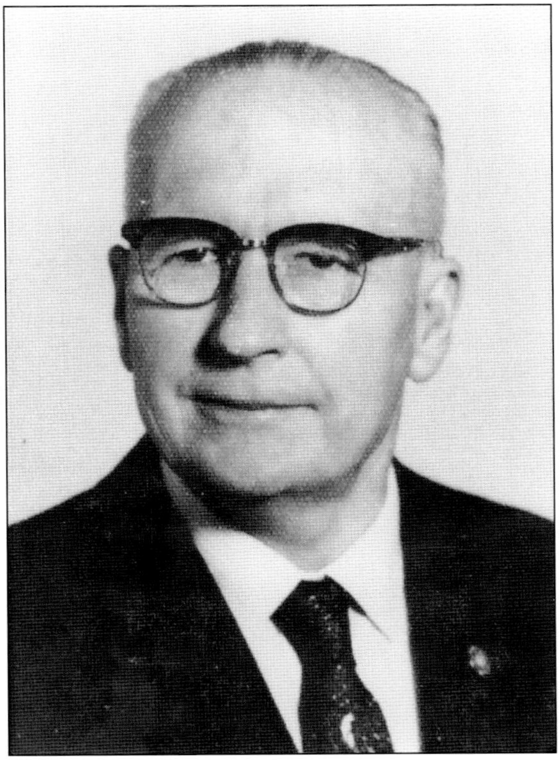

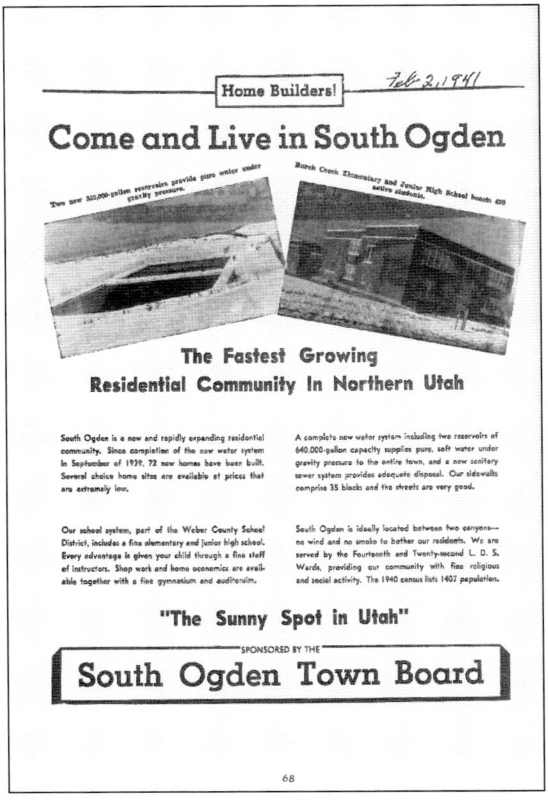

This advertisement, sponsored by the South Ogden Town Board, first appeared in February 1941. It encourages people to move into South Ogden and for builders to construct new homes there. It emphasizes educational opportunities, a modern water system, climate, and references the religious and social life of the area. Census figures show this advertising campaign may have been successful, as the population between 1940 and 1950 grew by 2,356 people, a 167 percent increase. Another 97 percent increase occurred between 1950 and 1960, when 3,642 additional residents made South Ogden their home.

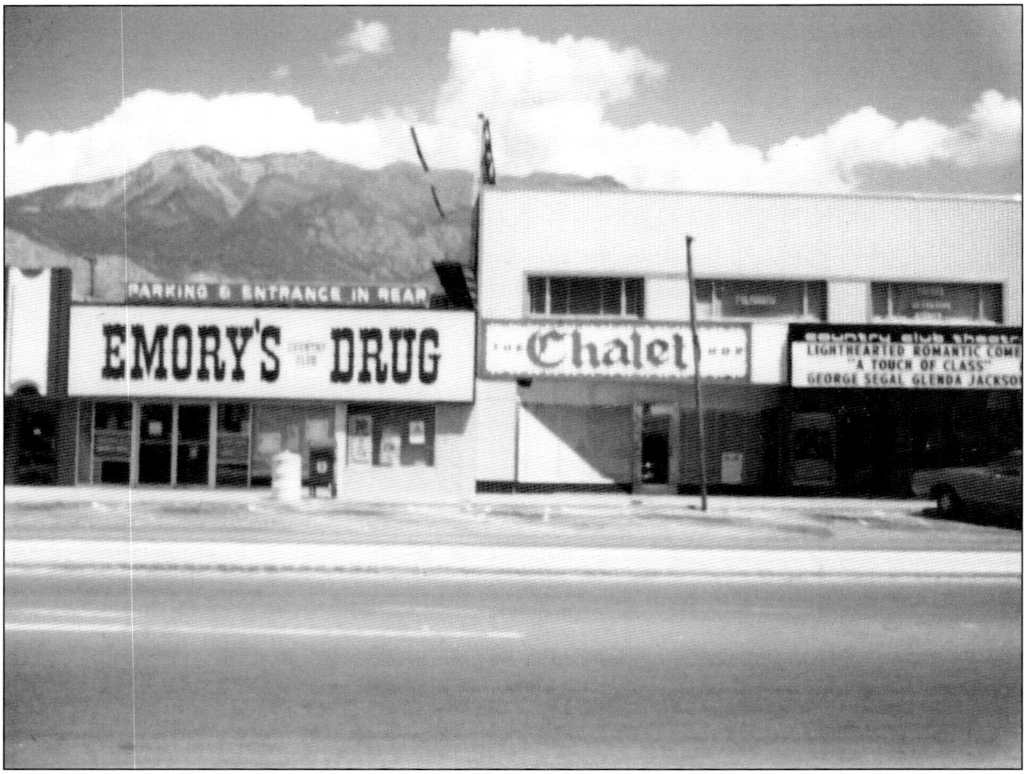

Emory's Drug store, 3986 Washington Boulevard, opened in 1947. Emory Herndon managed the shop for many years. It was a very popular stop off to load up on penny candy before seeing a movie at the Country Club Theater next door. In 1982, Emory Drug moved into the Bank of Utah building and became Country Club Drug.

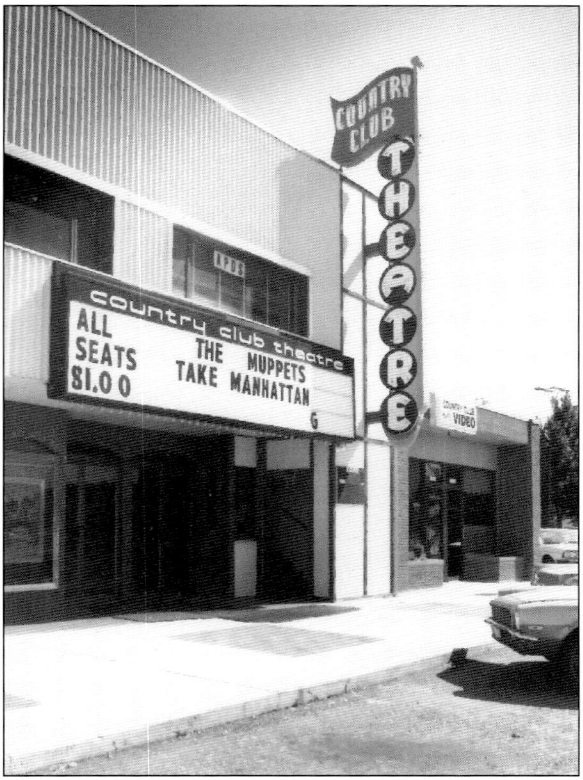

Country Club Theatre, located at 3930 Washington Boulevard, is pictured here. The Country Club opened to the public on November 11, 1948. The 500-seat theater was the first building on the east side of Washington Boulevard. It was built after 2,500 truckloads of soil filled the cattail swamp hole that was on the site previously. The theater showed new release movies for decades, then became a $1 theater; it is currently unused and for sale.

Two

1950s

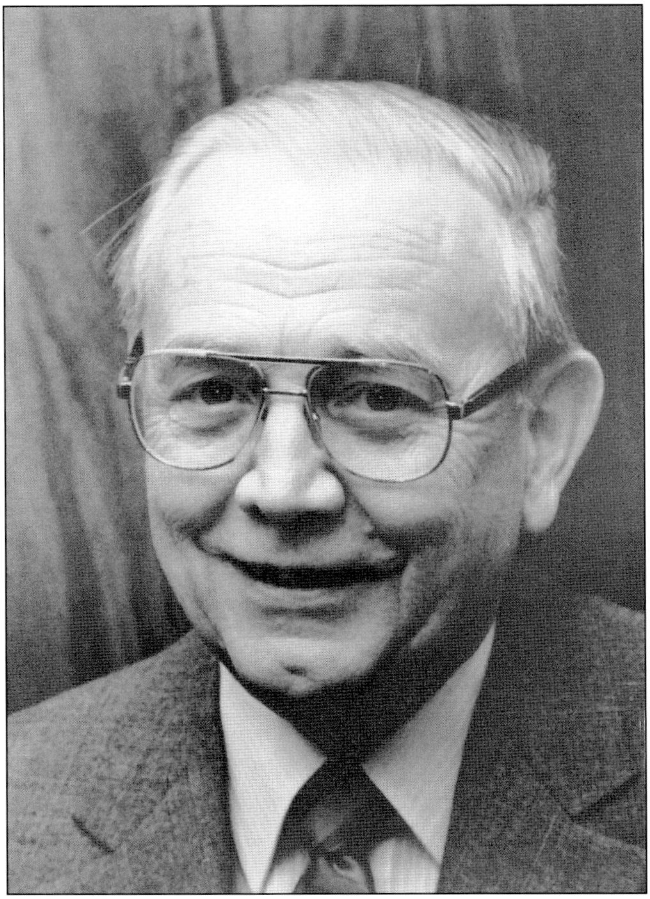

Doren Benjamin Boyce was the third mayor of South Ogden. Boyce served from 1950 to 1957. During his terms as mayor, greater police protection was authorized and land was acquired for a new municipal building on 39th Street. Boyce was also instrumental in getting mercury vapor lamps along Washington Boulevard, providing South Ogden with one of the first such systems in the area.

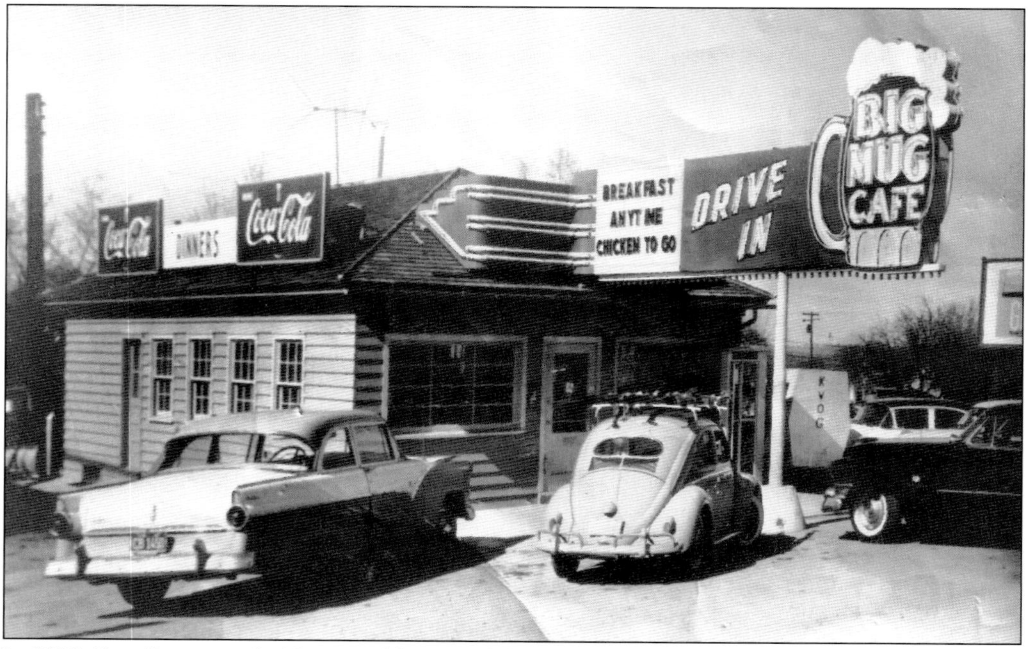

In 1950, Bert Empey, only 22 years old, opened the Big Mug Café at 3631 Washington Boulevard. It included car service, which had become popular in the 1950s, and served malts and mugs of beer. The building was torn down in 1965.

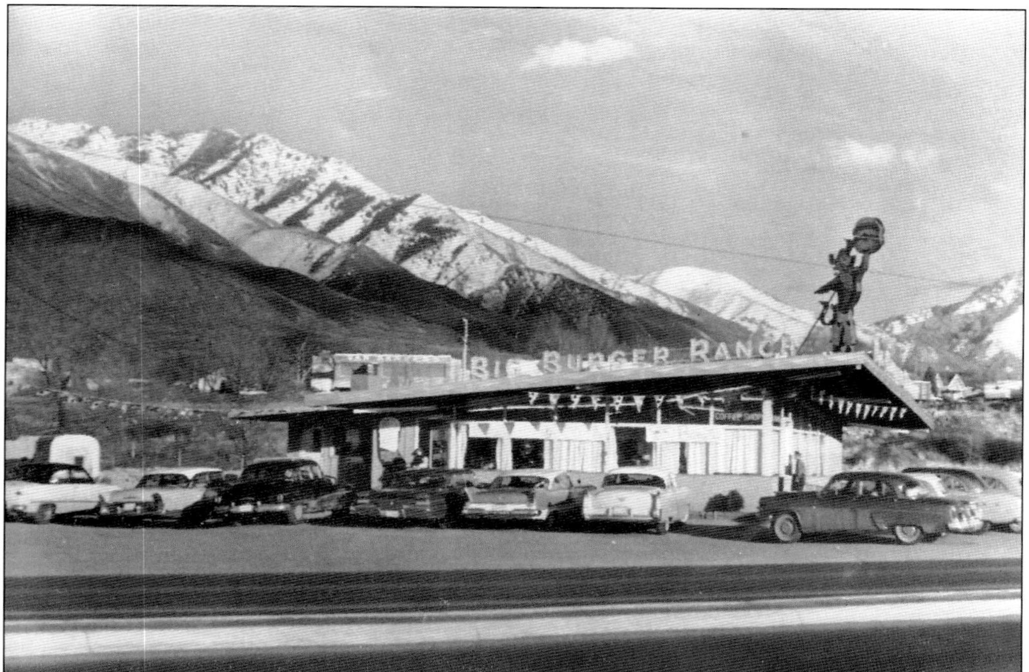

Bert Empey also opened the Big Burger Ranch on the southeast corner of 36th Street and Wall Avenue. In addition to being in the restaurant business, Empey served on the auxiliary police force and often helped with community projects, including boiling and coloring 1,000 eggs for the children to have an Easter egg hunt.

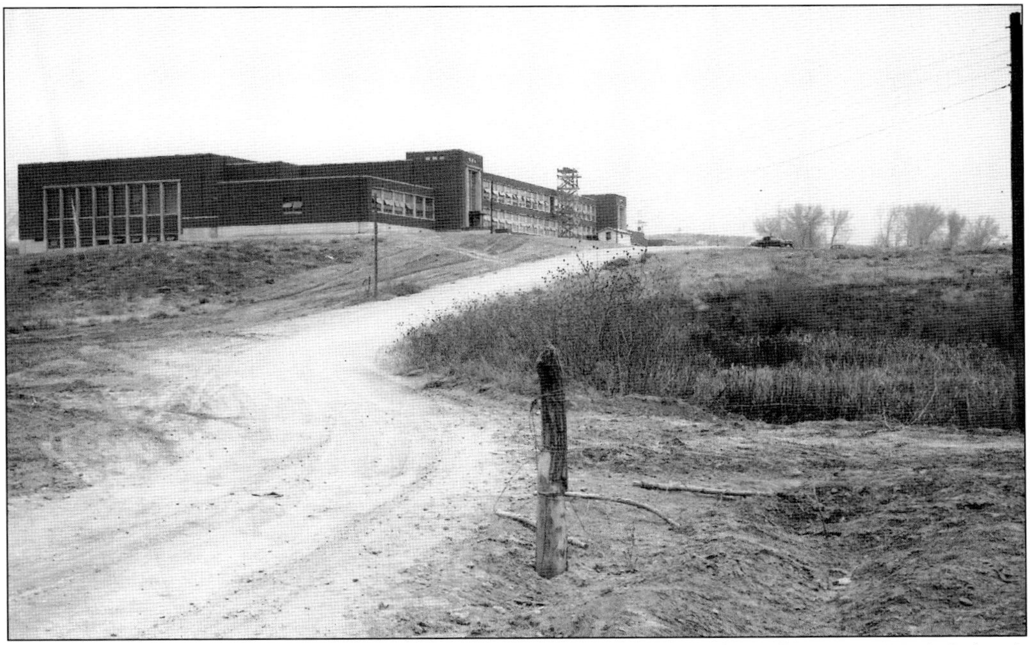

These photographs, taken in 1949, show the near completion of South Ogden Junior High School. The school, located at 4300 Madison Avenue, was built a cost of $750,000 by Whitmore & Sons Construction Company to accommodate 850 students. The building was dedicated November 2, 1950, with Rulon P. Peterson offering the dedicatory prayer. Lawrence Jenkins was the first principal of the junior high, and its students were known as the Spartans. In 1964, a new eight-classroom addition was completed at a cost of $300,000. Another remodel took place in 1978 when the cafeteria became the cafetorium, with an improved auditorium added. Further changes included new carpet on the floor and walls, all at a cost of over $1 million. The dirt road in the photograph is now the 4200 block of Madison Avenue. Below is the 1949 view of the nearly finished construction, looking north. (Both, courtesy Paul Woodin.)

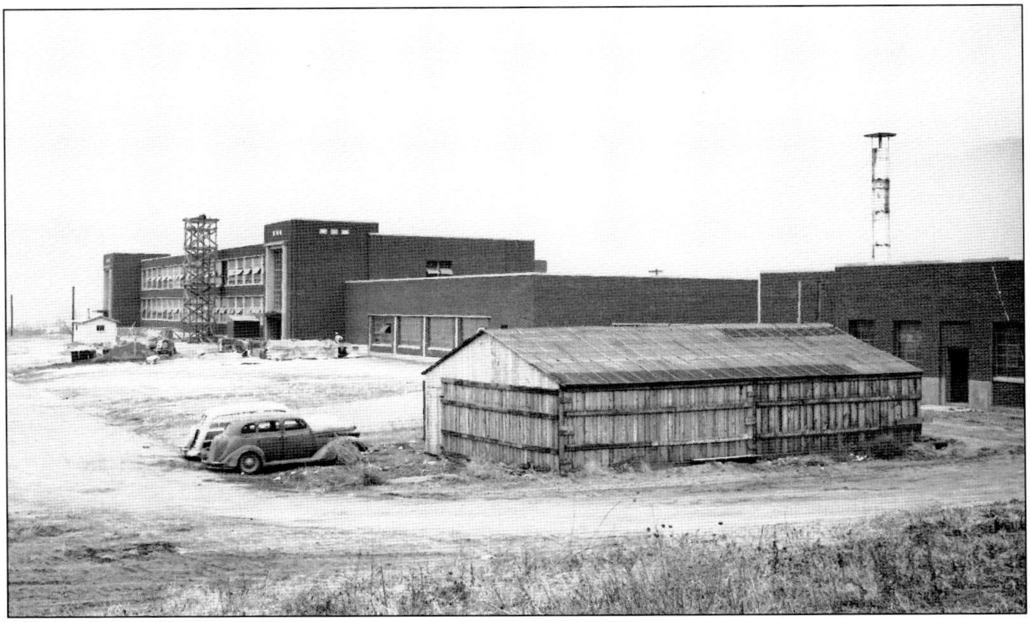

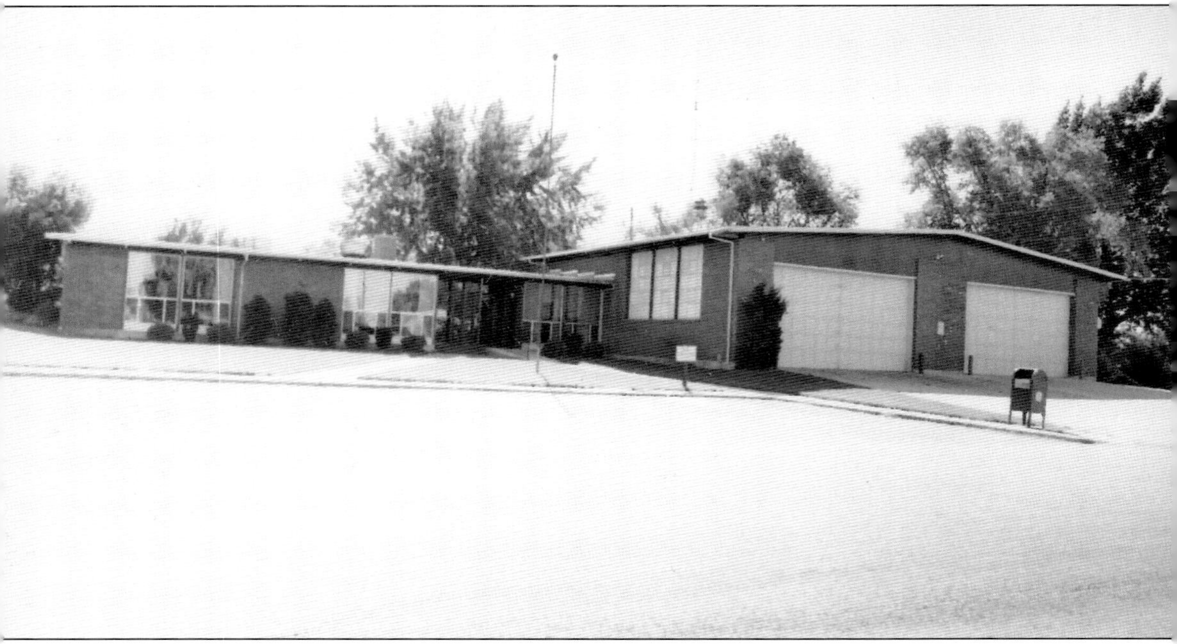

The second municipal building was located at 525 39th Street. The building was dedicated on November 15, 1953, while Doren B. Boyce was mayor. This new building had space for city offices, a council room, an apparatus room, and public restrooms. An expansion was completed in 1975 with a special program held for the occasion. Milton C. Meacham gave the dedicatory prayer, and the Bonneville High School band provided the music.

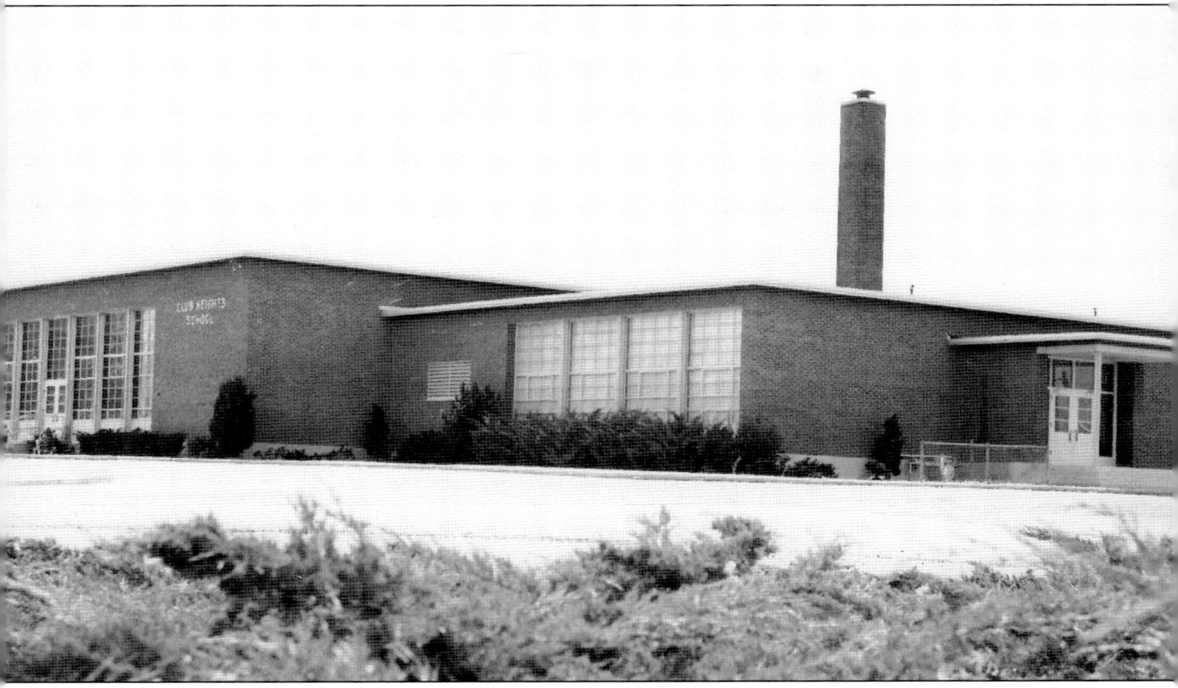

Club Heights Elementary School opened in the fall of 1952. The school was dedicated under the direction of A. Parley Bates, superintendent of Weber County Schools. It is located at 100 East 4150 South and continues to serve students in kindergarten through sixth grade.

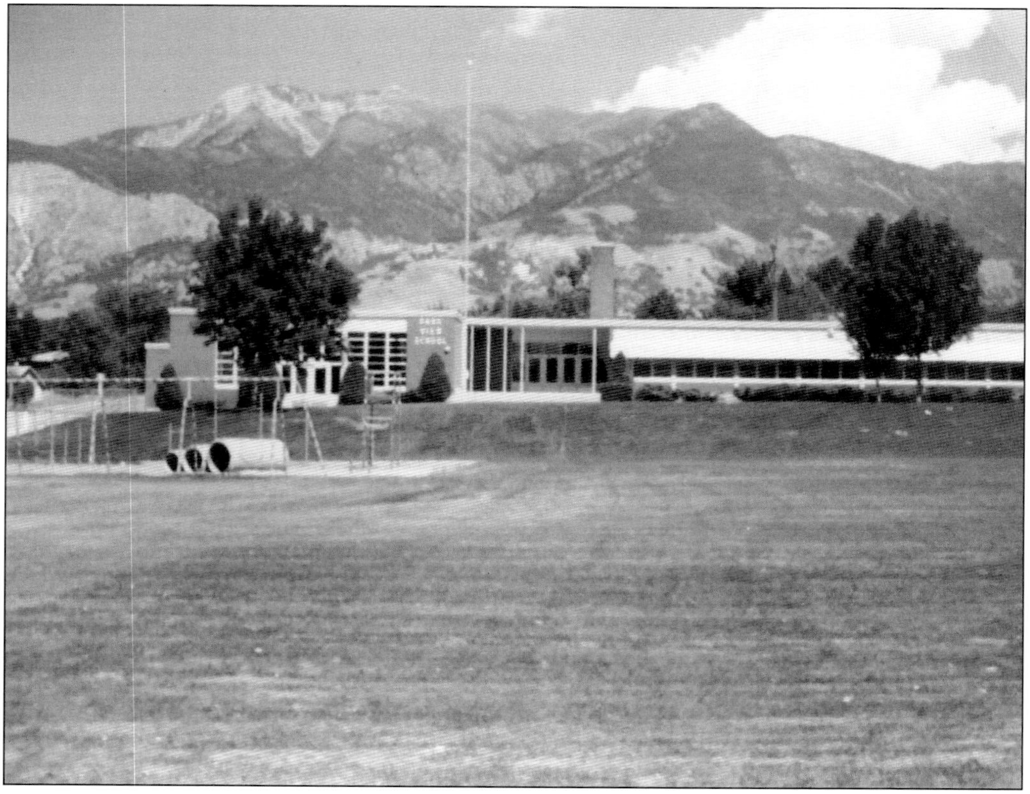

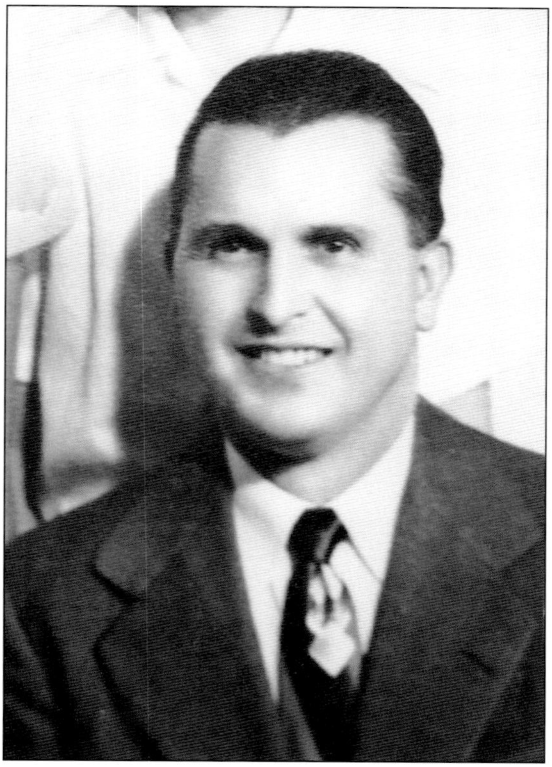

Park View Elementary School, at 40th Street and Jefferson Avenue, opened to students in September 1956. It was built to accommodate students in first, second, and third grades; the older grades attended Burch Creek Elementary.

Louis Hoggan served as South Ogden mayor from 1958 to 1961. During his tenure as mayor, city water lines were updated and improved and the city purchased a new pump for the recently dug well at a cost of over $9,000. Also, permanent street signs were installed throughout the city, and the streets were further improved with more curbs and gutters.

Three

1960s

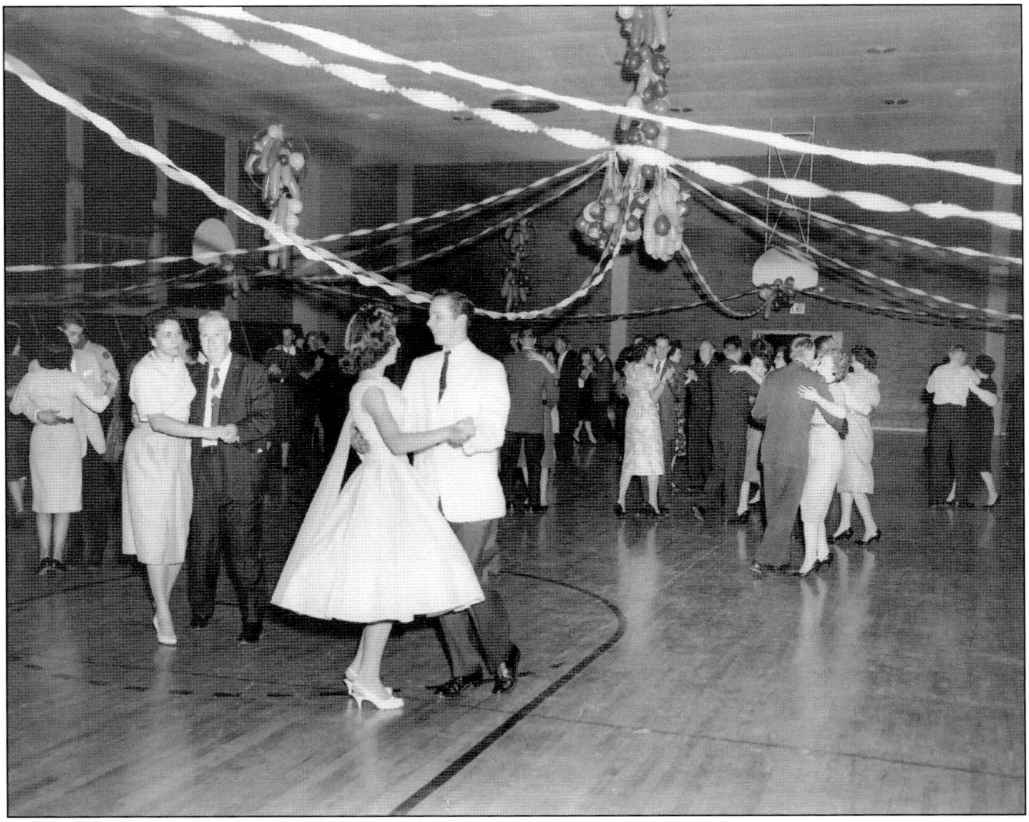

This photograph is of the annual Fireman's Dance in October 1962, inside the gymnasium of South Ogden Junior High School. This was just one of many events sponsored by the ladies of the South Ogden Firemen's Auxiliary. Besides planning many enjoyable parties, the women of the auxiliary provided much needed service to the community, such as sewing articles for the Thomas D. Dee Memorial Hospital and helping needy families at Christmastime.

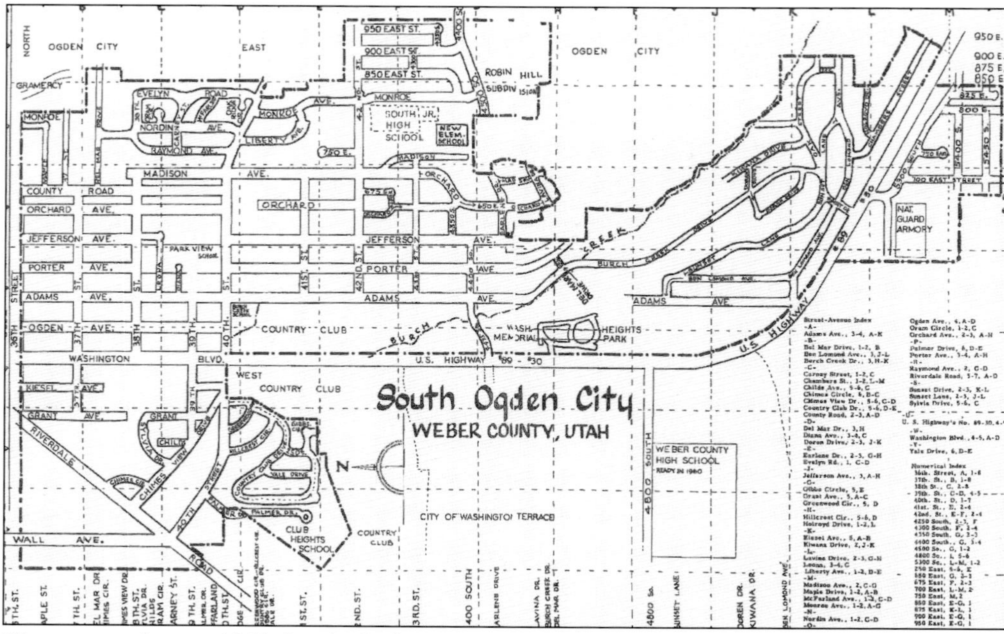

This map is from a 1960 South Ogden City Directory. Most of the modern city is not on the map, as much annexation and growth took place after 1960. The map makes reference to a new Weber School District high school. Bonneville High School was close to completion and became the high school for South Ogden's youth of that age. The directory included residents' names (including their children with ages listed), addresses, and phone numbers. Business names were also listed, including some advertisements. The cover listed a few government and emergency numbers; for police, just dial 2-9321. The nickname "the City of Homes" also appeared on the cover. The directory cost 50¢.

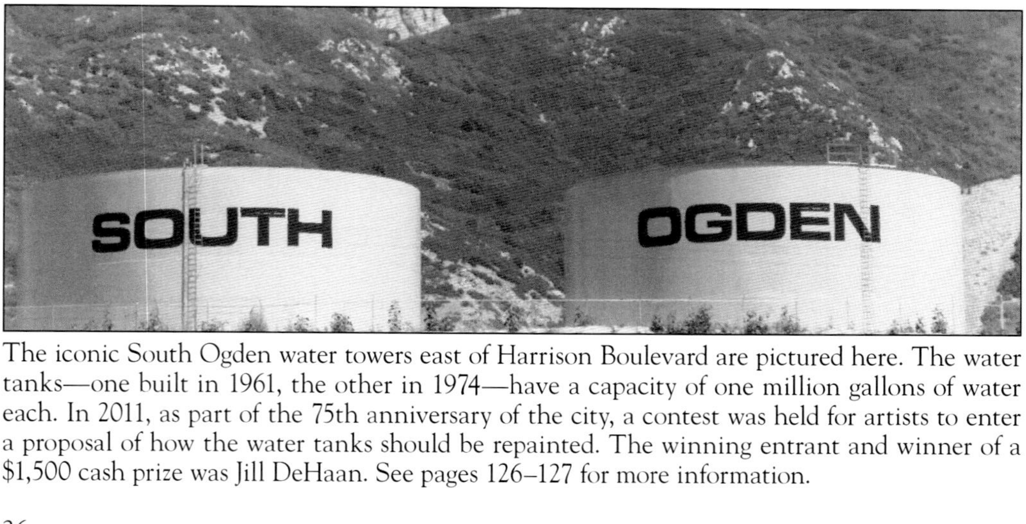

The iconic South Ogden water towers east of Harrison Boulevard are pictured here. The water tanks—one built in 1961, the other in 1974—have a capacity of one million gallons of water each. In 2011, as part of the 75th anniversary of the city, a contest was held for artists to enter a proposal of how the water tanks should be repainted. The winning entrant and winner of a $1,500 cash prize was Jill DeHaan. See pages 126–127 for more information.

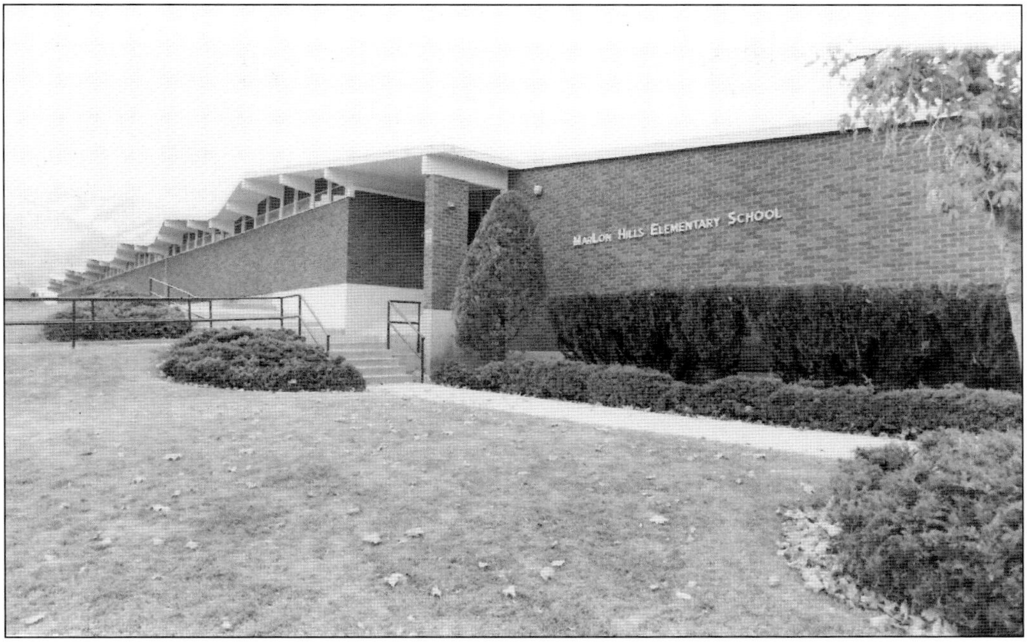

MarLon Hills Elementary School opened to students in 1961 at 4400 Madison Avenue. It was built on land owned by Marie and James Alonzo Stephens, thus the name combination of MarLon. Wallace M. Knight was appointed the first principal of the school. The school continues to serve kindergarten through sixth grade.

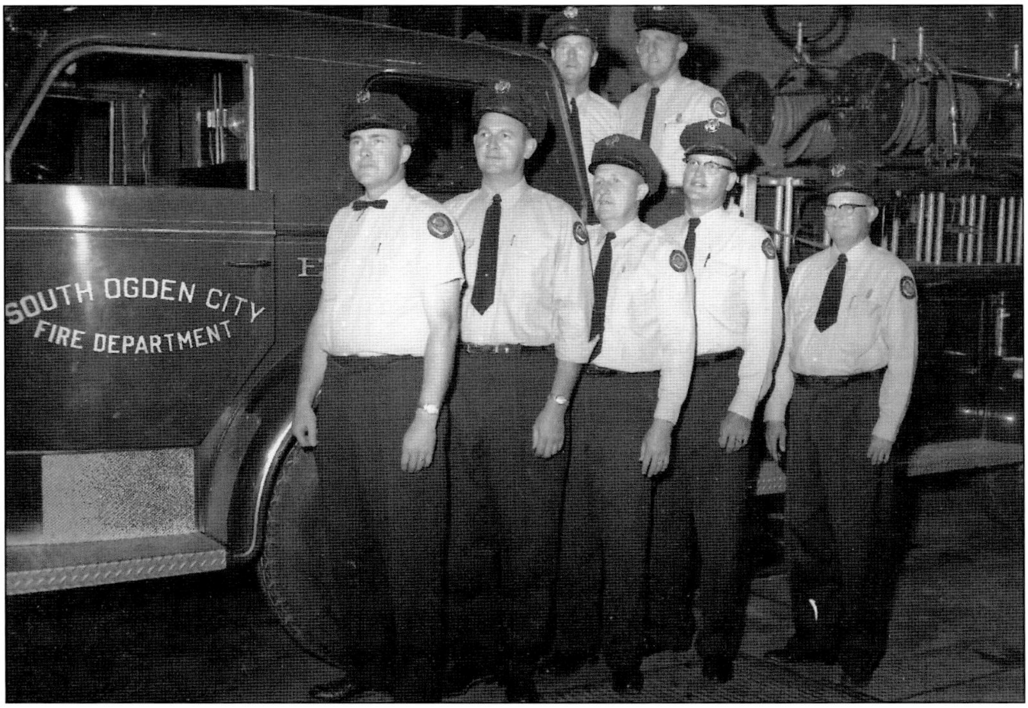

The new officers in the South Ogden fire department are pictured in 1962. They are, from left to right, (first row) Lloyd King, Roy Van Drimmelen, Paul Tesch, Gene Bateman, and William Brown; (second row) Vernon Barney and George Van Drimmelen.

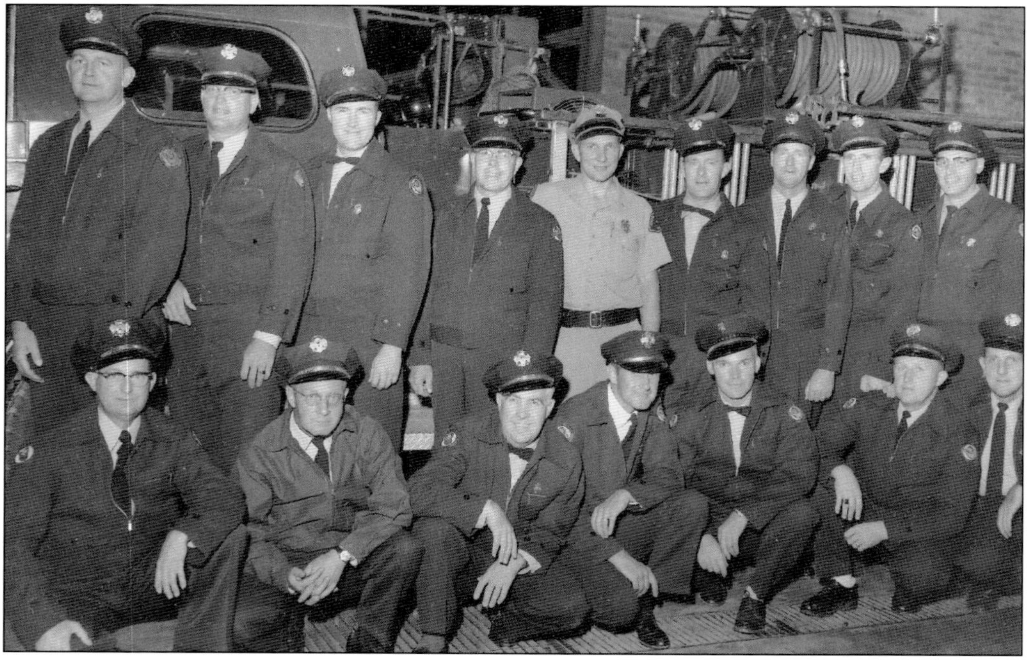

The complete South Ogden fire department is pictured in 1962. They are, from left to right, (first row) Bill Brown, Deb Burton, Ed Erickson, Don Wintle, Lenard Saunders, Paul Tesch, and George Van Drimmelen; (second row) Roy Van Drimmelen, Gene Bateman, Lloyd King, Dell Iverson, Joe Torman, Clint Peterson, Vernon Barney, Stan Bushell, and Lamar Scadden.

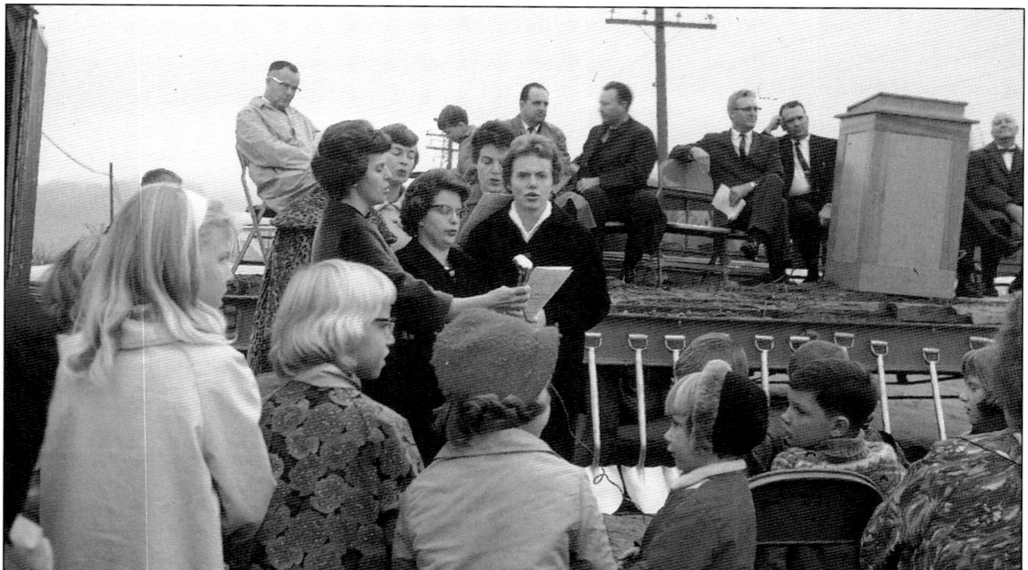

This photograph was taken during the ground-breaking ceremony of the 60th and 70th Ward building of the Church of Jesus Christ of Latter-day Saints (LDS), November 1963. The singers are, from left to right, unidentified, Gloria Rippon, Shirlene Thomas, Jessie Foster, and unidentified. The children in the photograph include two Wintle siblings, Sara Foster, Paula Foster, Rich Radmall, and the daughter of Bob and Emma Lu Draper. The site was at 4955 Adams Avenue. (Courtesy Jessie Foster.)

Fred L. Montmorency served the city as mayor from 1962 to 1969. He was instrumental in developing the city's first long-range plan for capital improvements. Land for what later became Friendship Park was also purchased from Ogden City during Mayor Montmorency's tenure. The name of the park was chosen to reflect the friendly relationship between South Ogden and Ogden.

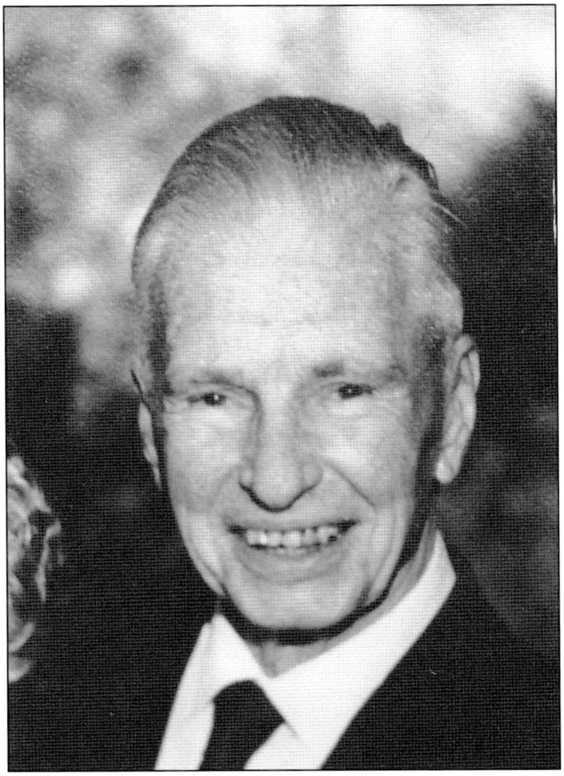

The Greek Orthodox Church of the Transfiguration, at 647 42nd Street, opened for worship on October 18, 1964. The first father was Sphyros Dyavatis. Archbishop Iakovos, who at the time was the Primate of the Greek Orthodox Church of North and South America, consecrated the building December 18, 1969. Besides a place of worship, the annual Greek Food Festival, held every September, draws hundreds of people to the church.

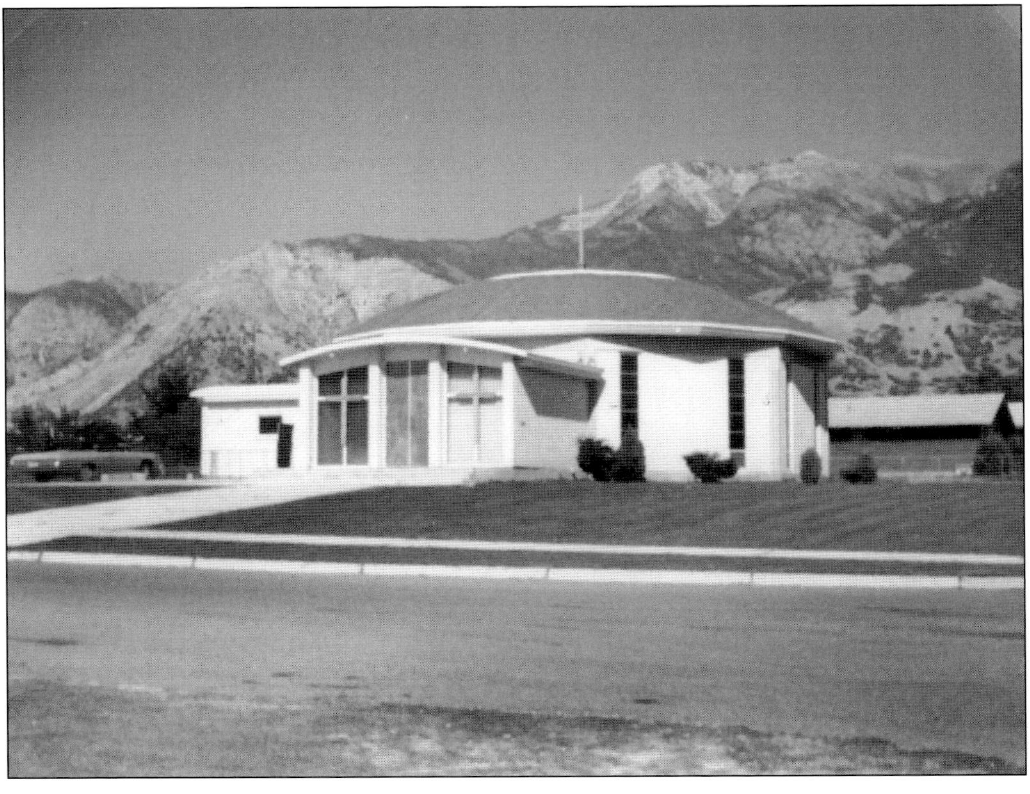

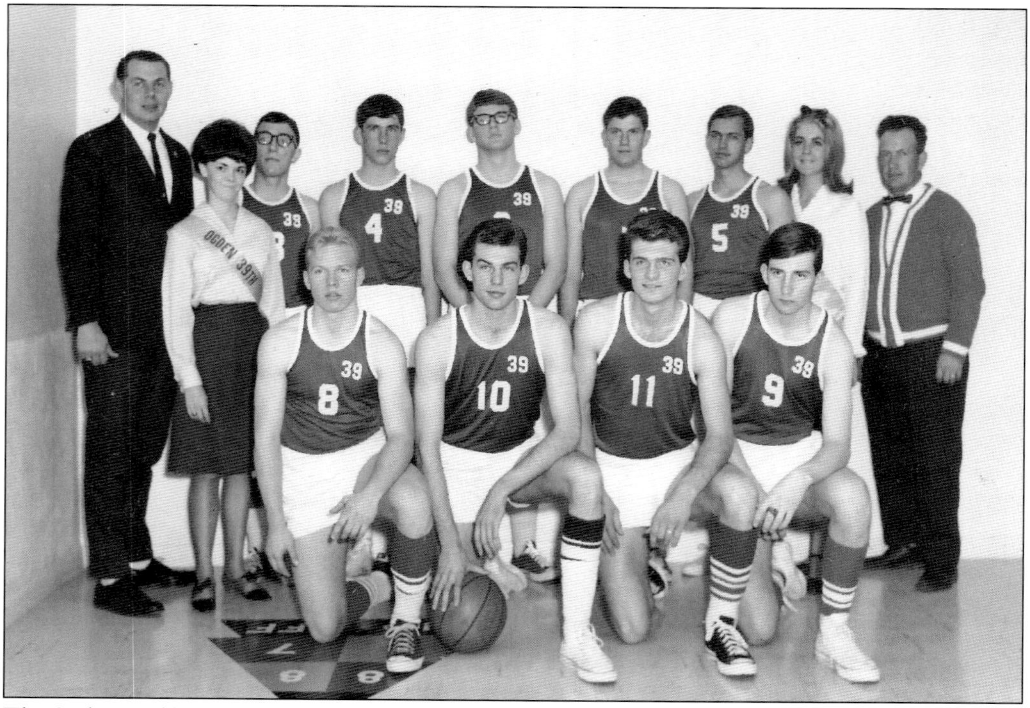

The 39th Ward basketball team participated in the All-Church Junior Basketball Tournament in Salt Lake City from February 28 to March 4, 1966. They are, from left to right, (first row) Glen Passey, Larry Campbell, Kirk Johansen, and Steve Carter; (second row) coach ?, tournament hostess ?, Bruce Shepherd, Larry Arbon, Ron Barney, Mike Fessler, Kenneth Henrie, tournament hostess ?, and coach Mark Porter. (Courtesy Barbara Porter.)

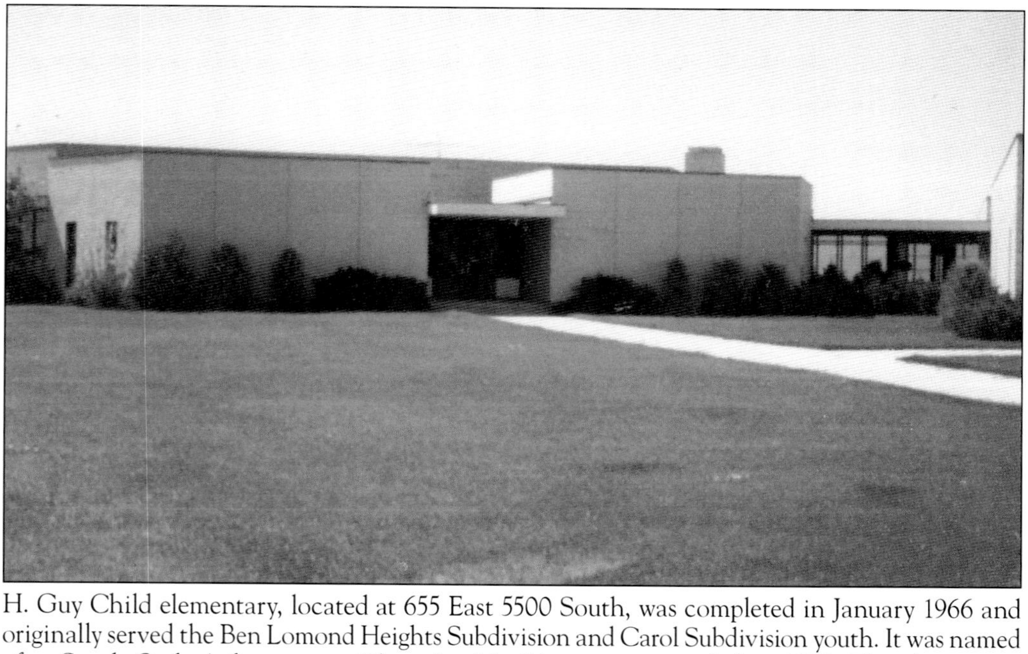

H. Guy Child elementary, located at 655 East 5500 South, was completed in January 1966 and originally served the Ben Lomond Heights Subdivision and Carol Subdivision youth. It was named after South Ogden's first mayor. The school building was expanded in 1978. The elementary continues to educate children in grades K–6.

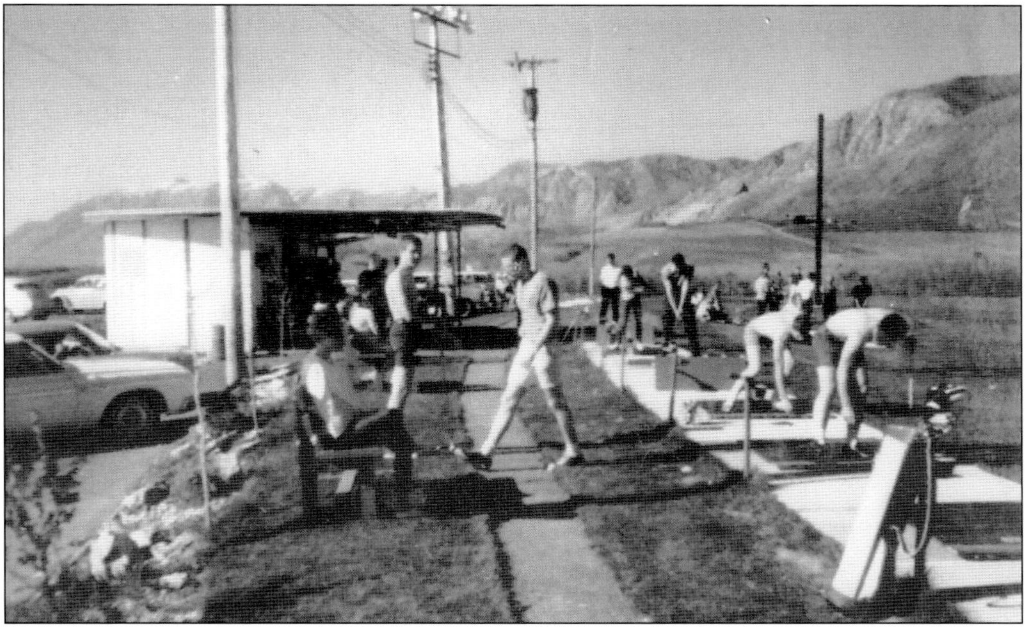

Golf City's driving range is seen above in 1965. Michael W. Farrell, while in his early 20s, purchased 25 acres at 1400 East and 5600 South, with the help of his father, Wayne P. Farrell. The land was used to build a golf facility, the realization of a dream Mike had since being a teenager. The driving range was completed in 1963, a par-3 course was added in 1965, and an "around the world" 18-hole mini-golf course was added in 1969. Many residents still have flashbacks of taking a score of eight or more on the Hawaii hole, trying to get the ball into the top of the volcano. Michael W. Farrell, along with his wife, Nancy Stanfield Farrell, and their children, Jeff and Jodi, tend the thriving Golf City Family Fun Center. Below is a similar view of the driving range in a 1995 photograph. (Both, courtesy Jodi Gale.)

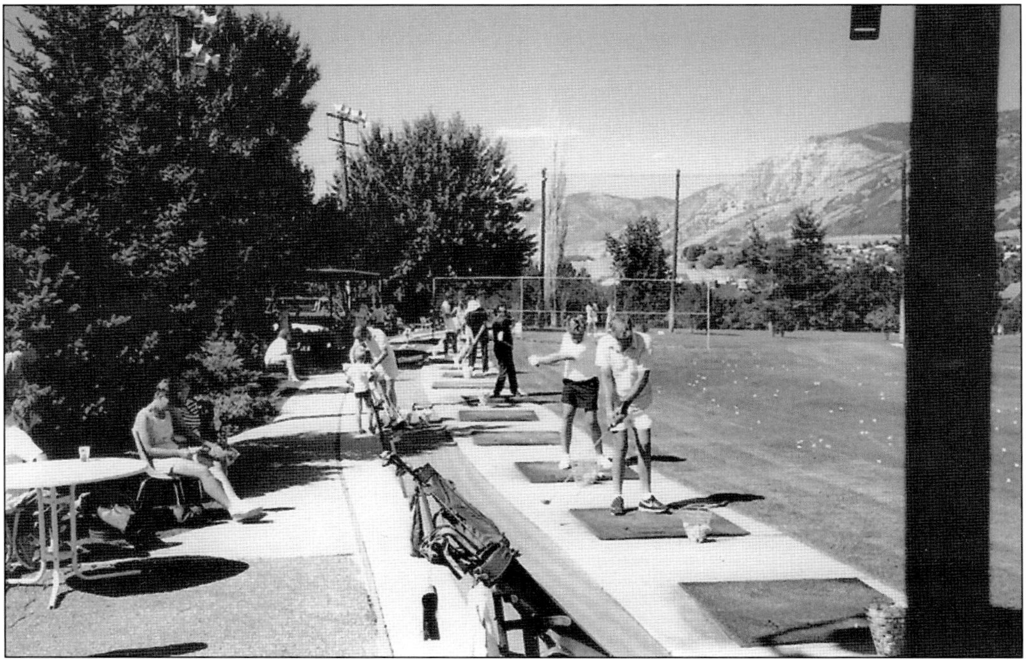

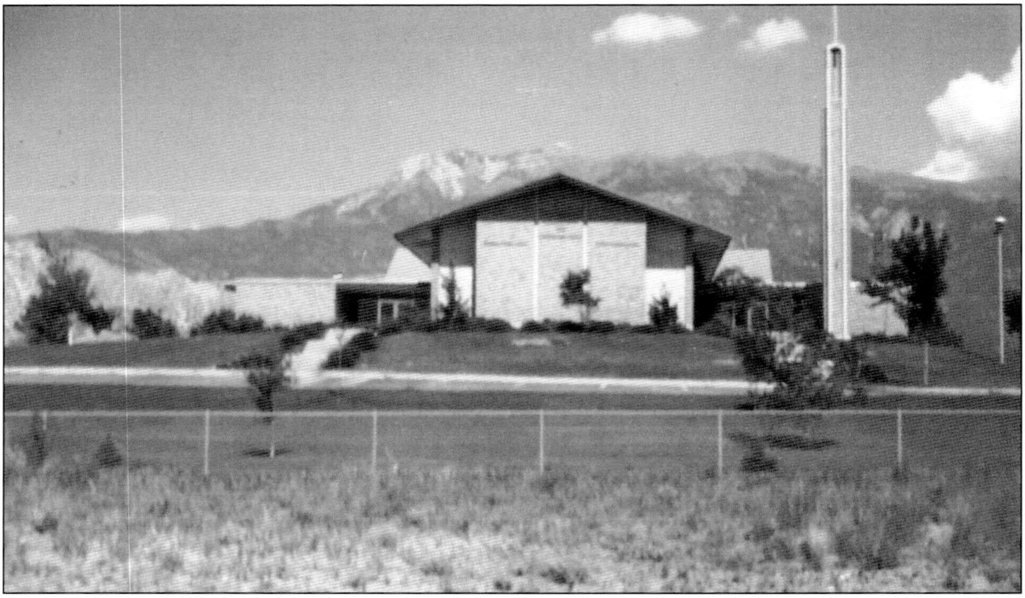

This LDS building, above, was completed January 30, 1966, at 4955 Adams Avenue for the 60th and 70th Wards. In recent years, names were changed, and it now houses the Fourth and Fifth Wards of the Burch Creek Stake. The building underwent remodeling and renovation in 2006 and 2009. The current bishops for the wards are Dan Dillingham and Brett Gray, respectively. Below, this building was completed February 1967 at 4380 Orchard Avenue for the Ogden 58th and 65th Wards. It currently houses the Fifth and Sixth Wards of the South Ogden Stake as well as the office for the Utah Ogden Mission. The current Fifth Ward bishop is Blake Sears, and the Sixth Ward bishop is Craig Scott. There are nine church buildings in South Ogden, where members of the LDS church make up approximately 60 percent of the city's population.

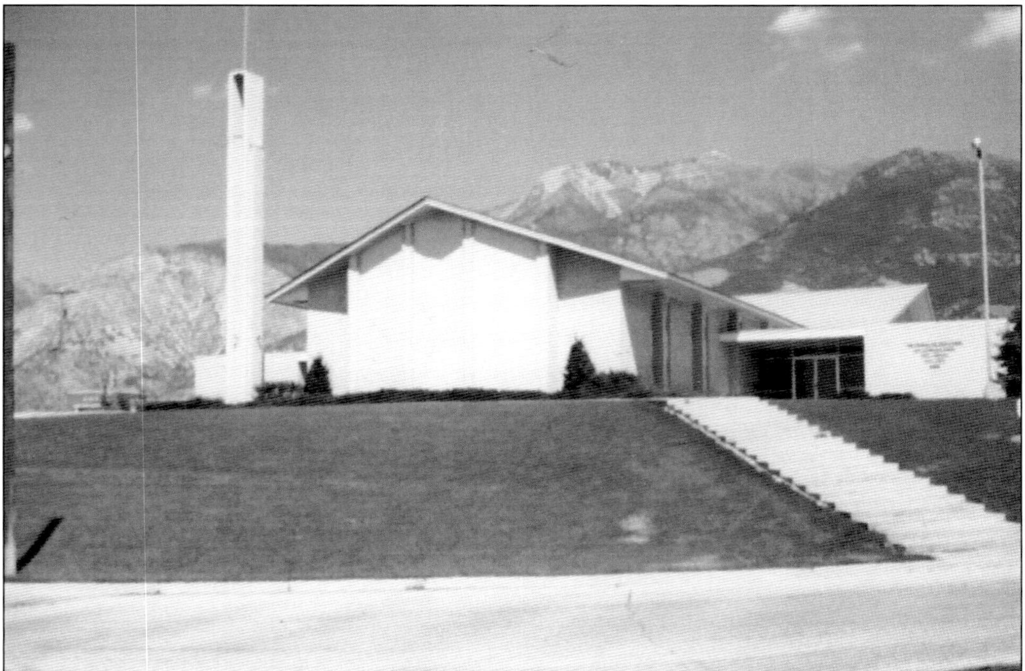

Four

1970s

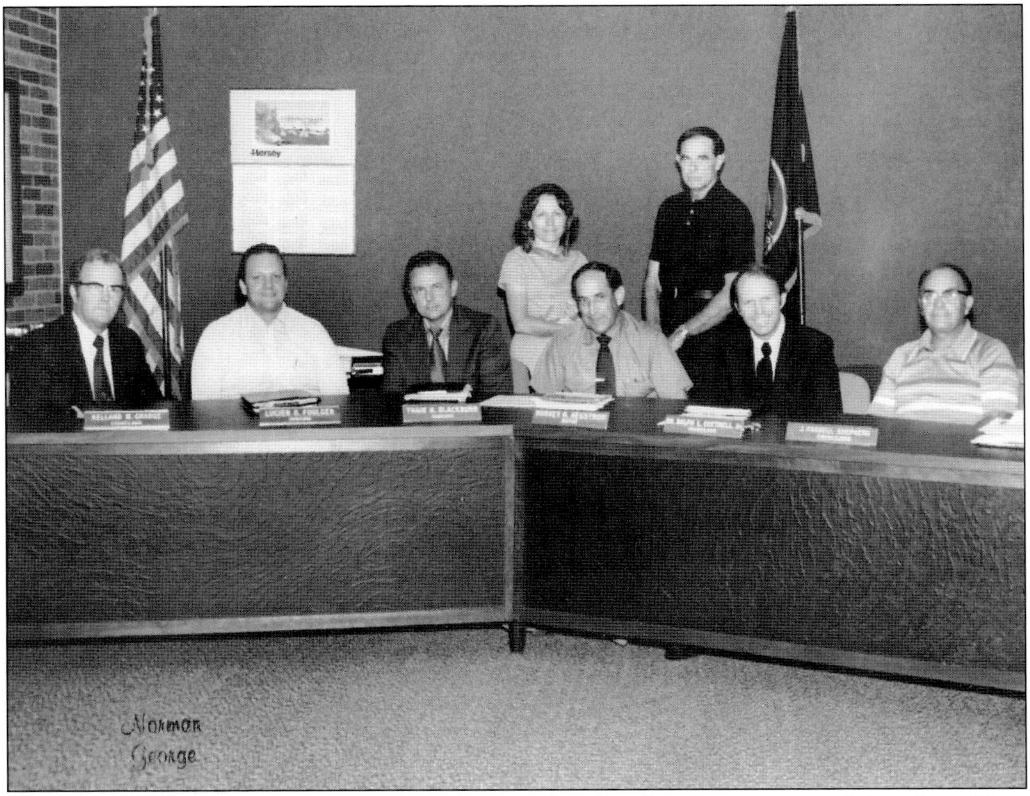

This early 1970s photograph is of the mayor council and staff in the city council chambers. They are, from left to right, (first row) Councilmember Kelland W. Grange, Councilmember Lucien O. Foulger, Councilmember Thair H. Blackburn, Mayor Harvey R. Hegstrom, Councilmember Ralph L. Cottrell Jr., and Councilmember J. Farrell Shepherd; (second row) council secretary Norrine Gardiner and city administrator Lee Stauffer.

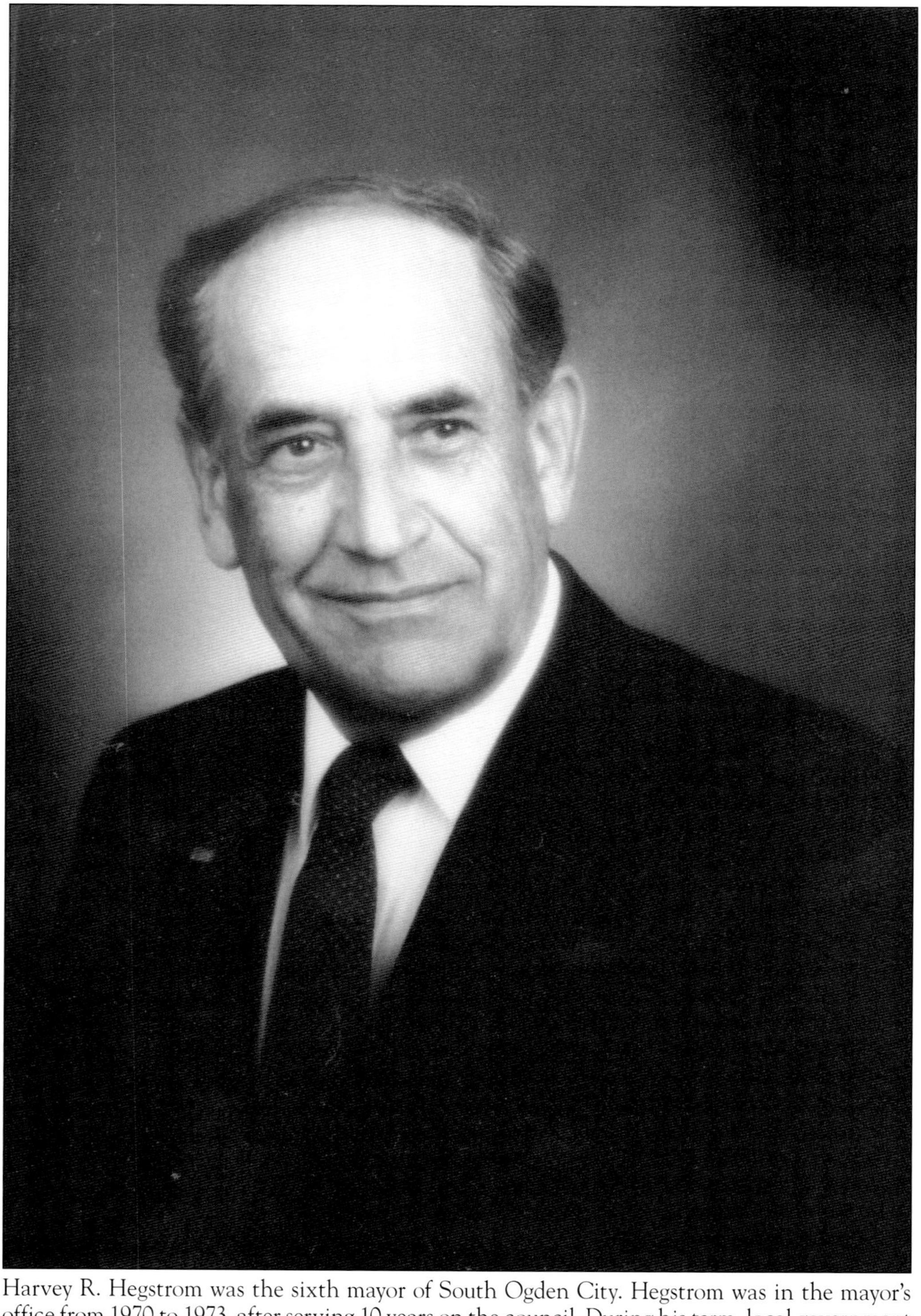

Harvey R. Hegstrom was the sixth mayor of South Ogden City. Hegstrom was in the mayor's office from 1970 to 1973, after serving 10 years on the council. During his term, local government was busy updating the water and sewer lines of the city as well as installation of many curbs and gutters in the residential areas.

Walker Bank, on the corner of Thirty-sixth Street and Washington Boulevard, was built in 1970. Most memorable was the colored lighting on the tower. If the weather forecast showed good conditions, the light would be blue. Poor weather in the forecast resulted in an orange light. Flashing blue or flashing orange represented weather conditions somewhere in between. In 1982, the building became First Interstate Bank. Wells Fargo Bank currently occupies the building, sans any weather forecasting.

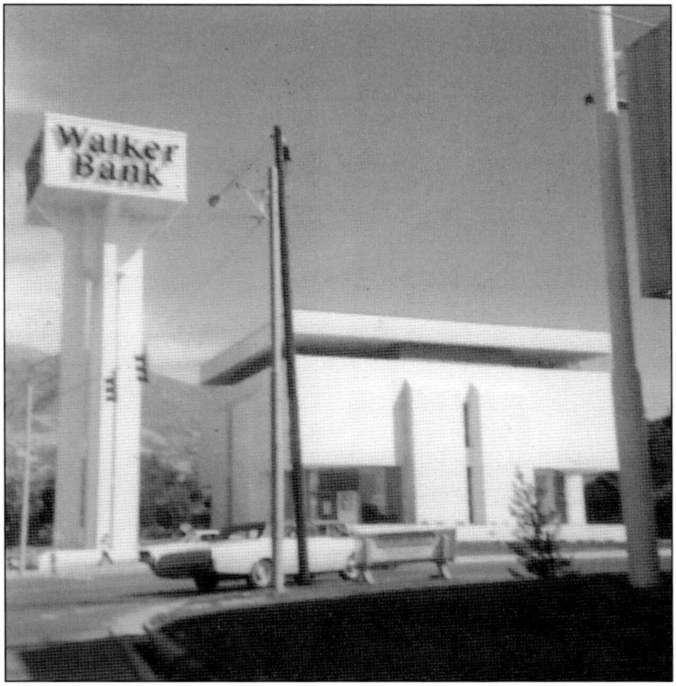

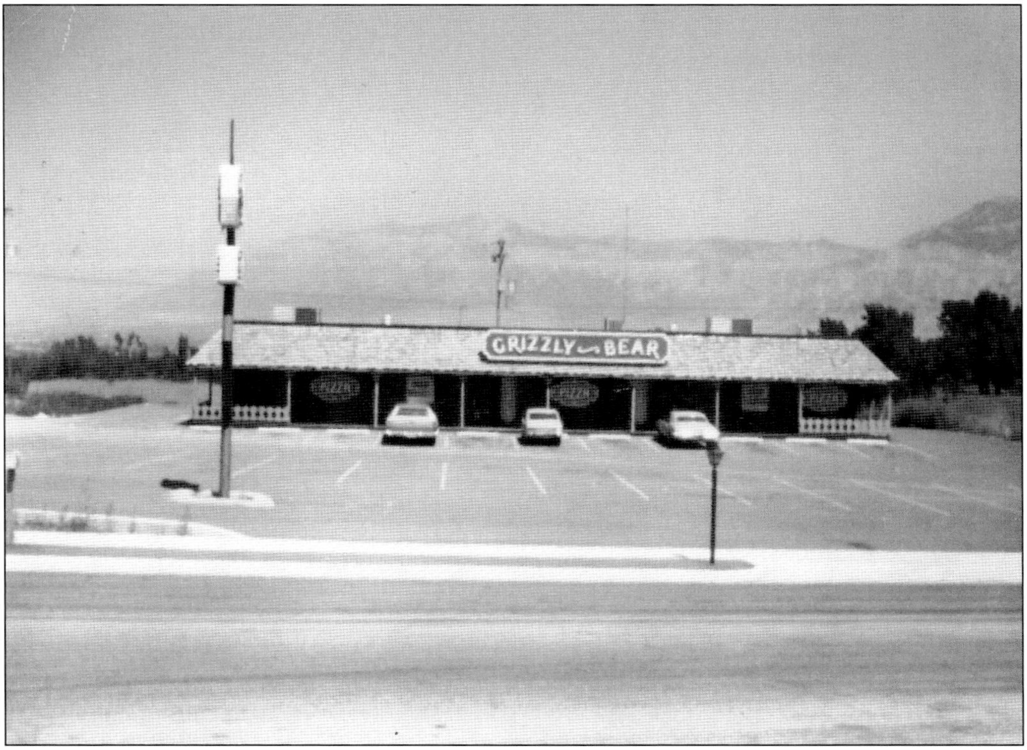

This is an August 1973 photograph of Grizzly Bear Pizza, located on the 400 block of Forty-fourth Street. The restaurant was in business until the early 1980s and was known for tasty pizza as well as a place to play the latest video games—*Asteroids*, *Galaga*, *Space Invaders*, and *Centipede*. The site was later home to the Shed restaurant and is currently the Mount Ogden Grill.

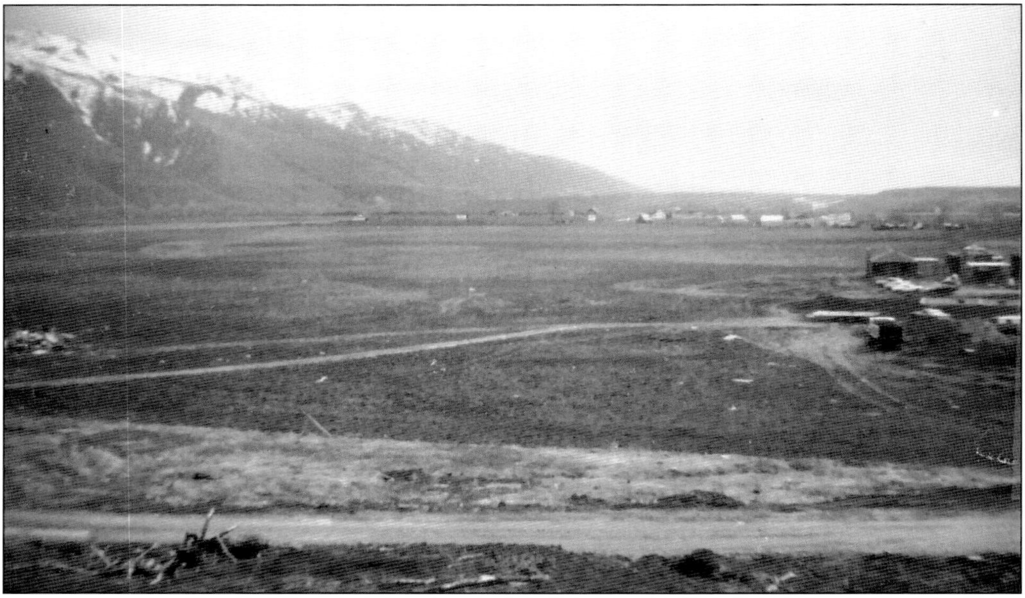

This area is being prepared for the building of the Yorkshire Meadows condominiums in 1971 (above). Noticeably absent in the photograph are the many condominiums, houses, trees, a school, and a park that fill the area today (below). The 35 percent growth the city experienced in the 1970s is due, in large part, to this area of the city. The modern Meadows includes the Meadows Park, a 1.5-acre grassy area with basketball courts and playground equipment. Land for the park was conveyed to the city by Robert D. and Sharon Rond. Some of the homes, particularly to the east and far south, including Uintah Elementary School, are not actually within the borders of South Ogden but are in unincorporated Weber County. The city border in the area is very inconsistent. (Below, courtesy Sherri Porter.)

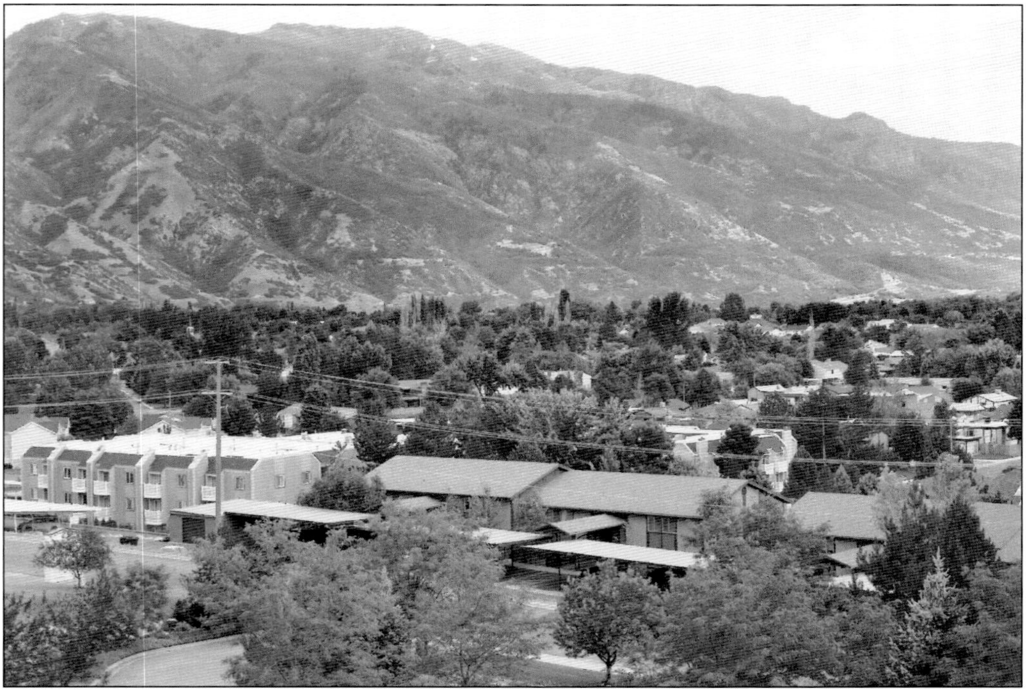

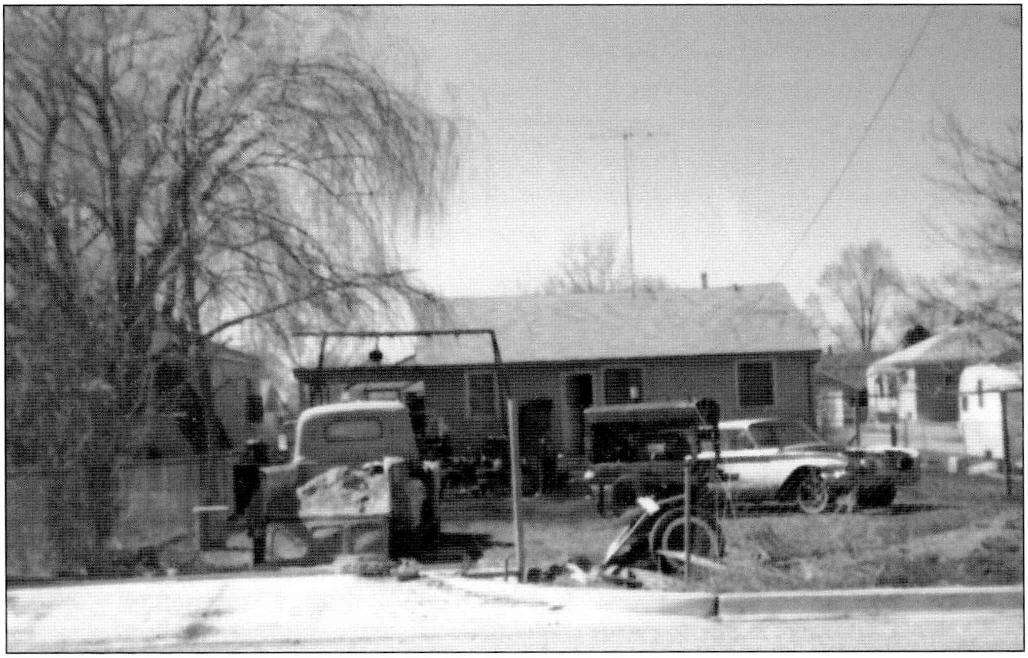

Before-and-after photographs show a South Ogden property that participated in and received an award for successful completion of Project WIN. Above is the home, as it appeared March 1972. Below, the same property is pictured after much effort in August 1973. Project WIN was a beautification project sponsored by Mayor Harvey Hegstrom and the city council to promote pride in the community and cleaner neighborhoods. The acronym WIN stood for "Work with enthusiasm, Involve everyone, and Never give up 'til the job is done." With or without government-sponsored competitions, there are many beautifully landscaped yards and conscientious homeowners in South Ogden.

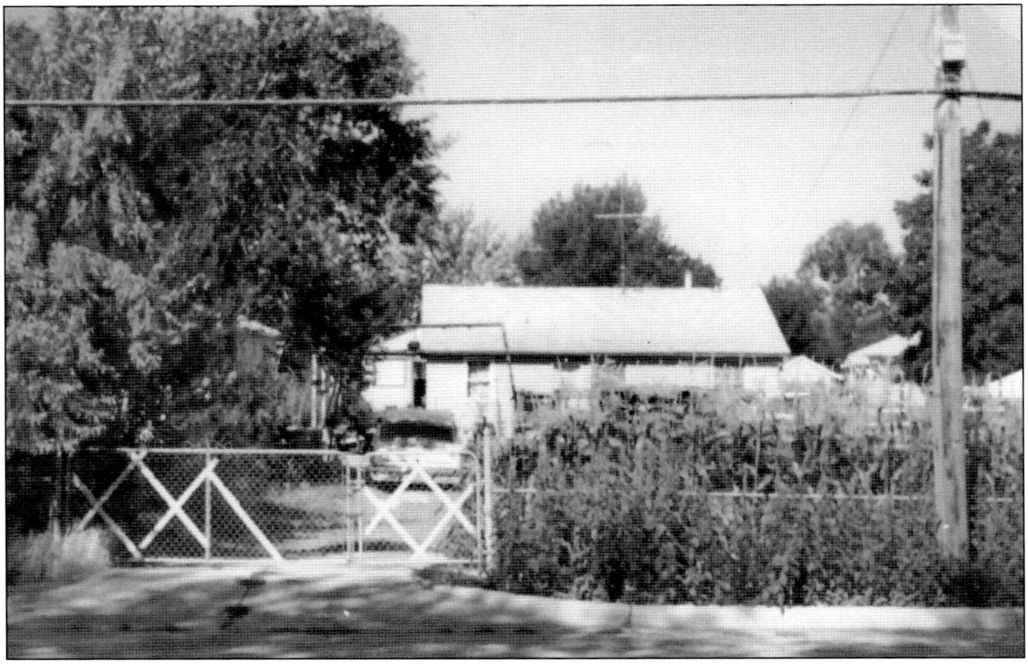

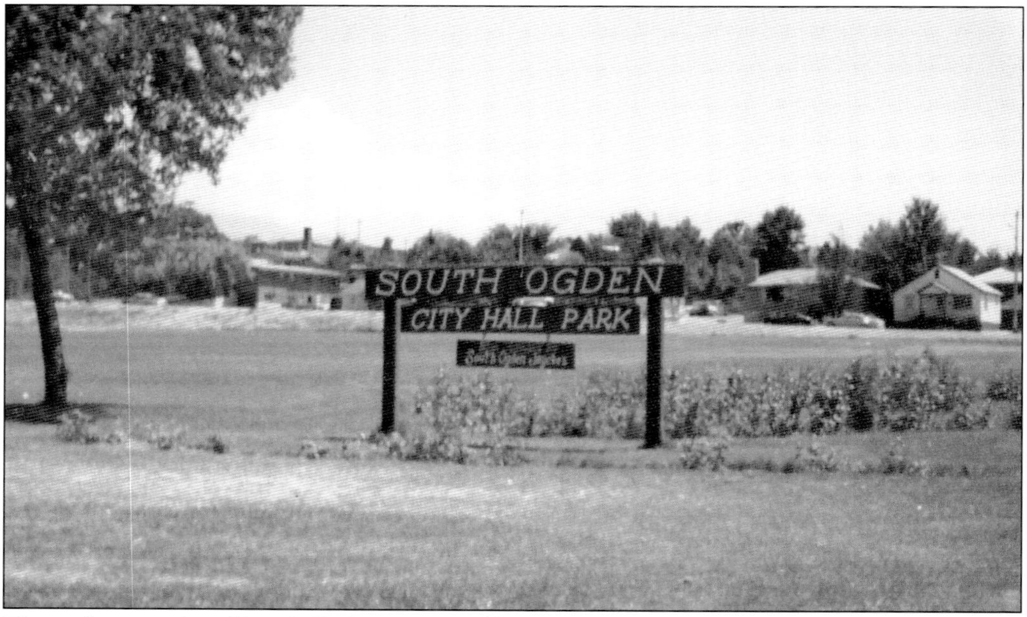

These photographs of South Ogden's City Hall Park were taken July 1973. The park is also called 40th Street Park, due to its location. Above is the view looking south toward 40th Street. Noticeably absent are the very tall trees that currently grow along the sidewalk of the street. Below, the view looks east to the bowery. Changing very little in appearance over the decades, the bowery, and area around it, has been a meeting place for generations. Family reunions have been held there since its inception, and city gatherings on Independence Day and after parades have filled the park with residents. Some annual events, such as the Old Fashioned Family Christmas and Night Out Against Crime, are still held in the park and bowery.

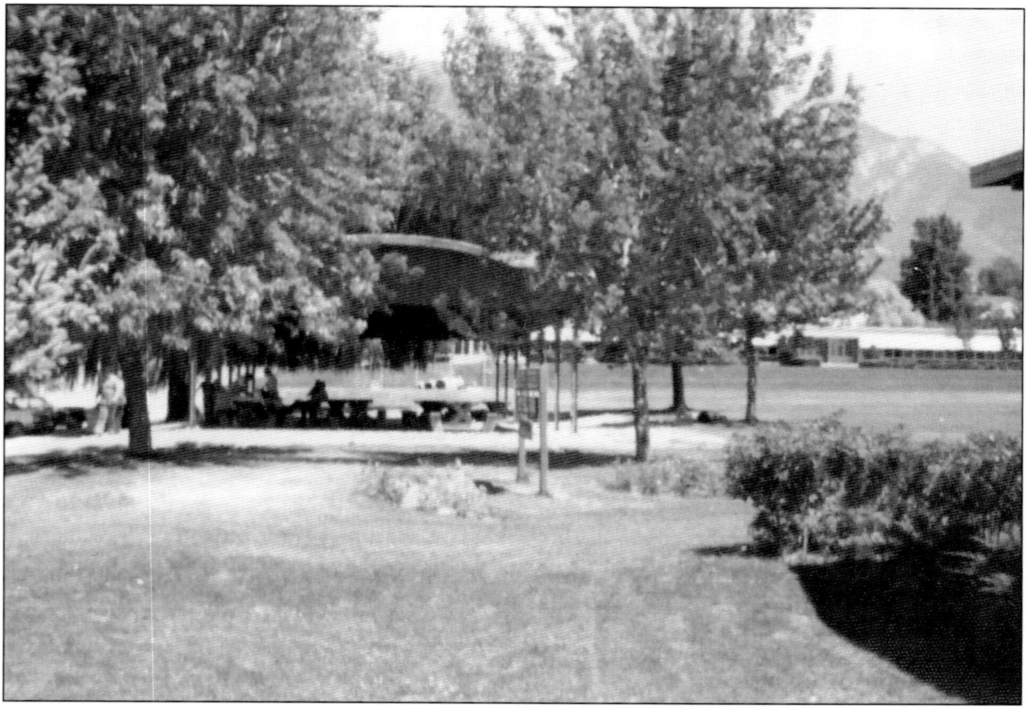

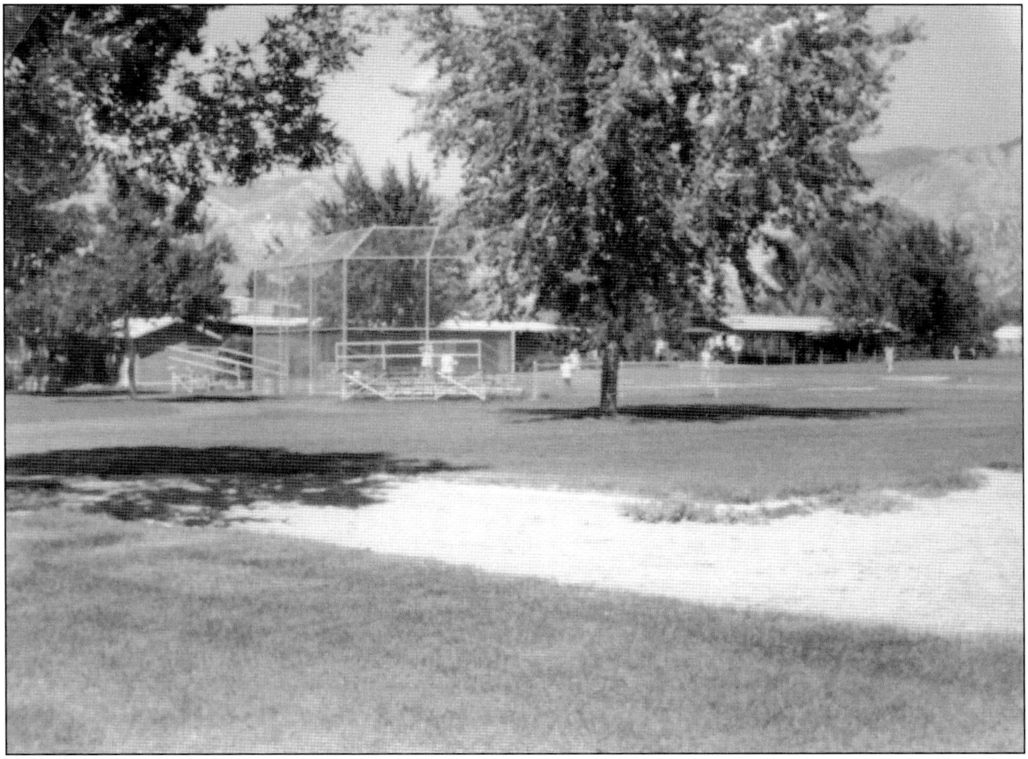

This 1973 photograph of City Hall Park looks northeast toward the sport's backstop and bowery. The park was the site of Little League baseball and T-ball games as well as girls' softball games. The small redbrick building to the left of the photograph was full of games and sporting equipment to be checked out during the summer months of the 1970s–1980s for youth who had signed up for "recreation." This part of the park is now the city hall and public safety building with a parking area.

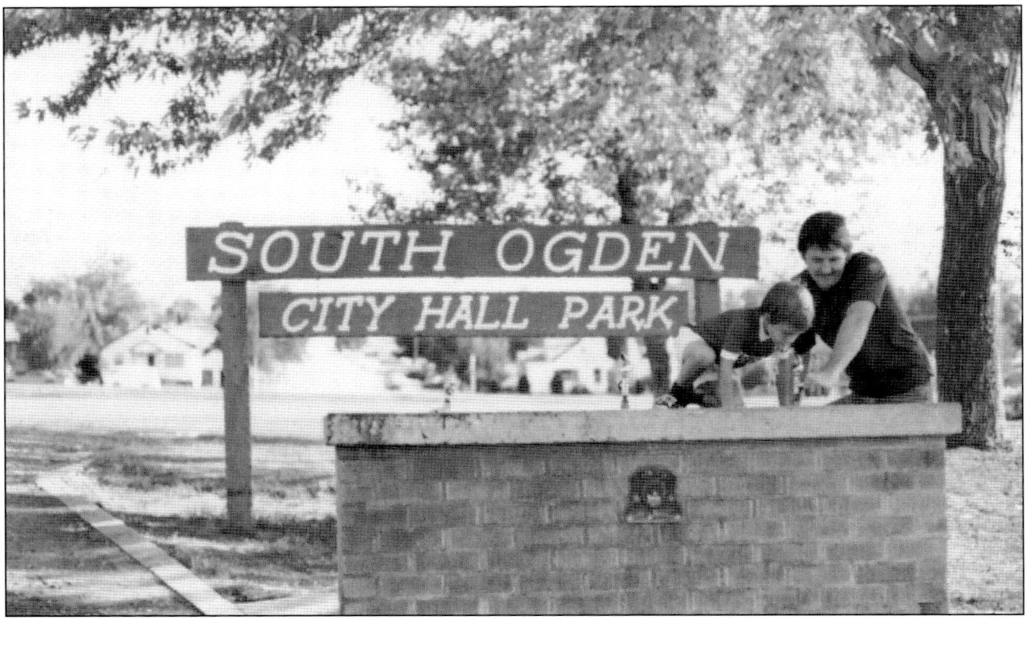

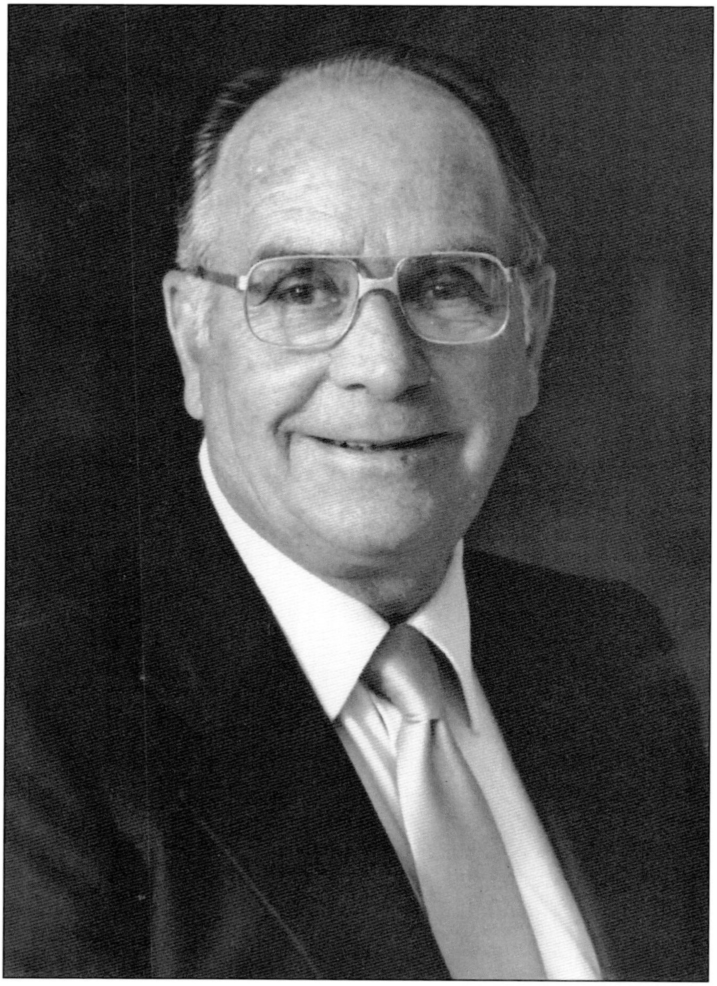

Joseph Farrell Shepherd was mayor of South Ogden City from 1974 to 1983. During his years as mayor, the city annexed over 100 acres of land, fire station No. 2 was completed, and the one-way streets west of Washington Boulevard were designed. The Union Building at Weber State University also bears his name.

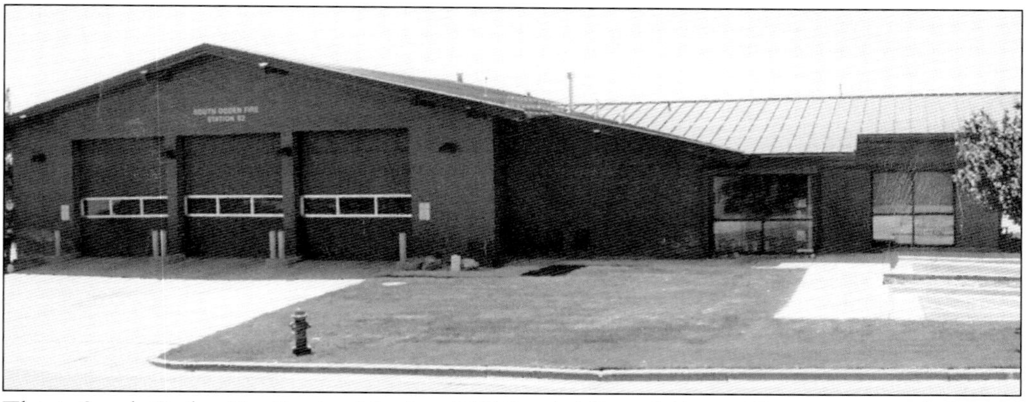

This is South Ogden Fire Station No. 2 at 5635 South Wasatch Drive. The station was dedicated September 13, 1975. In attendance and/or speaking at the dedication was US representative K. Gunn McKay, Mayor J. Farrell Shepherd, and fire chief Robert Marz.

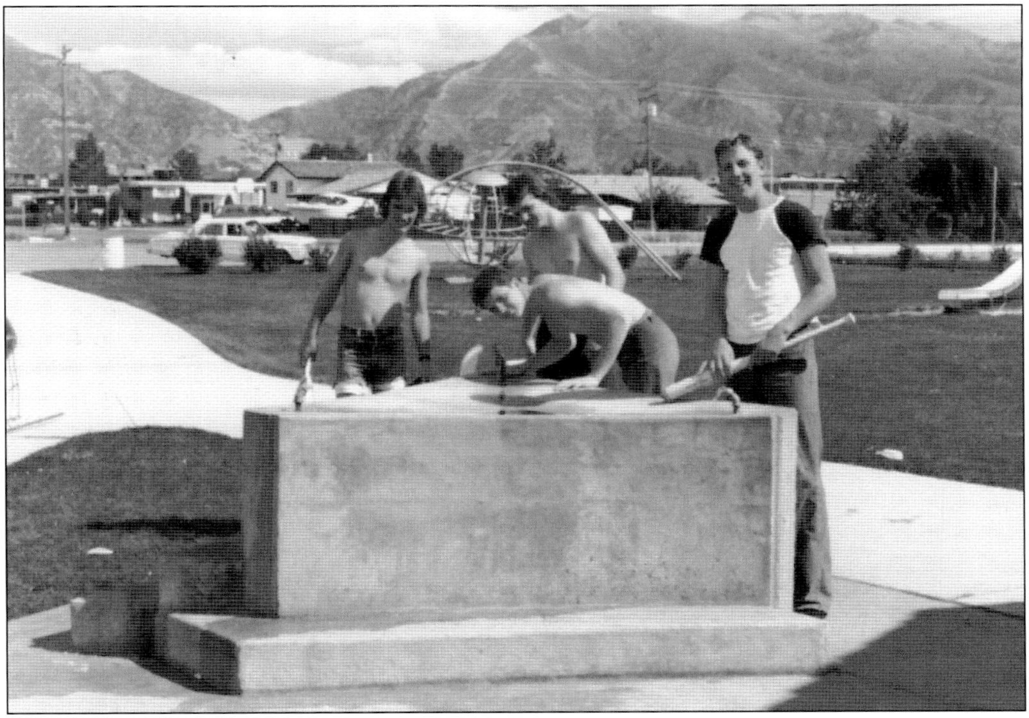

Four local youth enjoy the new water fountain at Friendship Park in 1978, above. Below is the view in July 1973, looking west at the playground equipment and storage/bathroom building. Friendship Park, at 11 acres, is the largest park in South Ogden. It was purchased in the 1960s from Ogden City for $3,000 and named Friendship Park because of the good relationship between the two cities. The park is home to soccer, baseball, and softball games, South Ogden Jets football practices and games, the annual South Ogden Days carnival and concert, and the Easter Egg Hunt held the Saturday morning before Easter each year. It also includes two tennis courts and a walking track.

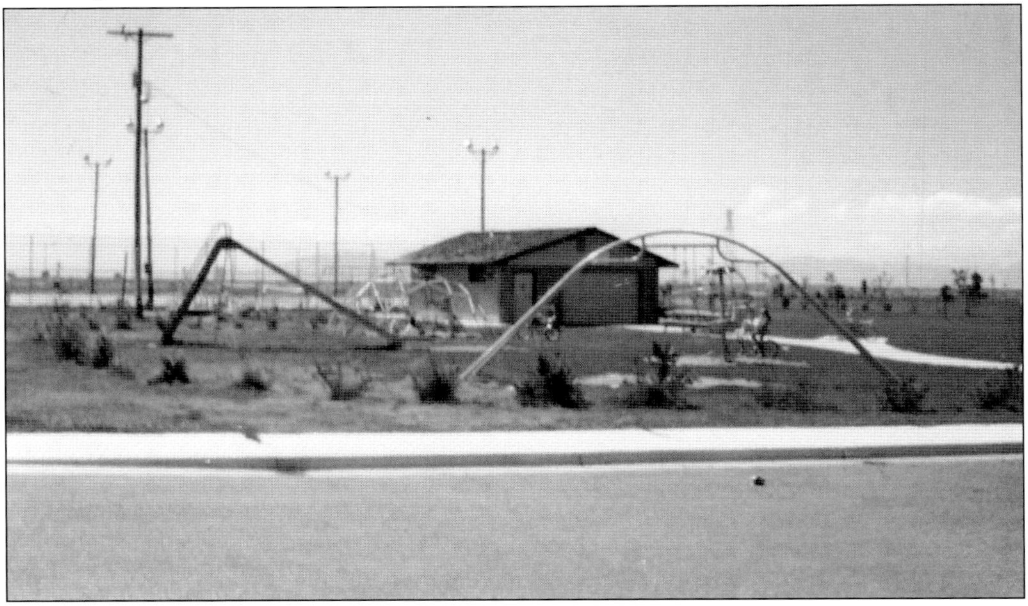

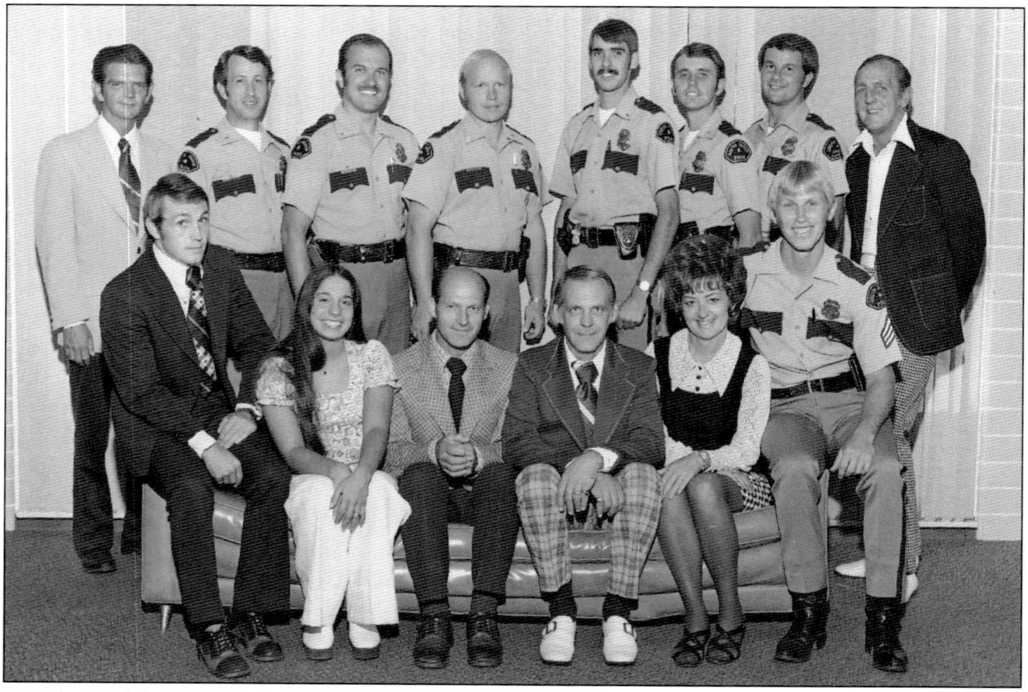

Members of the South Ogden City police force are pictured in 1975. They are, from left to right, (first row) Rich Noble, Peggy Barker, Chief Jim Wold, Sheldon Nelson, Elaine ?, and Darryl Jones; (second row) George Van Drimmelen, Brad Birch, Val Shupe, Jim Jensen, Glen Passey, Alma Richins, Bill Powell, and Bob Stephenson. Below is a 1975 photograph of the police force with their vehicles. The view is looking north across 39th Street.

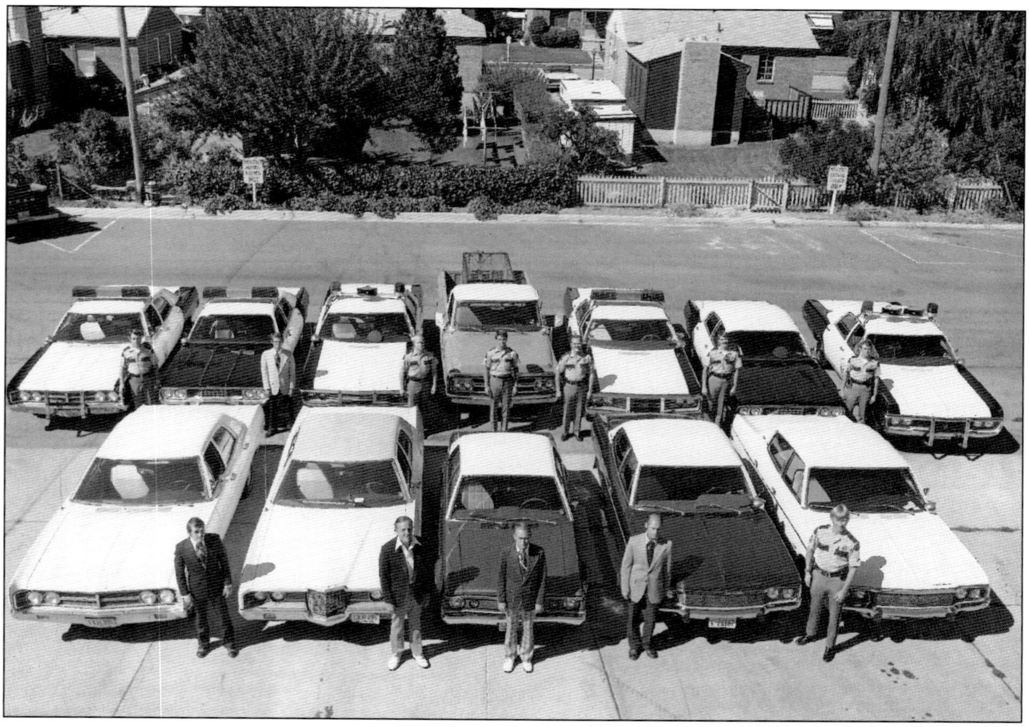

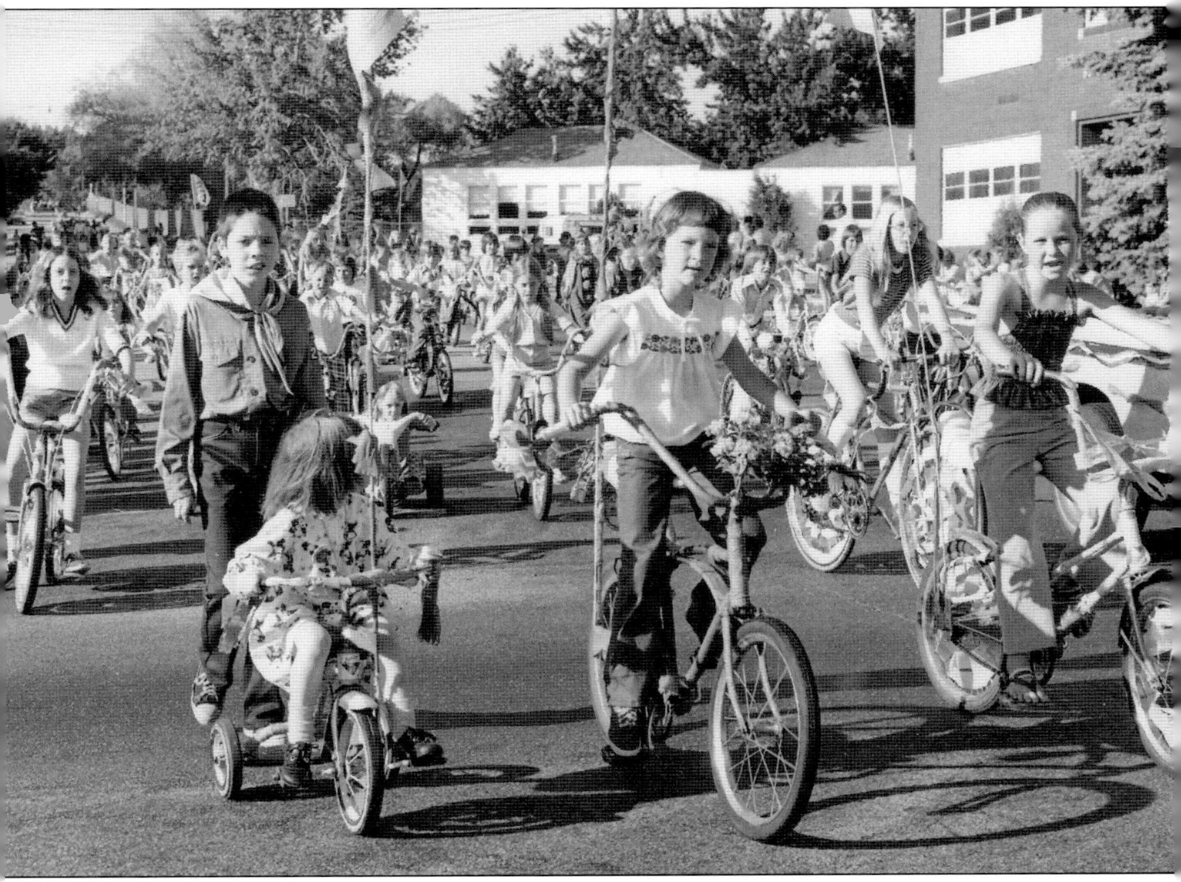

The 1976 Independence Day parade is pictured. These kids are on Adams Avenue, heading north in front of Burch Creek School. Local children were encouraged to decorate their bikes and participate in the parade.

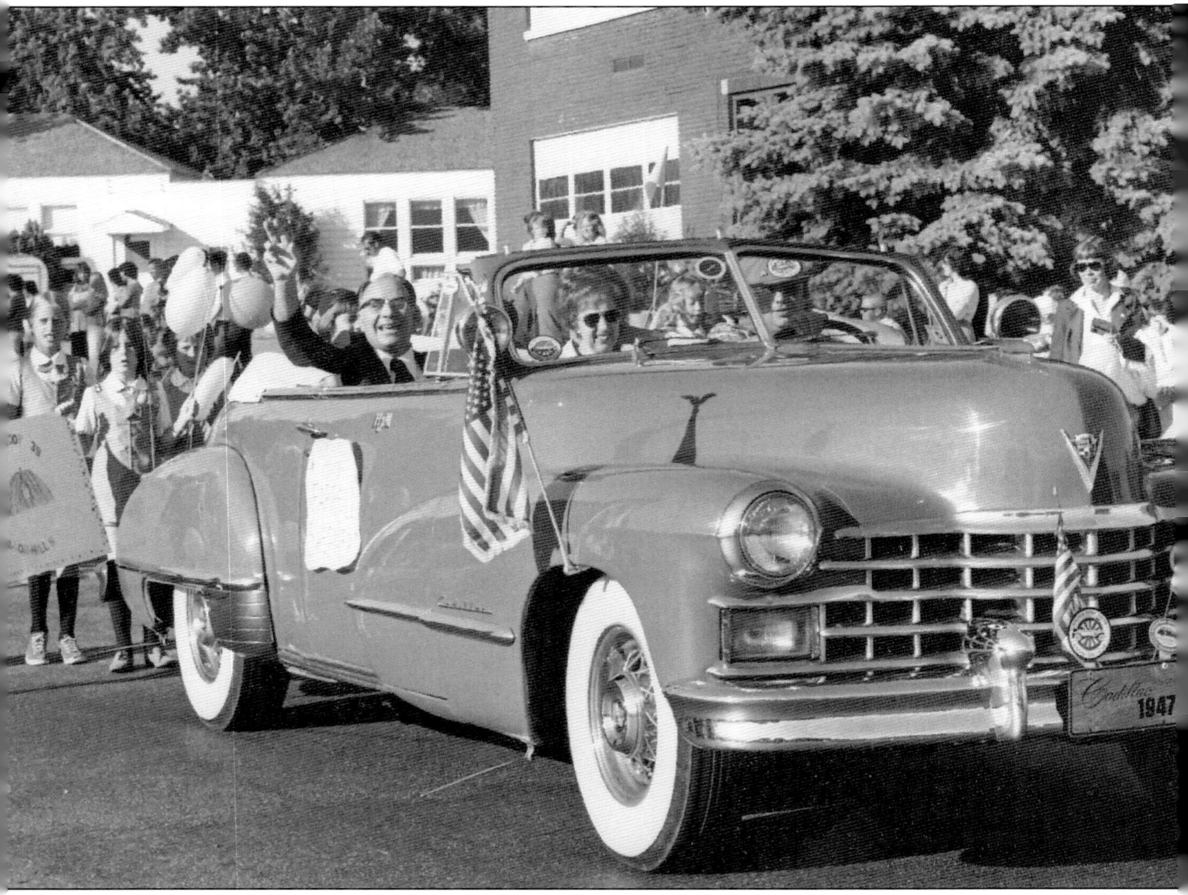

Mayor Joseph Farrell Shepherd is waving from a 1947 Cadillac on the Adams Avenue part of the 1976 Independence Day Parade route. His wife, Lois, is seated next to him, and they are being followed by Mar-Lon Hills Brownie Troop 39.

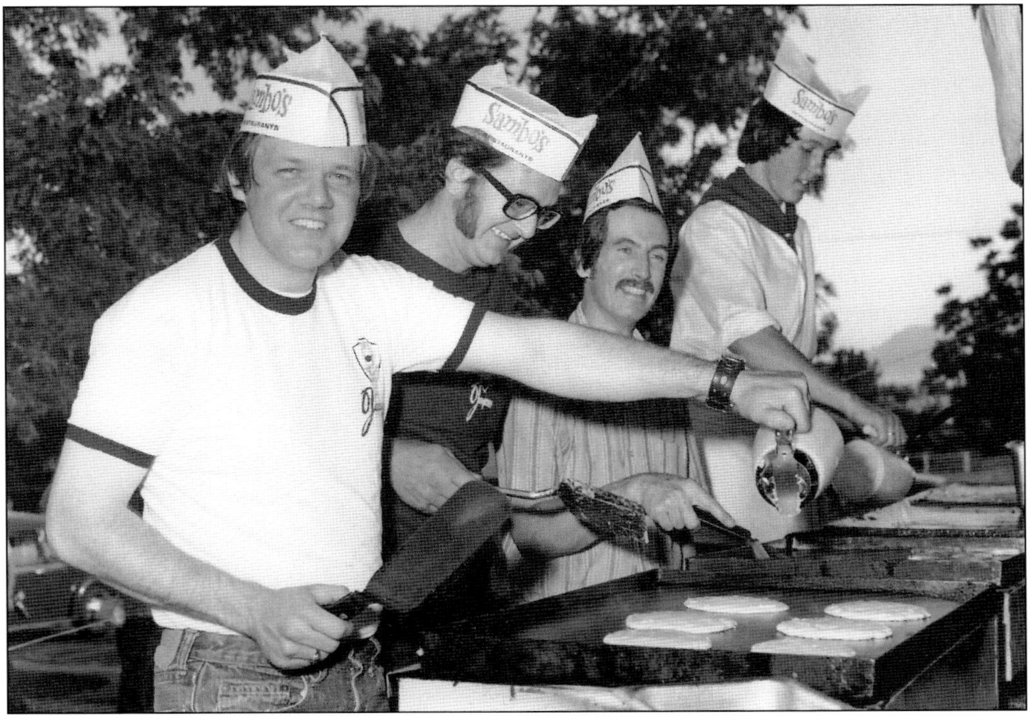

Four volunteers work the pancake section of the Independence Day breakfast, 1976. The annual event was held at 40th Street Park. The hats say "Sambo's," a restaurant that was located at 3670 Washington Boulevard during the 1970s and early 1980s.

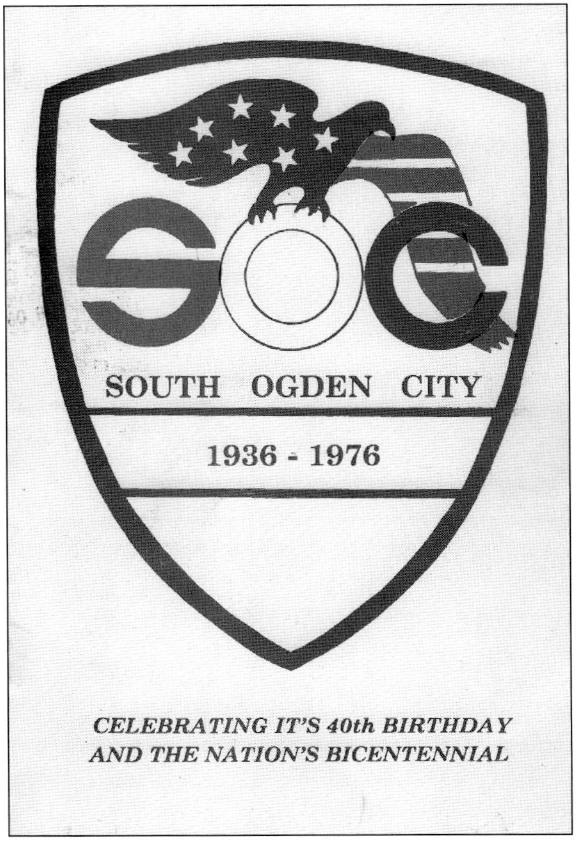

This logo was the winning entry of a contest held in conjunction with the city's 40th anniversary and the bicentennial of the United States. Kenneth Gardner, who was 19 at the time, was the contest winner and received a $25 prize. The red, white, and blue logo was displayed on city vehicles, police cars, and animal control arm patches.

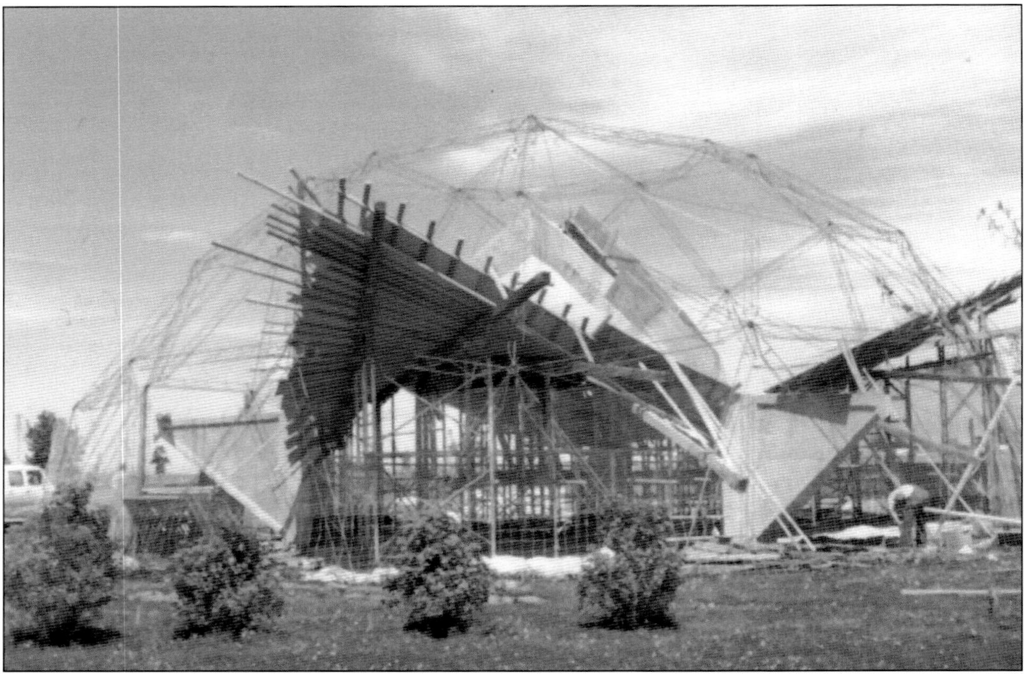

Photographs show the construction (above) and completion (below) of the Bicentennial Bowery at Friendship Park, 1976. The bowery was designed by former city councilman and architect Thair Blackburn and is officially a triaxial hyperbolic paraboloid. The goal was to build a large bowery that provides lots of shade while using a small amount of material. Built at a cost of $30,000, half of which came from the bicentennial celebration fund, the city got a bowery of a most unique design. Along with celebrating 200 years of America in 1976, city officials and residents celebrated the 40th anniversary of South Ogden being an incorporated city.

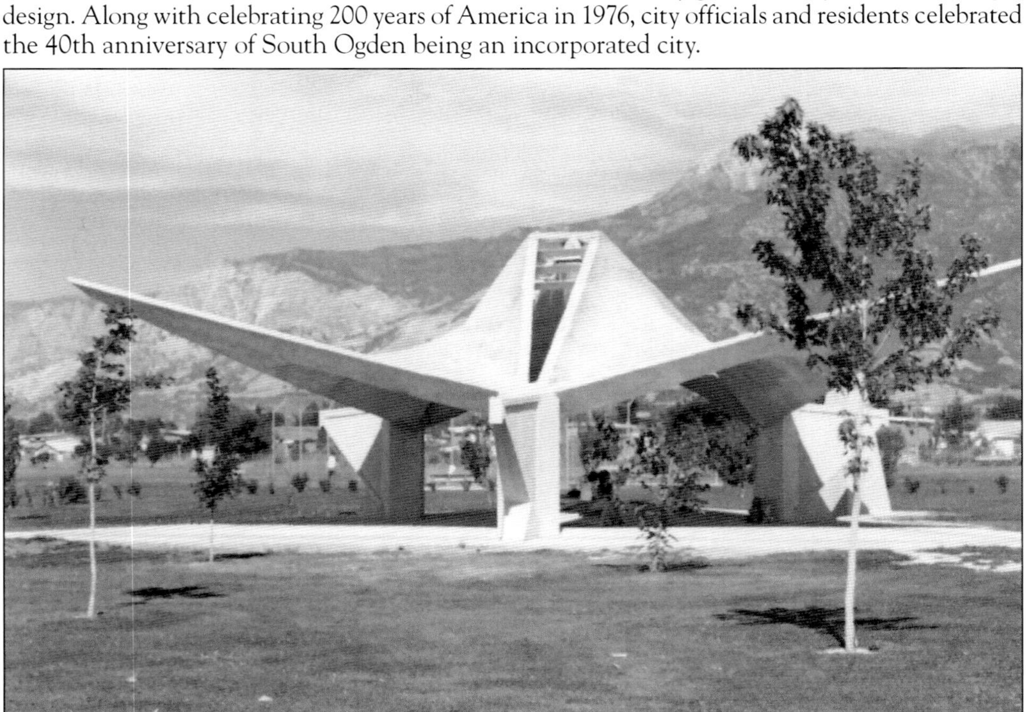

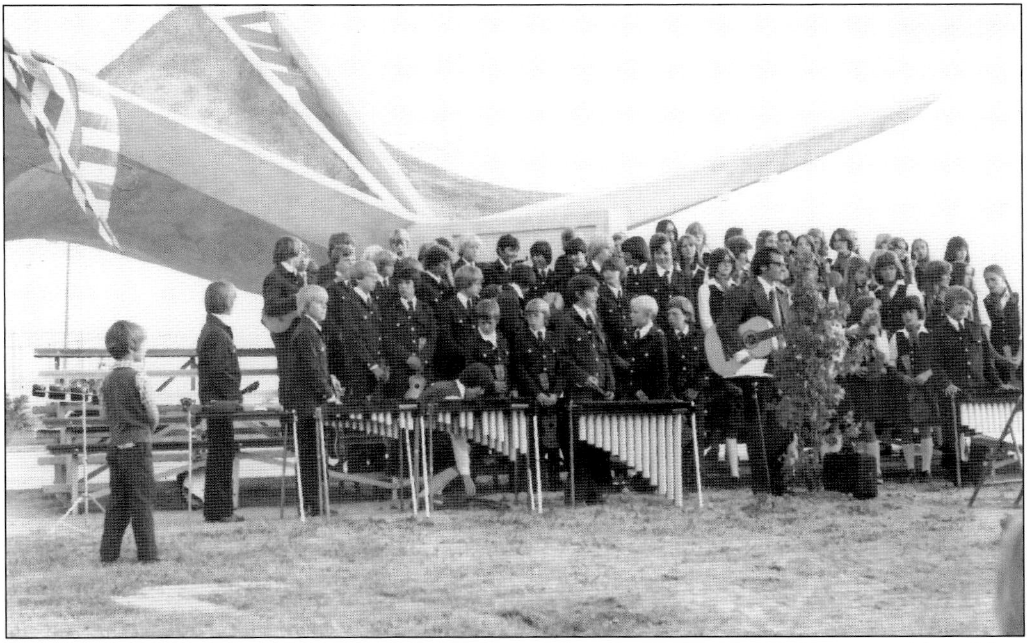

The Club Heights Bicentennial Singers are pictured at the Bicentennial Bowery in Friendship Park, July 4, 1976. The singers numbered 120 and had just returned from a weeklong trip to Washington, DC, where they had, among other things, sung on the Capitol steps. The picture was taken shortly after the group was presented with a flag that had flown over the US Capitol building the day they sang there. The students, mostly fifth and sixth graders attending Club Heights Elementary, were under the direction of Principal Thomas Littlefield and music directors Cordell Hull, David Grover, Nolan Wheelwright, and Nancy Moorman.

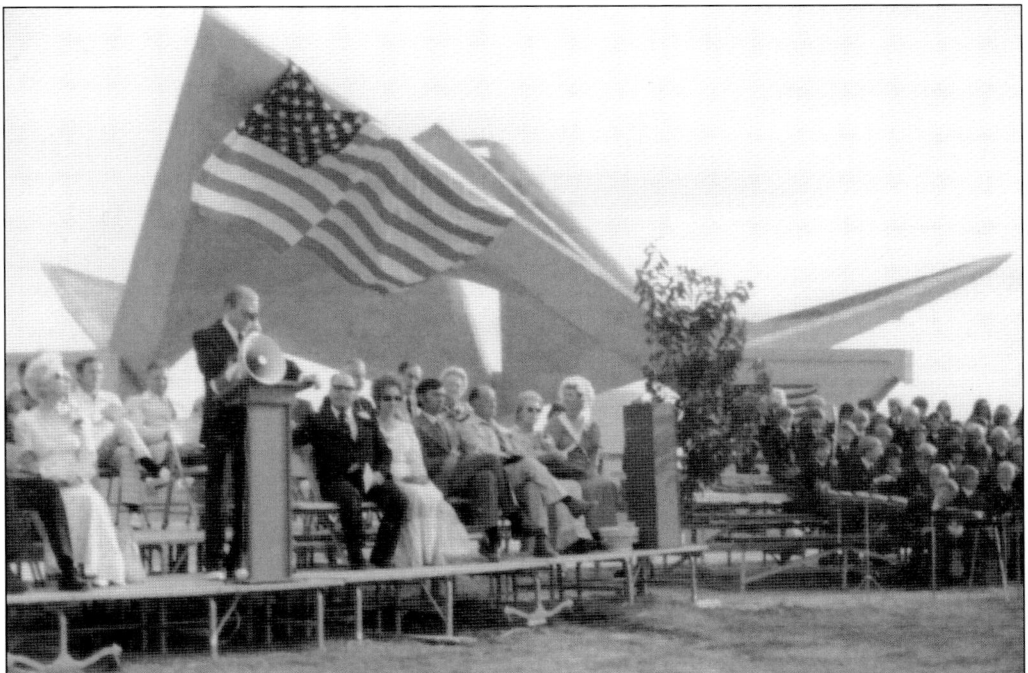

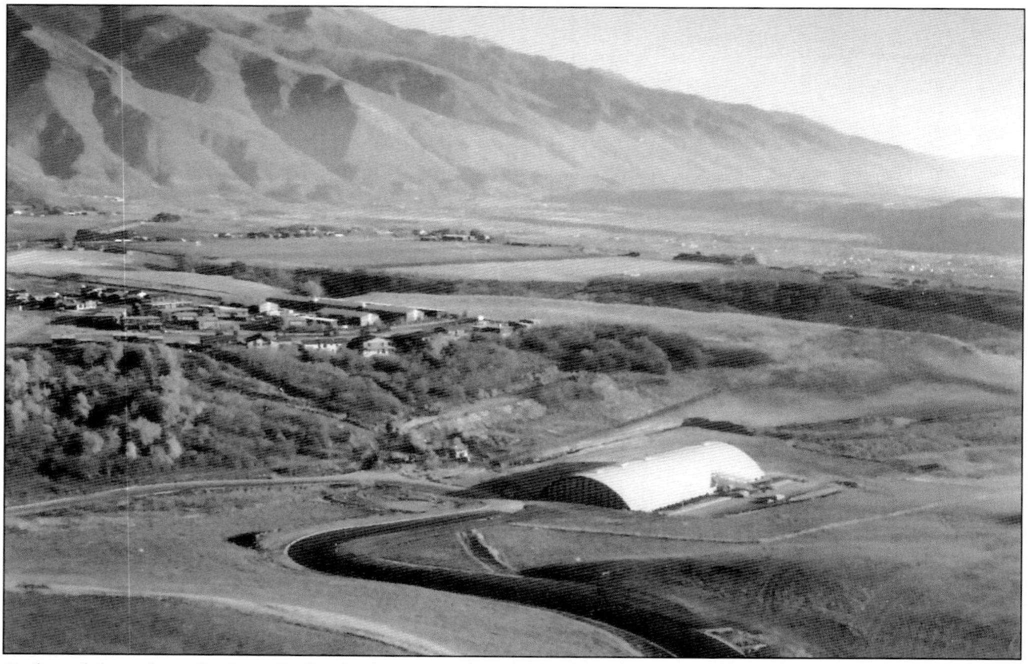

Before (above) and after (below) photographs show the Ogden Athletic Club and surrounding area. The OAC opened in March 1976 as a private tennis club at 1200 East and 5800 South, on land purchased by Michael Ritchie from the Douglas Stephens Development Co. The Ogden Athletic Club expanded in 1980 and 1983 and now has much more than just tennis. It is a family-friendly fitness and recreation center with something for everyone, including indoor and outdoor swimming pools, basketball, tennis, racquetball, and 16 different fitness centers. It is now such a part of South Ogden, it is referred to as simply "the Club." (Both, courtesy Travis Dugger.)

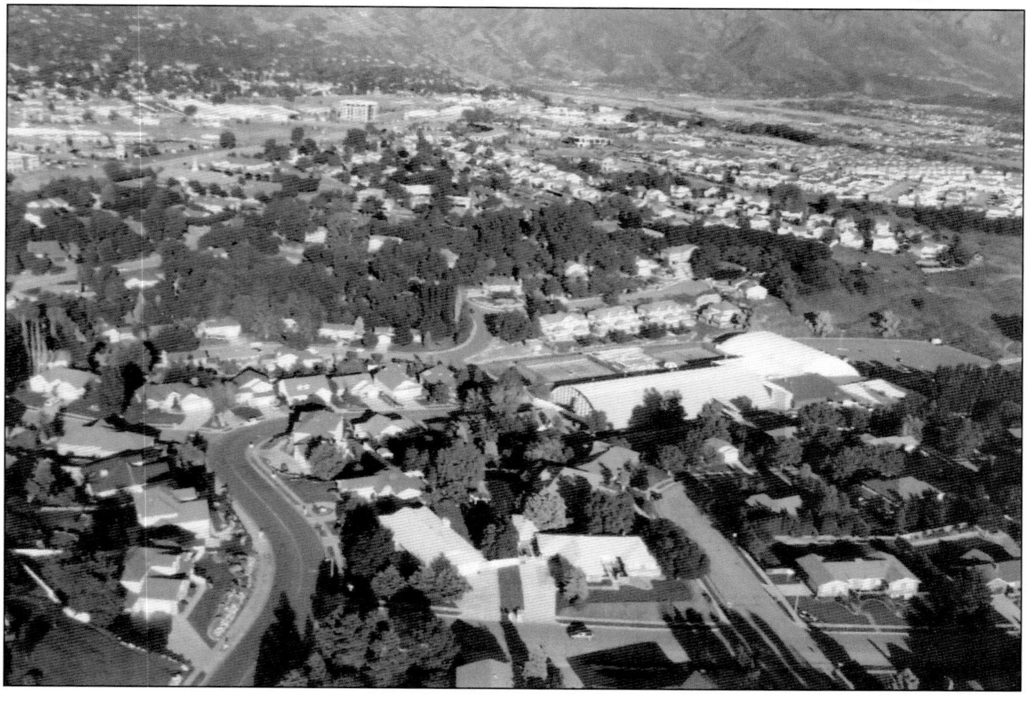

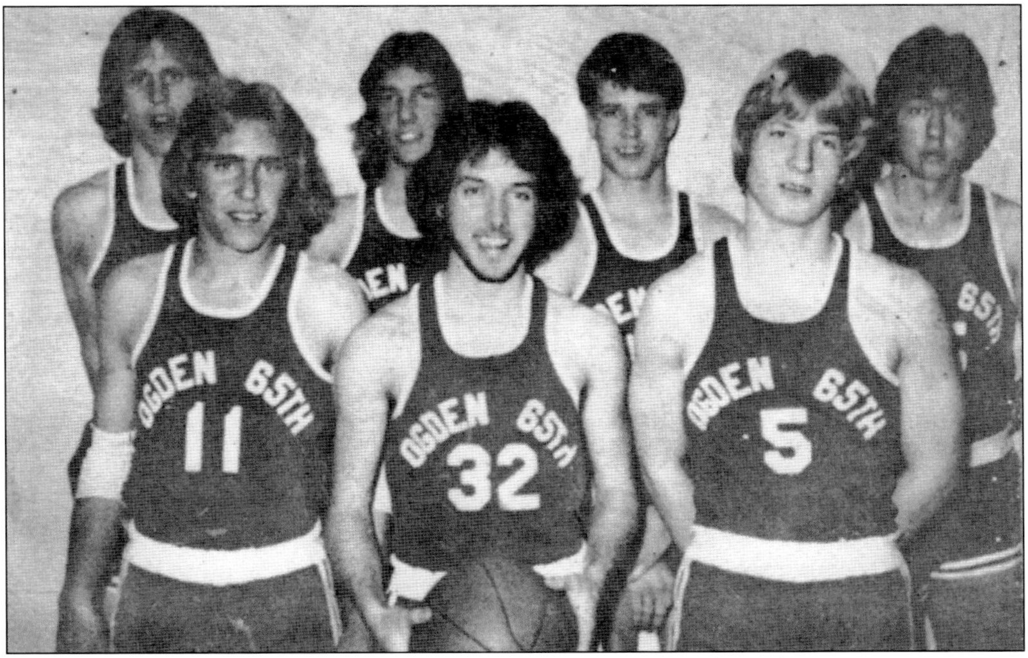

The South Ogden 65th Ward basketball team finished first in stake and region competition in 1978. The players are, from left to right, (first row) Greg Stimpson, Fred Schmidt, and Brad Lund; (second row) Dan Rich, Alan Davis, Brent Castlemain, and Chris Perry.

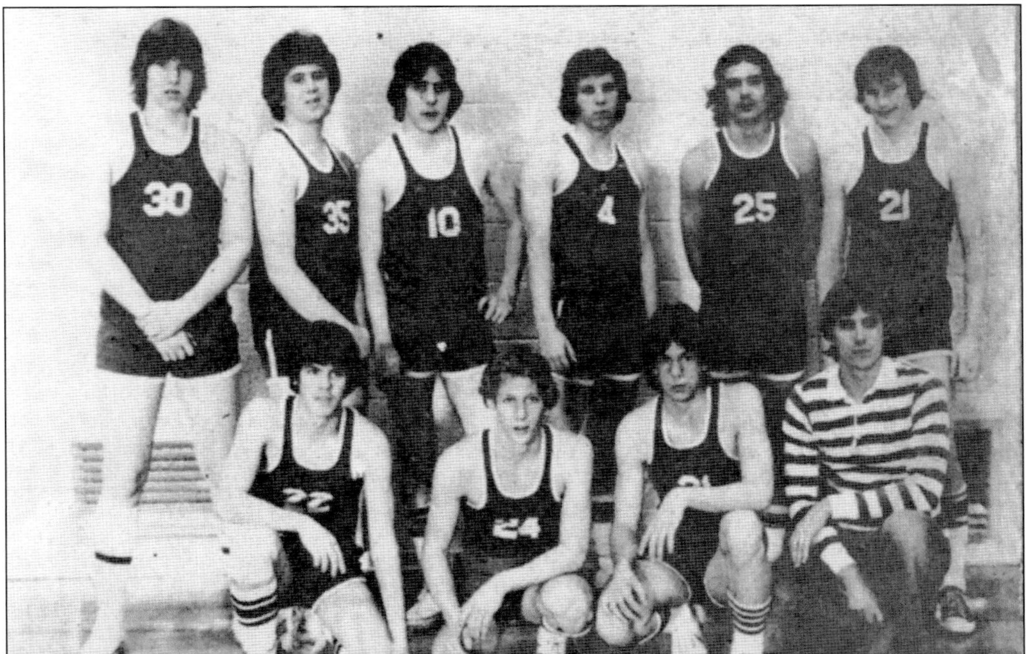

The South Ogden 38th Ward basketball team finished second in stake and region competition in 1978. The players are, from left to right, (first row) Kirk Hanni, Doug Clark, Kerry Moffett, and coach Karr J. West; (second row) Chris Hayball, Ricky Bateman, Keith Hess, Richard Rounds, Kerry Jensen, and Brian Carter.

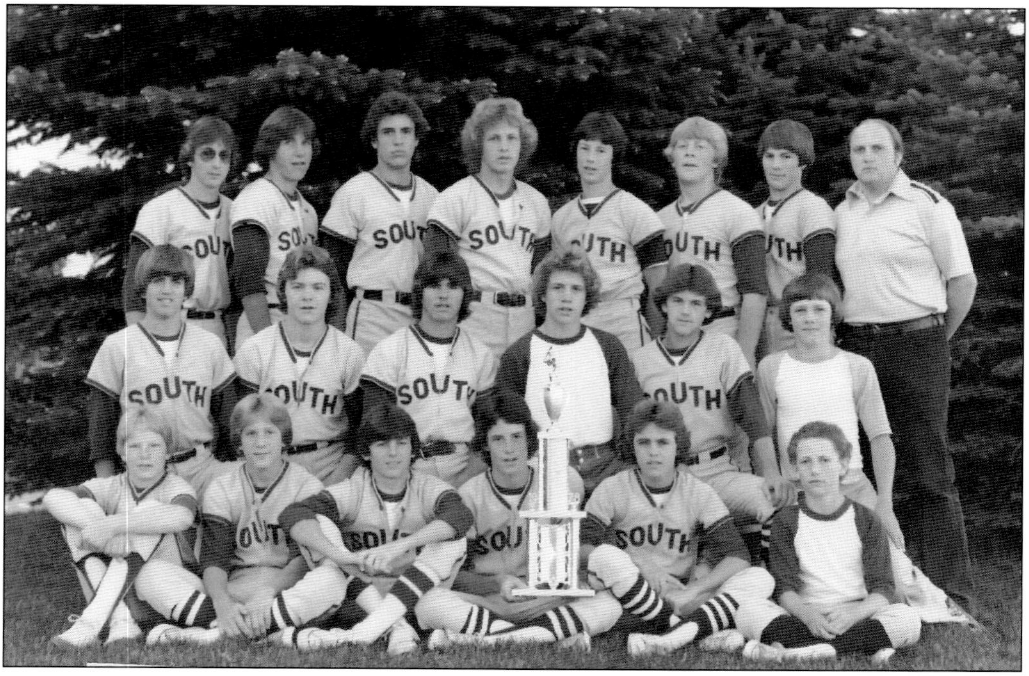

Pictured are the South Ogden Junior High School district baseball champs of 1978. They are, from left to right, (first row) Mark Rhead, Steve Draney, Jeff McFarland, Paul Booth, Ken Engeman, and Glade Porter; (second row) Jamie Hawkins, Kelly Larson, Tommy Land, Kevin Hadley, Kevin Bybee, and Greg Engeman; (third row) Doug Shepherd, Mike Wilson, Cory Buckway, Derk Sawley, Robb Hunt, Dan Hunter, Matt Roush, and coach Jerry Nelson. (Courtesy Paul Woodin.)

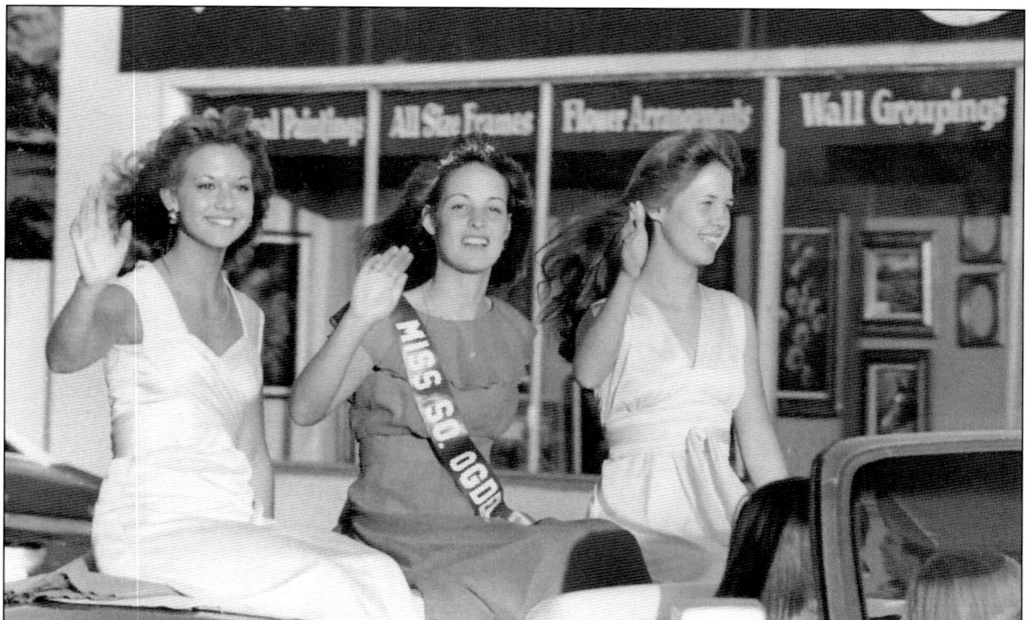

This photograph was taken during the July 4, 1978, parade down 40th Street. Pictured are, from left to right, Toni Van Houten, first attendant; Mary Ann McBurnie, Miss South Ogden; and Rebecca Fuller, second attendant.

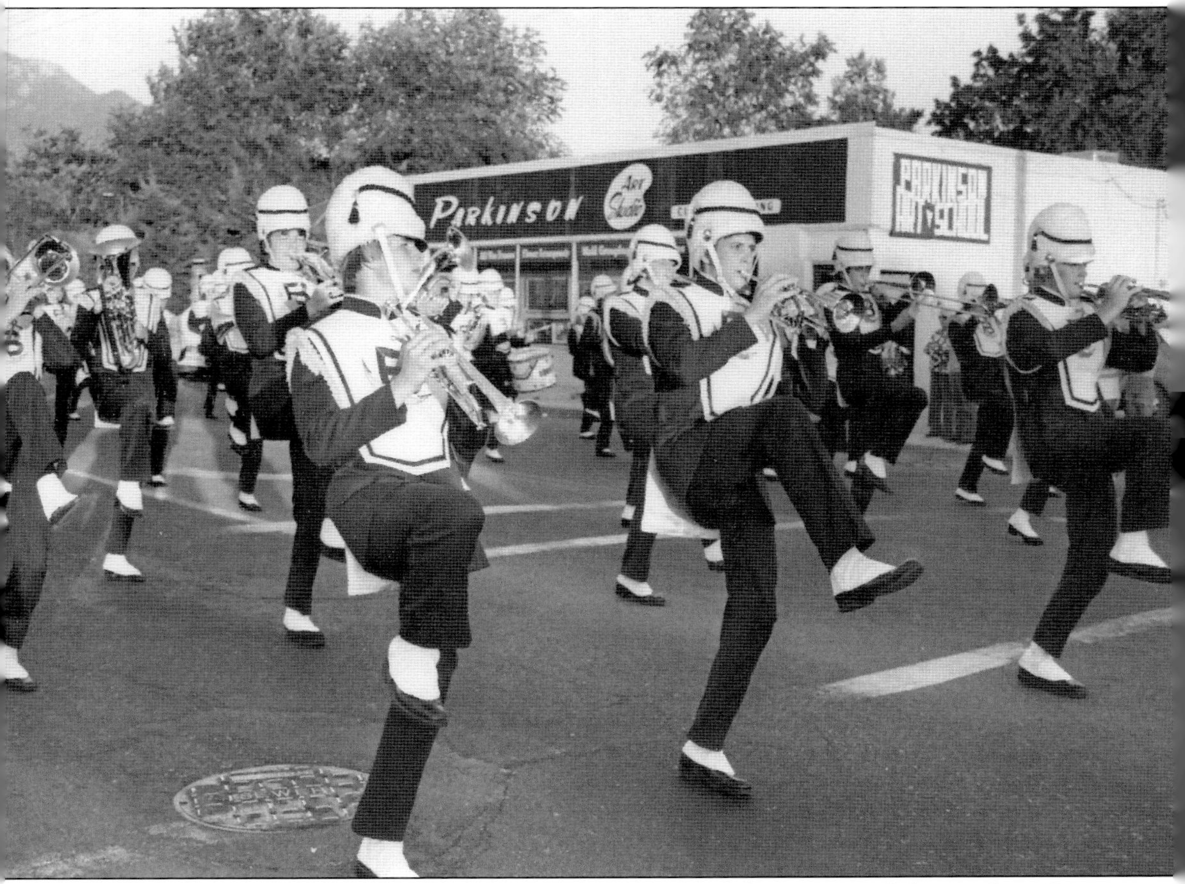

Members of the Bonneville High School Laker marching band are pictured during the 1978 Independence Day parade. In the background is Parkinson Art School, a city icon that stood on the corner of 40th Street and Adams Avenue from 1972 to 1990. A person driving on 40th Street has been able to see beautiful nature-style paintings in the windows from the early 1970s to the present. Prior to Parkinson's, Frost Market, owned and run by Ivan Frost and his wife, Edith, did business on that corner, beginning in 1944. The Frosts loved having the kids from Burch Creek School come in to buy candy and toys and selling dairy products and groceries to the locals. The Frost Market slogan was, "Where Friends Meet." The site is currently home of Artist Touch, an art and framing business owned by mother and son team, Sandra and Don Ashby.

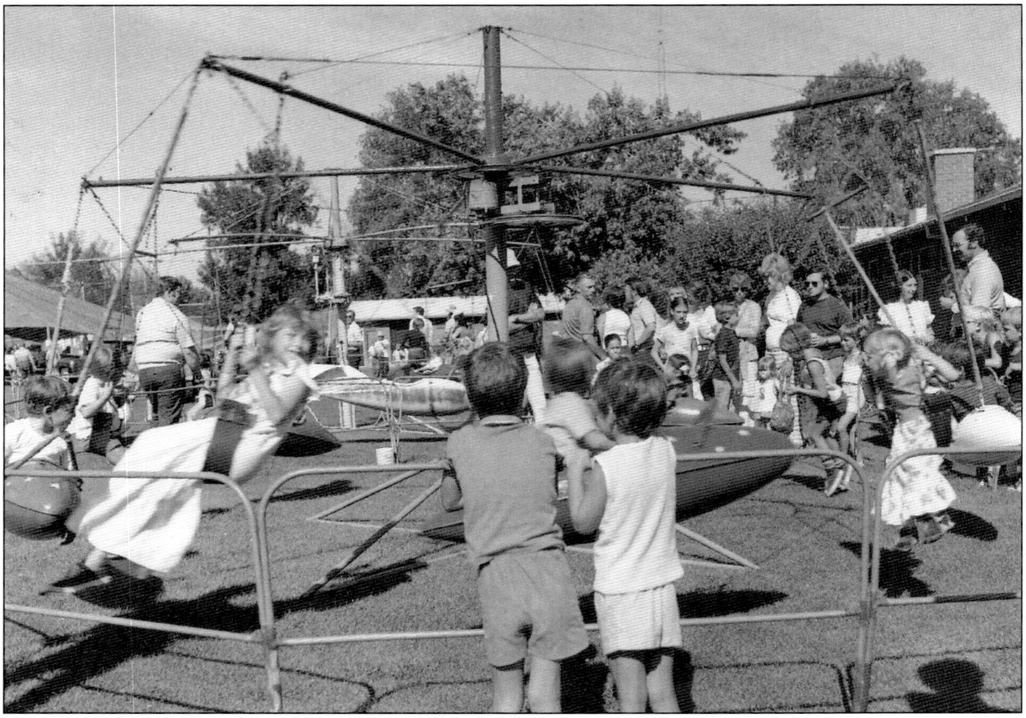

Area youth are photographed in 40th Street Park after the Independence Day parade. A South Ogden tradition for decades was for the parade to finish at the park, where people of all ages enjoyed the many games, rides, concerts, various booths, and nighttime fireworks. These photographs from the late 1970s are typical of the fun activities available on a yearly basis. Currently, the festivities are held at Friendship Park during South Ogden Days, generally the fourth week of June. It is a much anticipated week of events. "Where Summer Begins" is the slogan, and not only have the booths and concerts continued, but car shows, movies in the park, three-on-three basketball, and mud volleyball have been added.

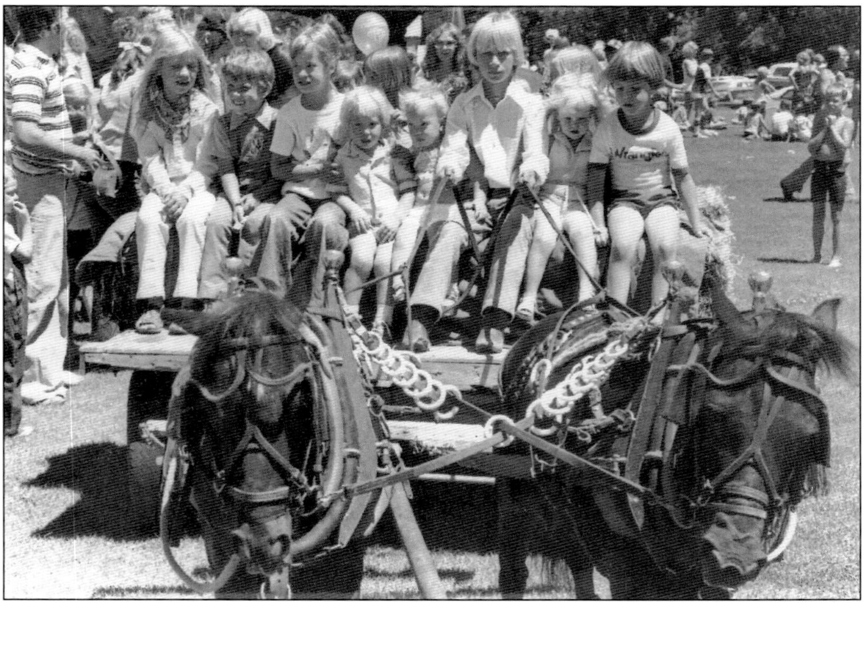

Five

1980s

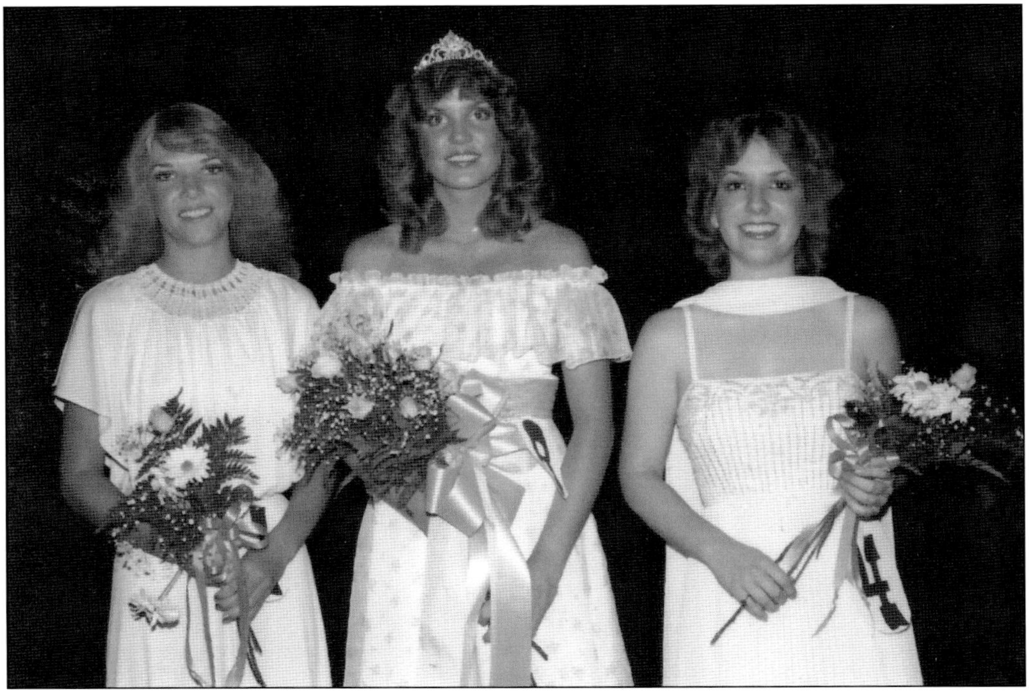

This is the royalty of the June 27, 1980, Miss South Ogden Scholarship Pageant. The girls are, from left to right, first attendant, Linda Burdett, daughter of Dr. Fred and Helen Burdett; Miss South Ogden 1990, Lisa Matthews, daughter of Mr. and Mrs. Jesse Matthews; and second attendant, Jan Richards, daughter of Richard and Annette Richards.

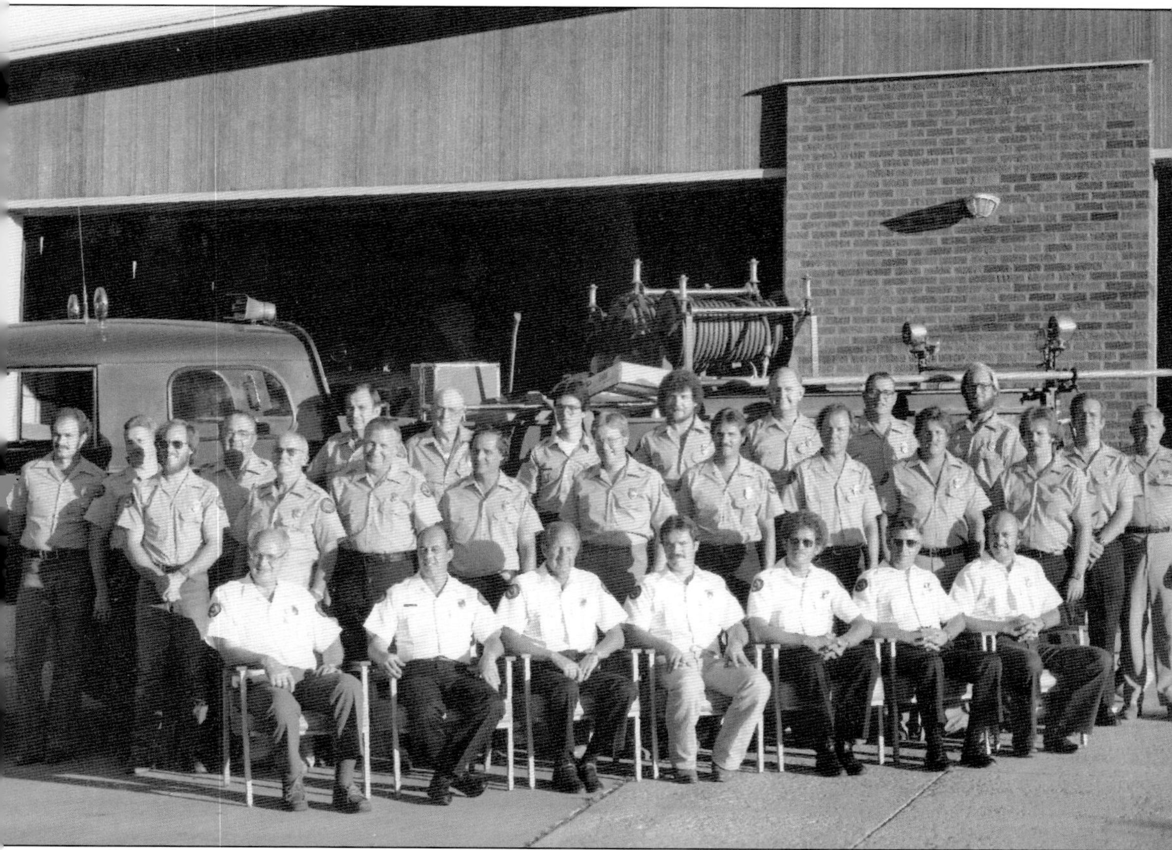

This July 10, 1980, photograph is of the South Ogden Fire Department outside the station on 39th Street. They are, from left to right, (first row) Chief Lamar Scadden, Jim Minster, Don Wintle, Steve Taylor, Don Nye, Bill Powell and Joe Hill; (second row) Jim Harris, Leonard Fox, Bob Marz, Val Hale, Steve Porter, Randy Blackett, Steve Bideaux, unidentified, and Ray Gilbert; (third row) Alan Bybee, Don Bateman, Eldon Checketts, Alvin Carter, Emory Taylor, Dave Hales, Gary Evans, Roy Van Drimmelen, Gene Bateman, Lynn Scadden, Jim Tenney, and Paul Tesch. These following men had been or would be fire chief: Robert Marz, Lamar Scadden, Eldon Checketts, Roy Van Drimmelen, and Paul Tesch. (Courtesy Denise Taylor.)

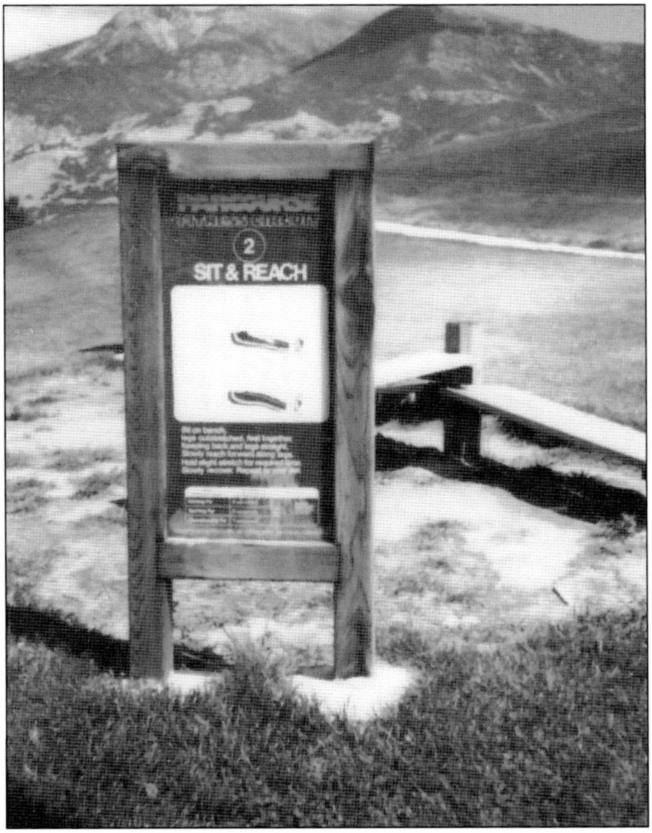

This photograph is of stop No. 2 on the "par course," a one-mile exercise and jogging track with 10 stations at intervals along the way. The course was built on the South Ogden Junior High School grounds and was used by students as part of their physical education course and by community members. Sherm Smith, chairman of the Marlon Hills community council, spearheaded the project, getting much help from his council members and the newly formed senior citizens council.

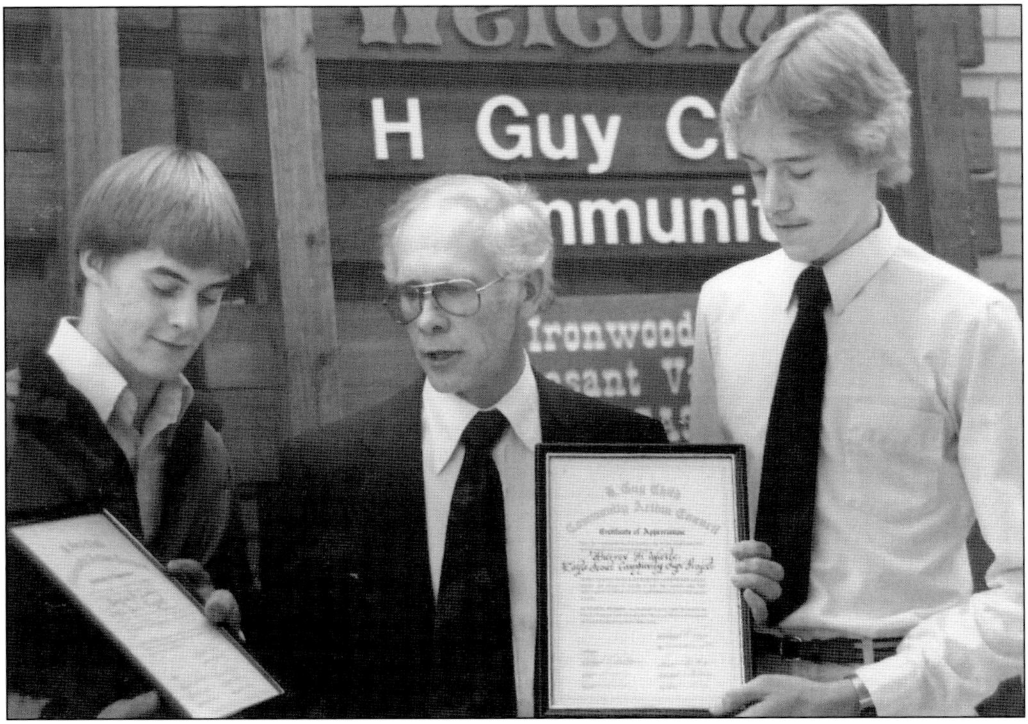

H. Guy Child Community Council president David Terry presents plaques to Doug Elwood (left) and Darin Waite (right) in 1982. The young men had recently completed Eagle Scout projects that benefitted the local community. South Ogden City has always had a strong relationship with the Boy Scouts of America.

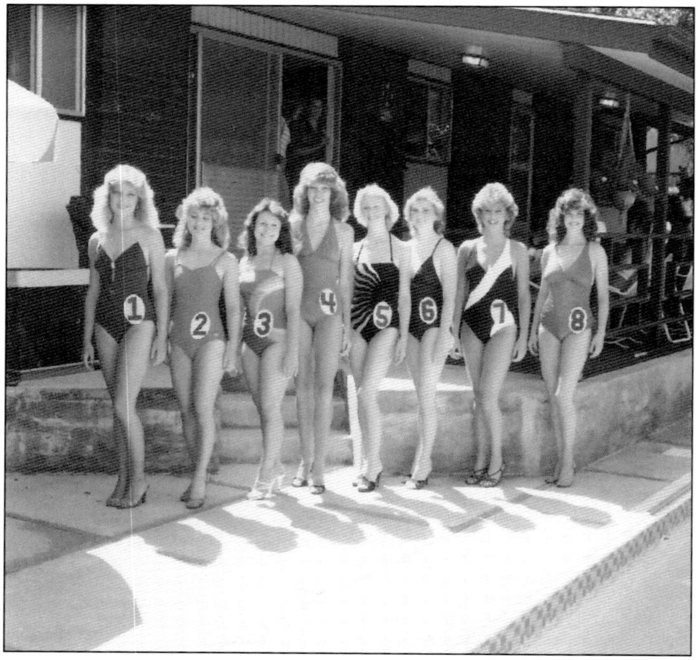

These eight candidates are vying for Miss South Ogden 1982. This photograph was taken on June 30 next to the pool at the Evertson home. The girls are, from left to right, Jodi Jones, Jeannie Larsen, Dorie Richards, Sandy Pettigrew, Judy Olson, Bonnie Stevenson, Lisa Rothey, and Michelle Terry. At pageant's end, Michelle Terry was named Miss South Ogden, with Lisa Rothey and Jodi James first and second runners-up.

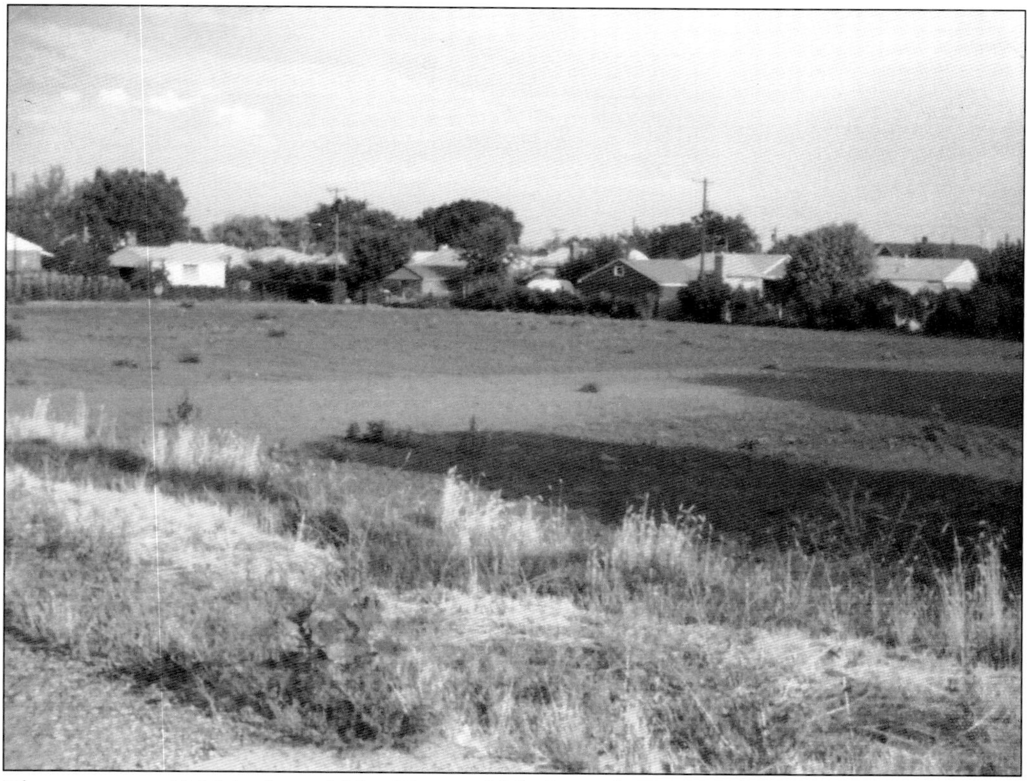

The property of Makinojo and Ishi Oka, on 39th Street between Adams Avenue and Orchard Avenue, is pictured in 1983; it would be the eventual site of a new city hall. The Oka vegetable farm was 10 acres at one point in history, stretching between Adams and Jefferson Avenues from 38th to 39th Streets. People traveled from near and far to buy vegetables grown on the Oka Farm.

Ida Mae Bankhead stands by the construction site of the city's third city hall in March 1983. Bankhead worked for the city for over 20 years, as a clerk from 1972 to 1980, then as city treasurer from 1980 until 1993. It was through her scrapbooking at city hall that many of the images seen in this book were saved and made available.

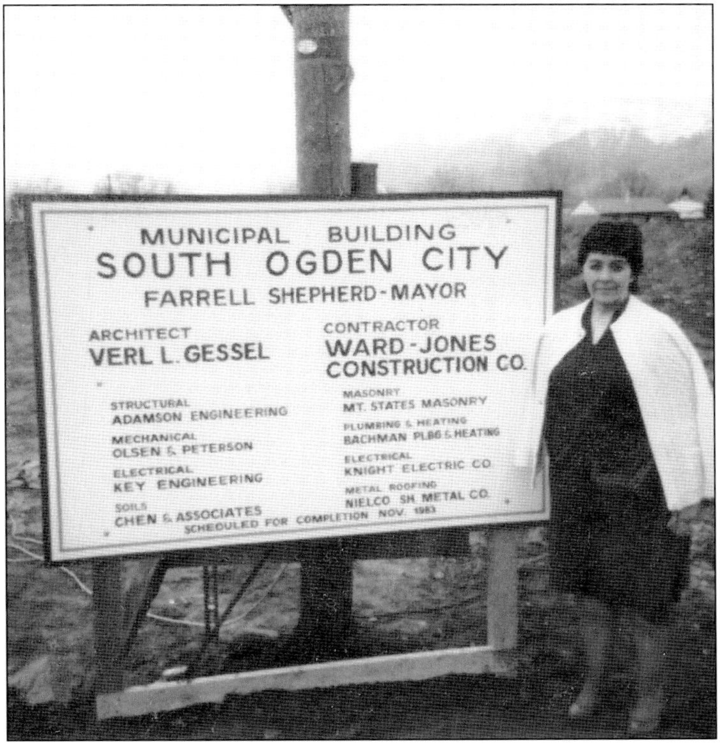

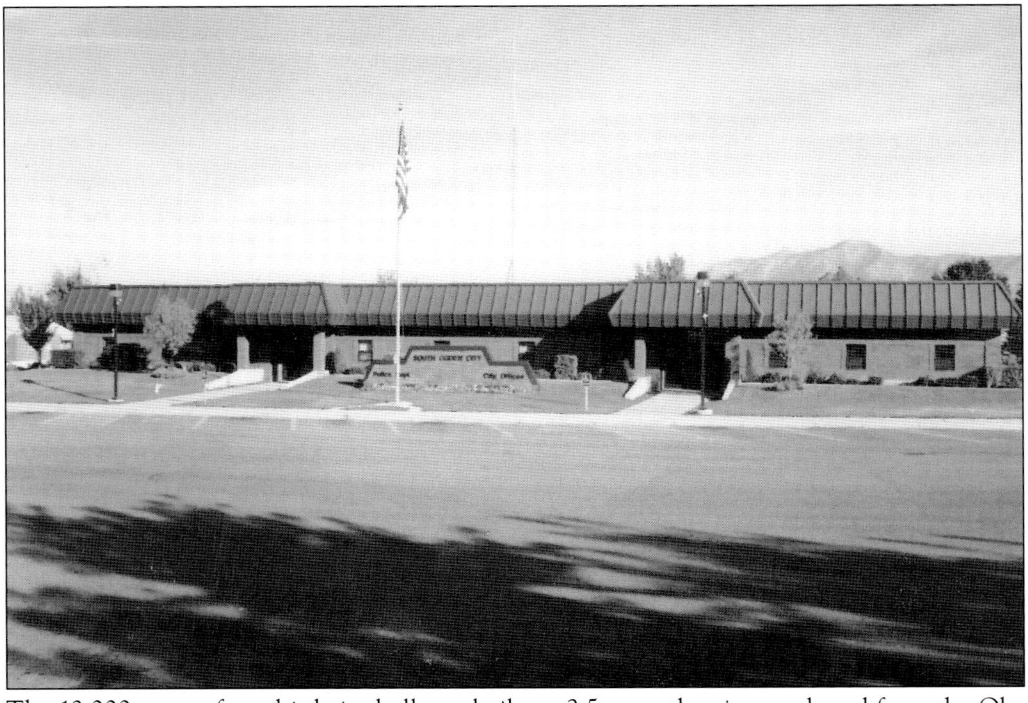

The 12,000-square-foot third city hall was built on 2.5 acres the city purchased from the Oka family in 1978. The structure housed the administrative offices, city council chambers, city court offices, planning and zoning offices, and the police department rooms and lab. The offices officially opened on November 24, 1983.

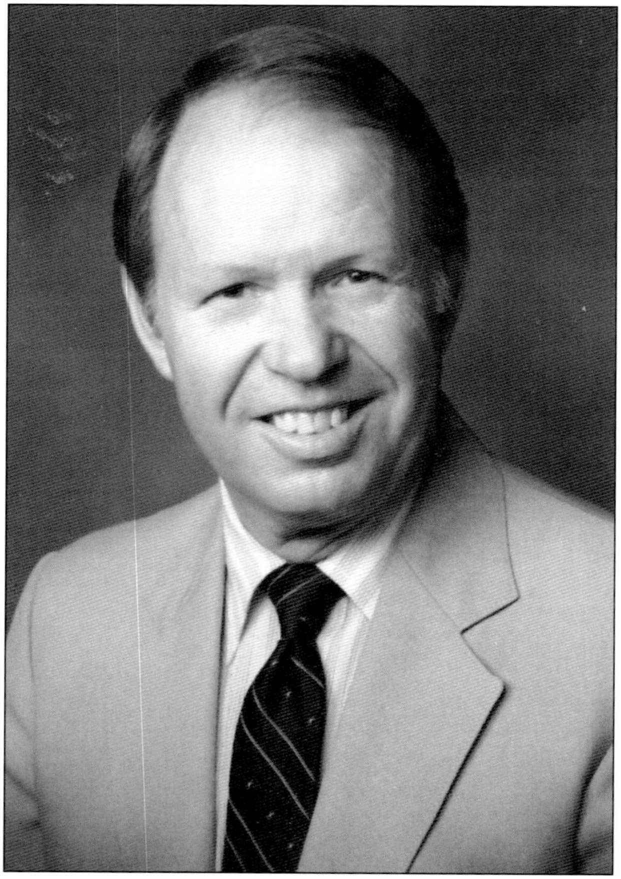

After 12 years on the city council, Ralph L. Cottrell Jr. was appointed mayor in 1984. The appointment was made necessary when Mayor Shepherd left before his term ended to serve a mission for the Church of Jesus Christ of Latter-day Saints. Cottrell served the remaining two years of the term, leaving elected office with the election of Lew A. Wangsgard in 1985.

This photograph taken in May 1985 is of some of the city staff; the group was also serving as the parade committee for that year. They are, from left to right, (first row) Kathy Van Drimmelen, Cheryl Rankin, Linda Miller, and city treasurer Ida Mae Bankhead; (second row) city manager F. Stanley Nielsen, recreation director Ken Cottle, and Wesley Coates.

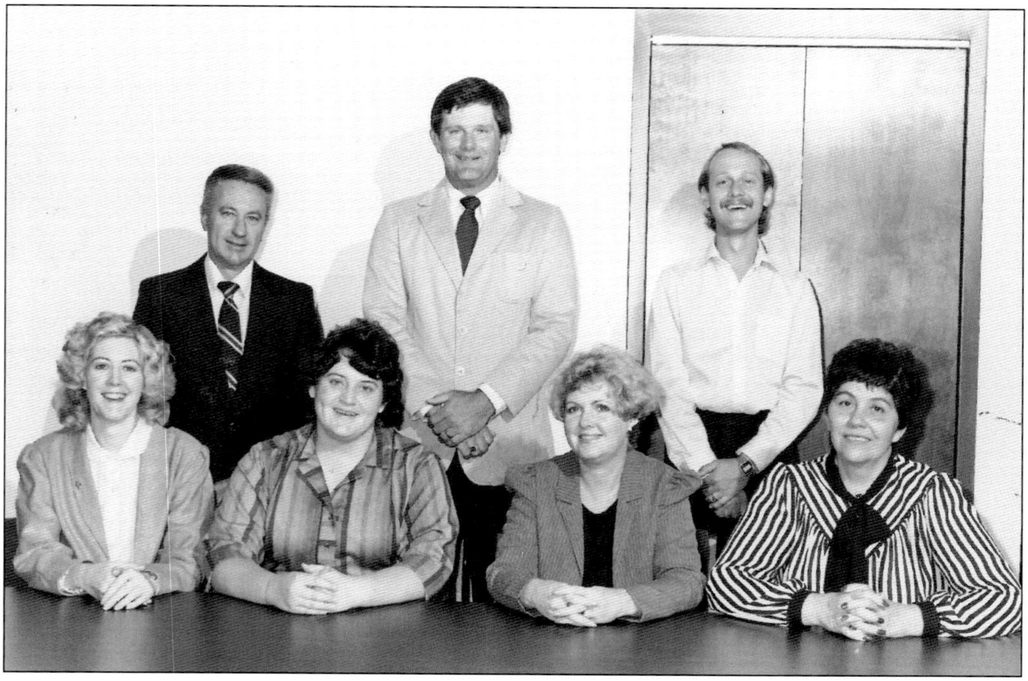

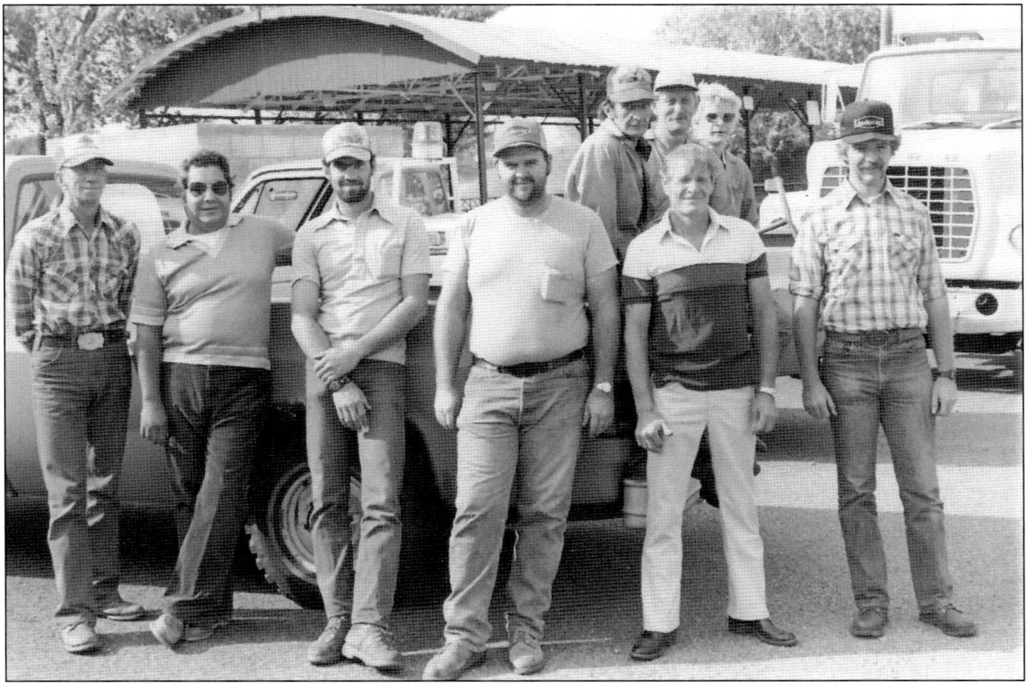

South Ogden City maintenance crew is pictured in May 1985. From left to right are (first row) Bill Shafer, Lorenzo Garcia, Raymond Hinds, Randy Rochell, public works director Glen Moore, and Bruce Miller; (second row) Vern Kilfoyle, William Pont, and Greg Layton.

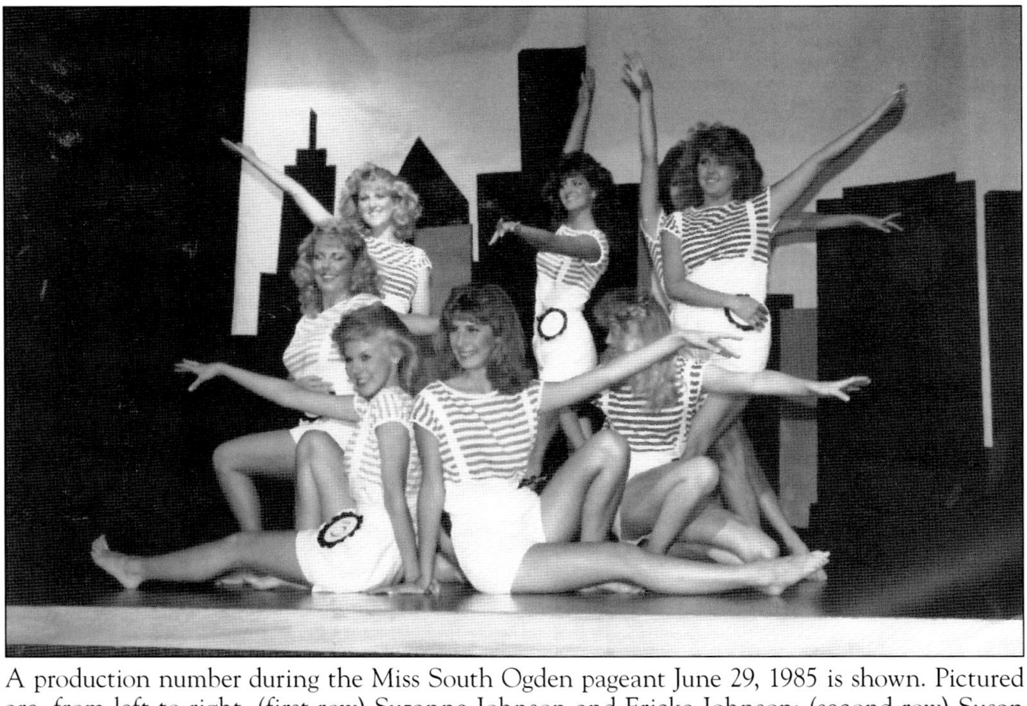

A production number during the Miss South Ogden pageant June 29, 1985 is shown. Pictured are, from left to right, (first row) Suzanne Johnson and Ericka Johnson; (second row) Susan Swenson and Shelly England; (third row) Julie Webber, Nicole Sylvester, Camille Hodson, and Dina Engeman. Nicole Sylvester was named Miss South Ogden at the end of the night.

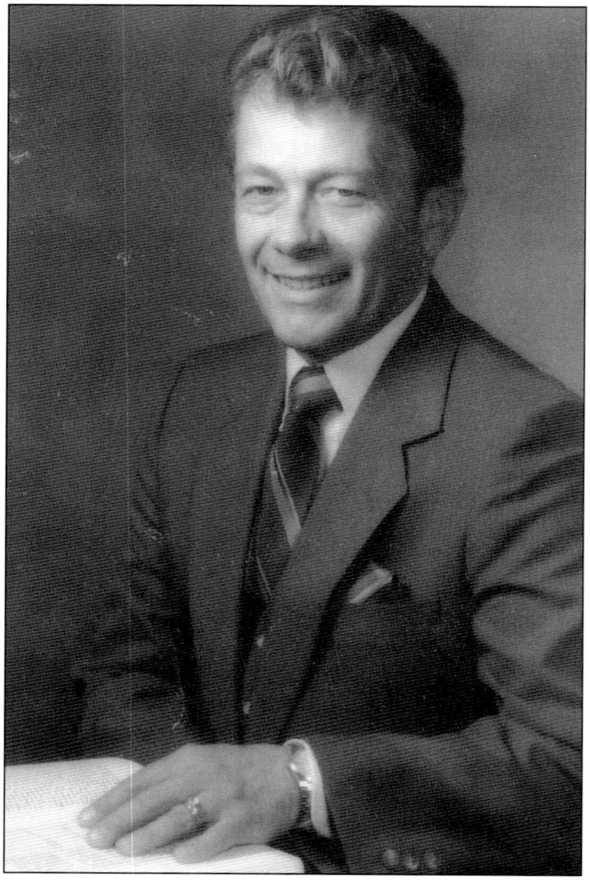

Lew A. Wangsgard was South Ogden mayor from 1986 to 1989. Wangsgard, a native of South Ogden, had never been in politics before being elected mayor. He just considered himself a civil engineer who had an interest in his community. Early in Wangsgard's term, he also served as city manager until one was hired. One thing accomplished through Wangsgard's time in elected office was the inviting redbrick bridge built over the Burch Creek on 44th Street.

Seven contestants for Miss South Ogden are pictured during the formal wear portion of the June 27, 1986, scholarship pageant. The girls are, from left to right, Suzanne Johnson, Natalie Weathers, Amber Bryan, Pam Wright, Nancy Moyle, Julie Beesley, and D'Ann Evans. At night's end, Suzanne Johnson was named queen, D'Ann Evans first attendant, and Nancy Moyle second attendant.

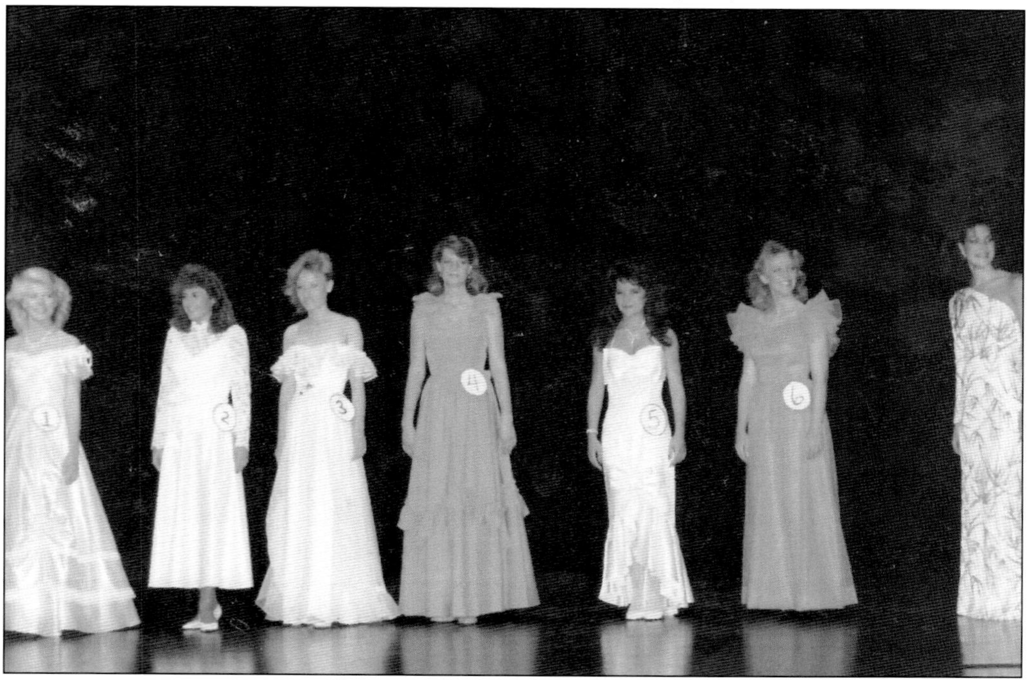

Six

1990s

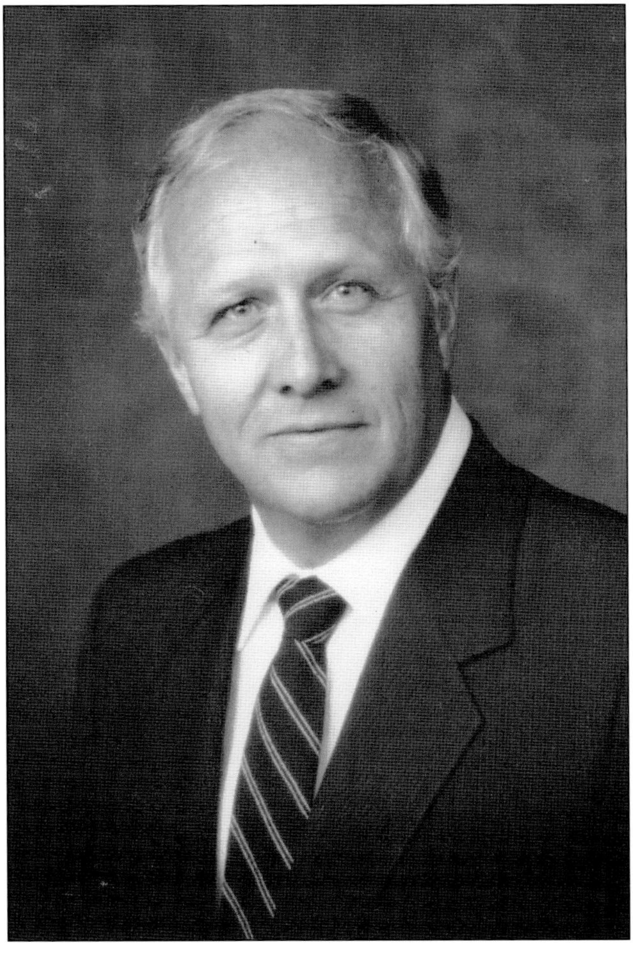

Brent H. Frost was South Ogden mayor from 1990 to 1993. During Frost's time as mayor, a ballot measure was proposed to consolidate South Ogden and Washington Terrace into one city, Bonneville City. Proponents often cited the hundreds of thousands of dollars that would be saved by the merger, as services would be consolidated. Opponents generally did not want to change traditional names or boundaries. The ballot measure failed during the November 1992 election.

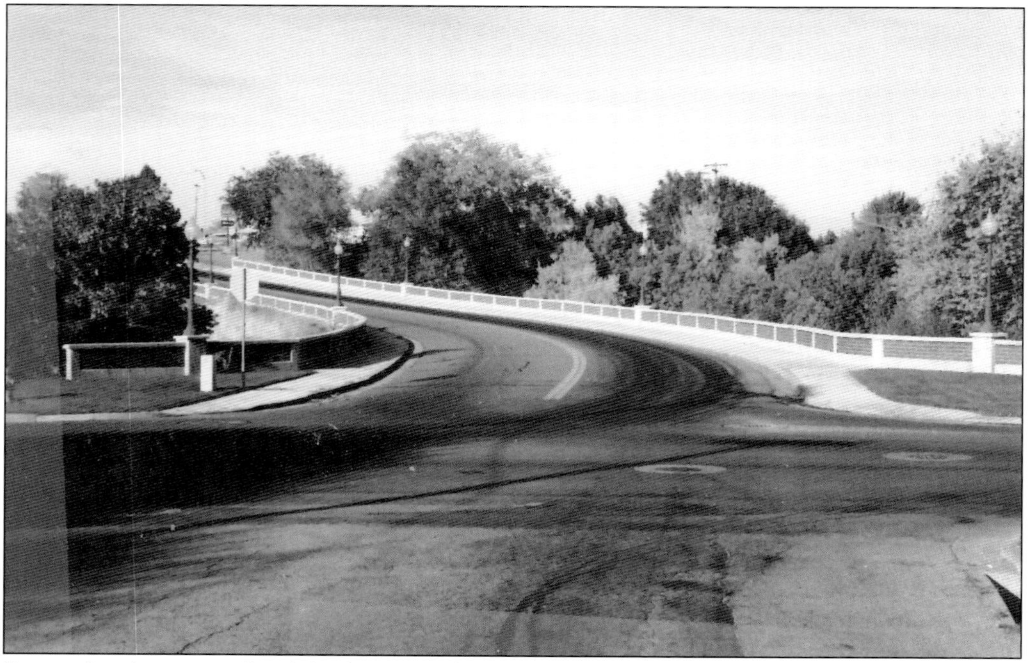

Pictured is the new redbrick bridge on 44th Street between Washington Boulevard and Adams Avenue. The bridge spans Burch Creek, a waterway that begins in Strong's Canyon, east of the city in the Wasatch Mountain. The creek is named for Daniel Burch, a Mormon immigrant who, in 1848, was one of the first to settle the area that became South Ogden.

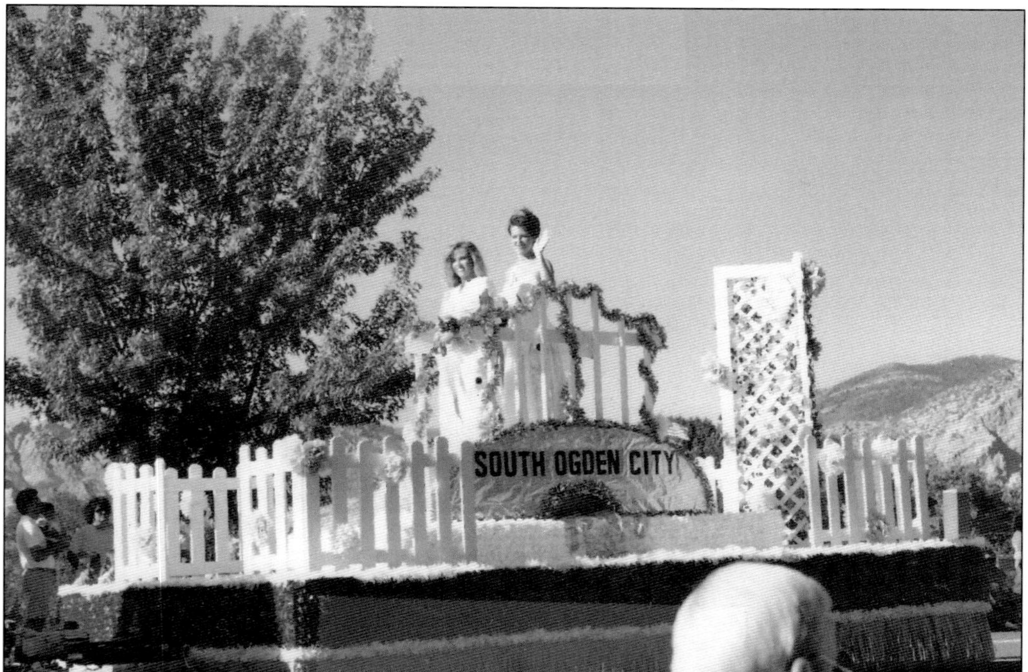

South Ogden City float is pictured during the 1991 Independence Day parade. The float is carrying Miss South first runner-up Ogden Darcie Quist (left), the daughter of Larry and Jay Ann Quist and the 1991 Miss South Ogden Stacie Edwards (right), daughter of Scott and Kris Edwards.

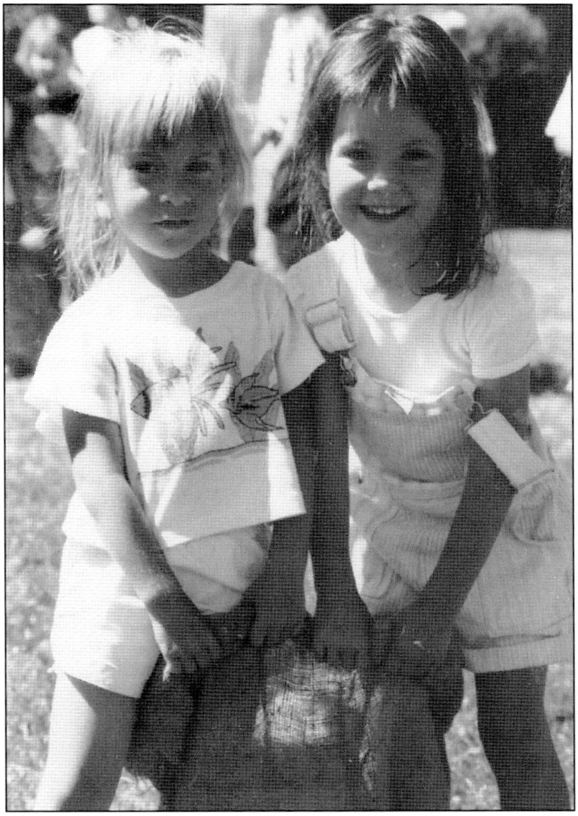

Two cute girls (pictured on the right) get ready for the three-legged gunny sack race across 40th Street. Below, other girl teams race south across the park grass toward the finish line. Before South Ogden hired a full-time special events coordinator, different city employees and community volunteers would serve on the South Ogden Days committees. This led to varied and unique activities every year. No matter who was in charge, the festivities in the park were highly anticipated by the kids in the city.

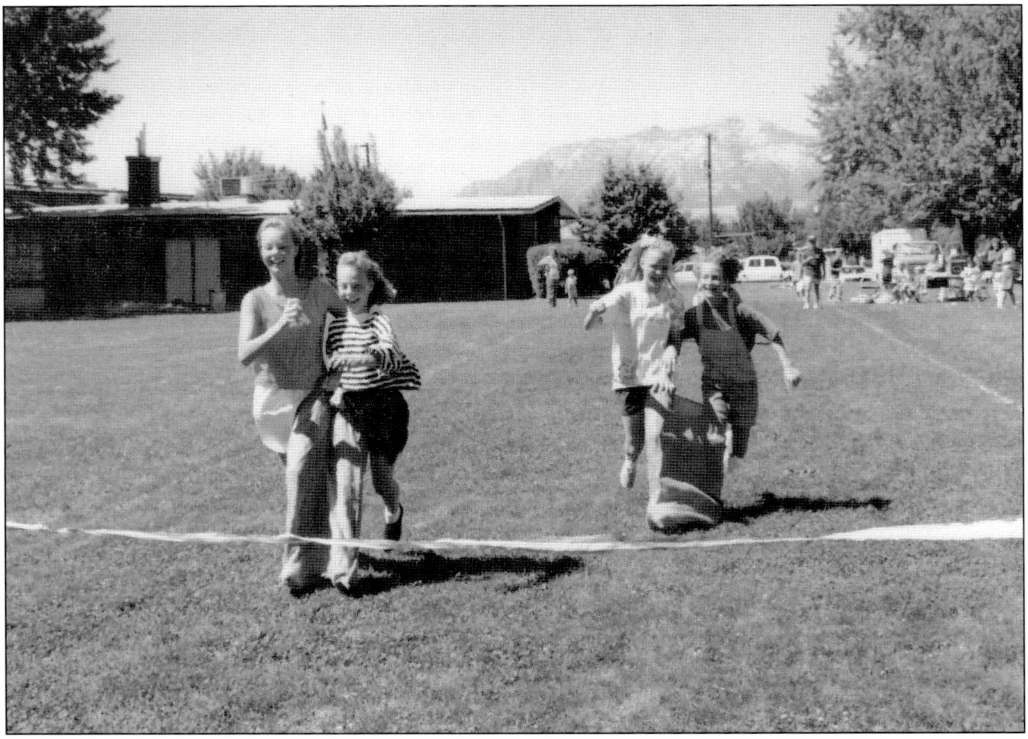

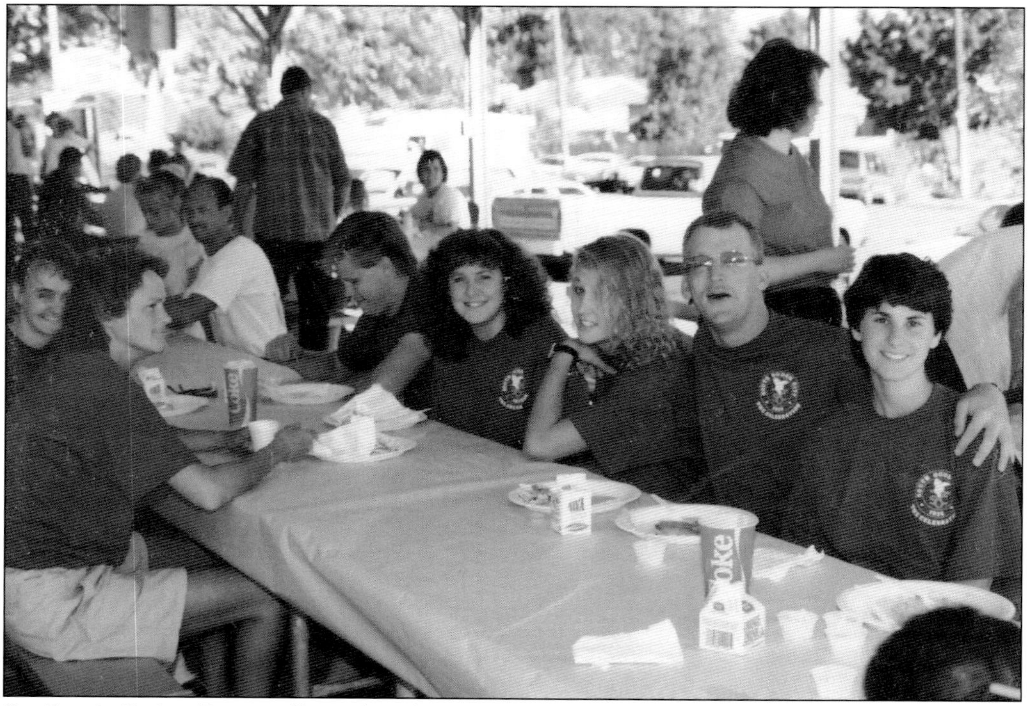

Six South Ogden Days staff members have lunch together wearing matching blue shirts in the bowery of 40th Street Park in 1991 (above). Below, a staff member judges a youth pie-eating contest. The best part about a pie-eating contest is even the losers are winners because they get to eat pie.

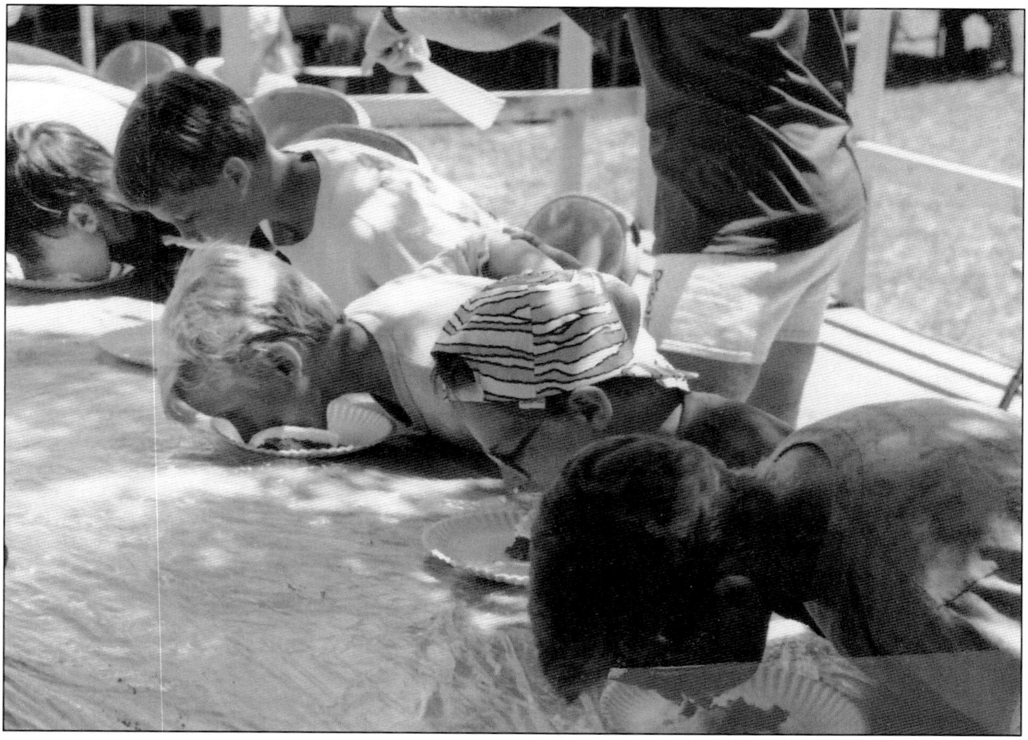

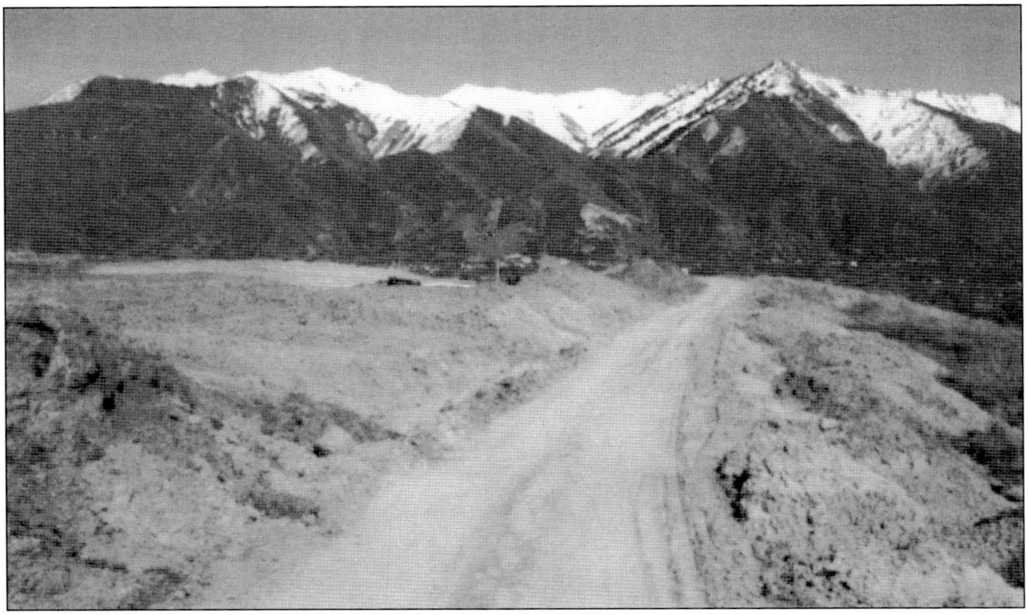

These are before and after photographs of Chimney Hill. Above, construction on the private residential use development (PRUD) began in 1992 with Steven D. Bailey as the general contractor. Below is a 2006 view of some of the 78 units in the development. (Both, courtesy Bill Parker.)

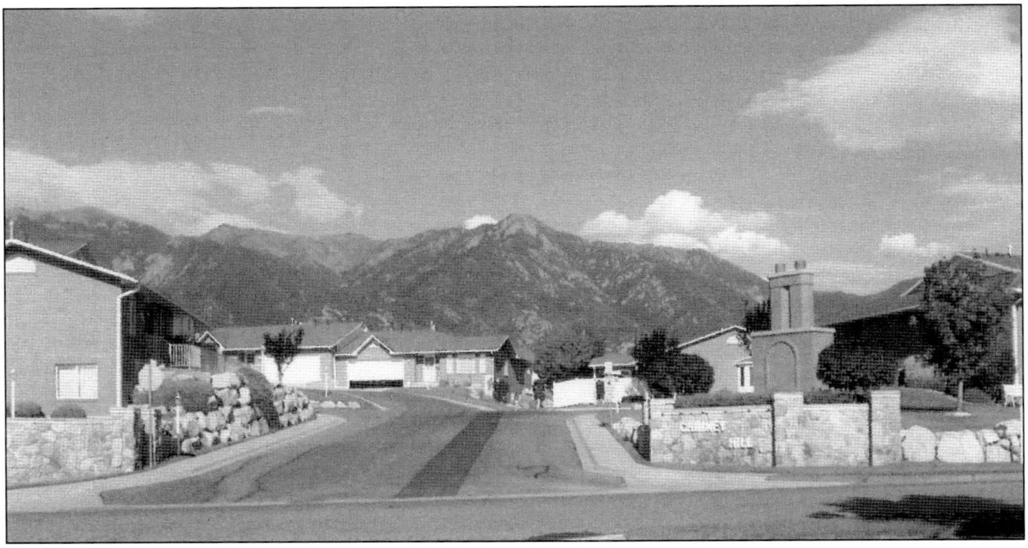

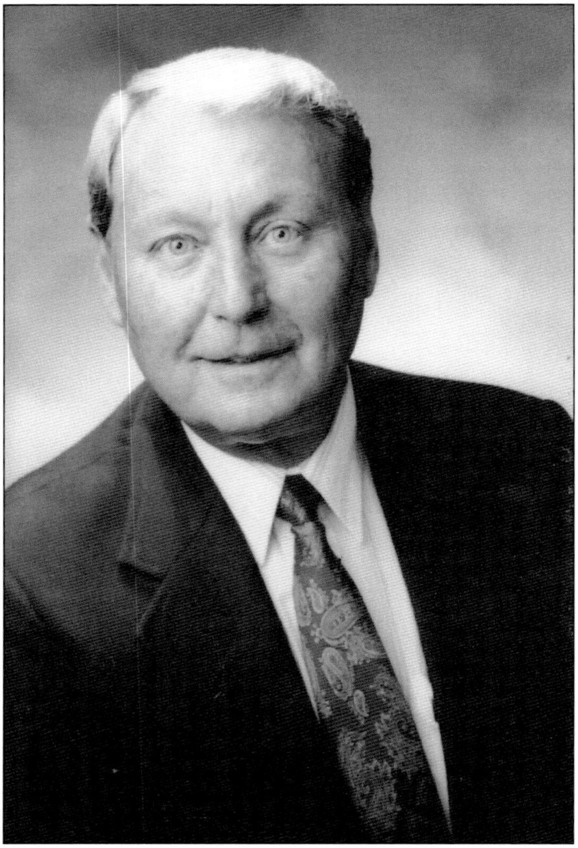

George Goodell was elected mayor in 1993 and served from 1994 to 2001. Goodell was elected mayor without previously being on the city council. Goodell was an Air Force veteran of the Korean War. Georgia Goodell, his wife, said his serving as mayor was one of the highlights of his life.

Pictured are the five members of the city council on inauguration day January 1996. From left to right are (seated) Kathy Van Drimmelen; (standing) Sandy Wright, George Garwood, Randall Parkinson, and Alma Richins. (Courtesy Denise Taylor.)

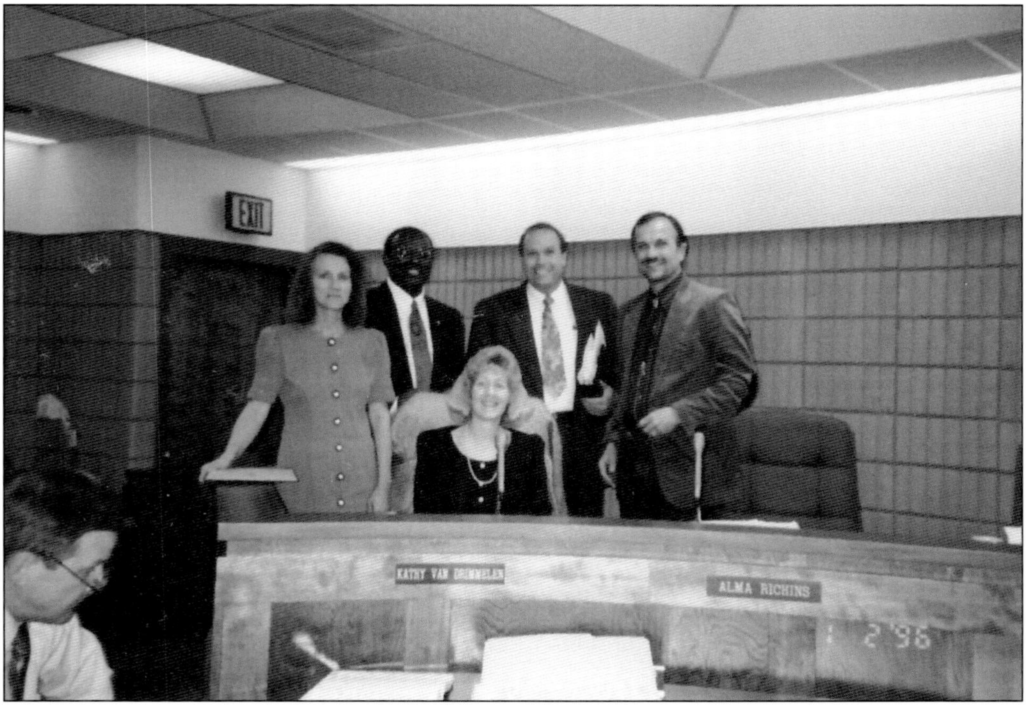

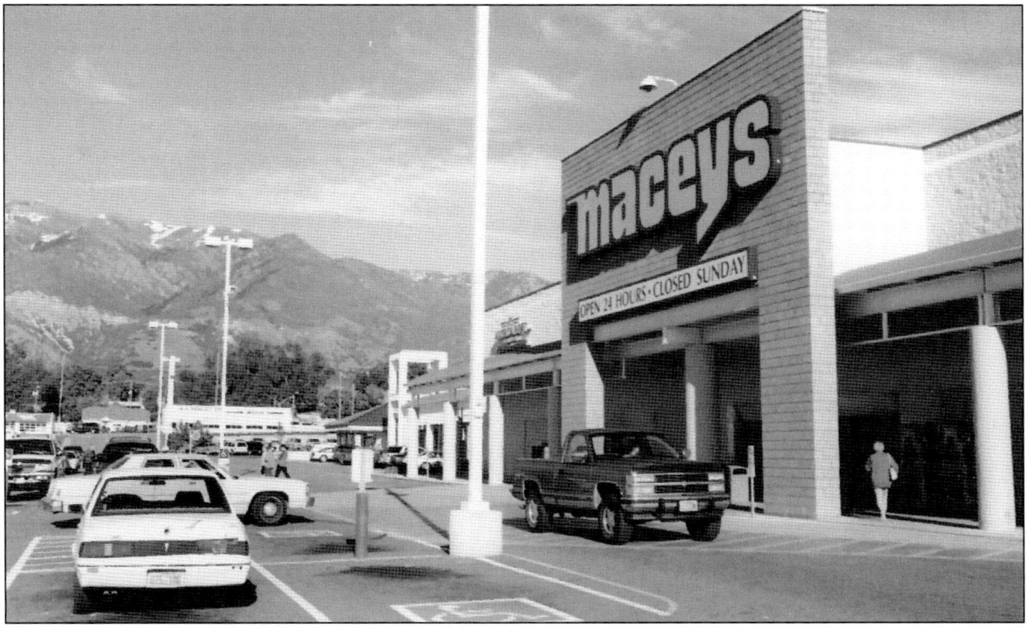

Macey's Grocery store opened at 36th Street and Riverdale Road in June 1996. Built in a Redevelopment Agency area, it has been a positive for the city since day one, being constructed in a previously blighted area. The store is also a big sponsor of South Ogden Days and other city events and is well known for the giant American flag that flies above the parking lot. (Courtesy Karen Kupfer.)

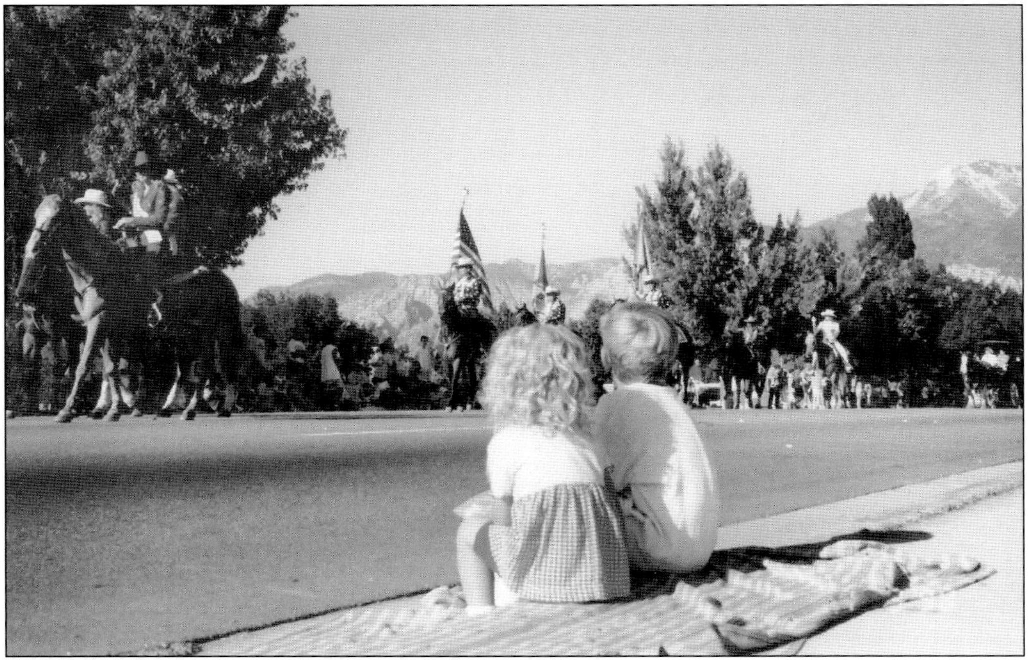

Cortney Porter (left) and her older brother Nicholas sit on the curb at 555 40th Street staring at the horseback-riding parade participants. This was the Independence Day parade, held on the evening of July 3, 1990. This was the last parade to be held on the evening before the Fourth of July. Starting in 1999, the parade is held on the fourth Wednesday of June. (Courtesy Sherri Porter.)

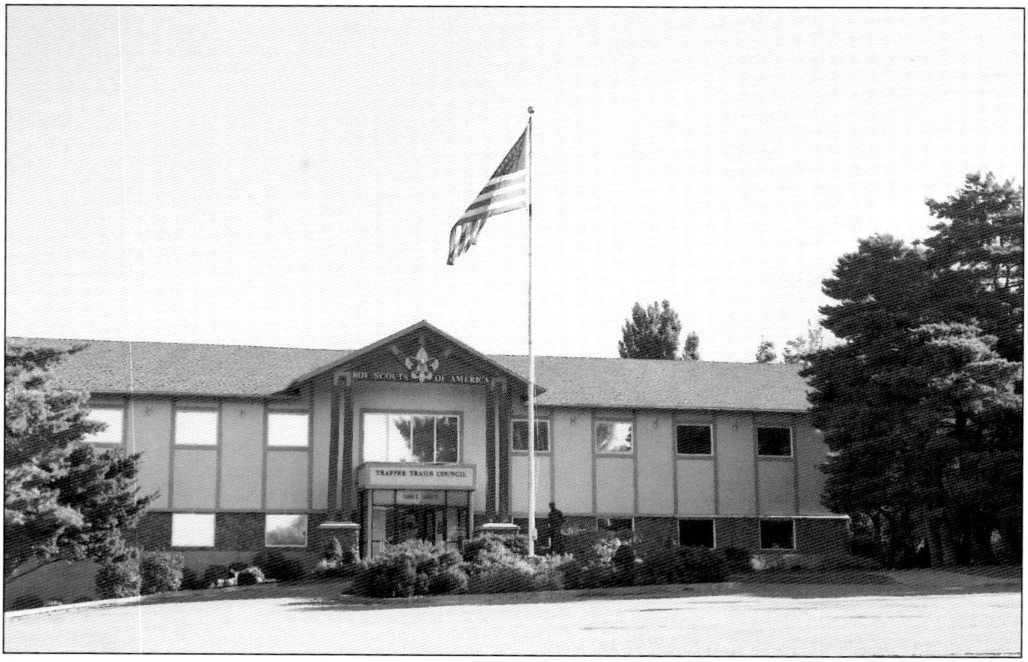

Above, a recent photograph shows the Trapper Trails Council service center for the Boy Scouts of America. This South Ogden landmark, located at 1200 East and 5400 South, was opened in 1965 as the Lake Bonneville Council service center. Frank M. Browning donated $100,000 to finance construction. Browning spoke at the dedication and Elder Thomas S. Monson gave the dedicatory prayer. Below is a recent photograph of the John M. Browning Armory, another longtime city landmark. Named in honor of the famous gun inventor and Ogden native, it is located at 625 East 5300 South. The armory was built in 1958 and is used by the Utah National Guard. Community functions and basketball leagues are also held in the building. (Both, courtesy Sherri Porter.)

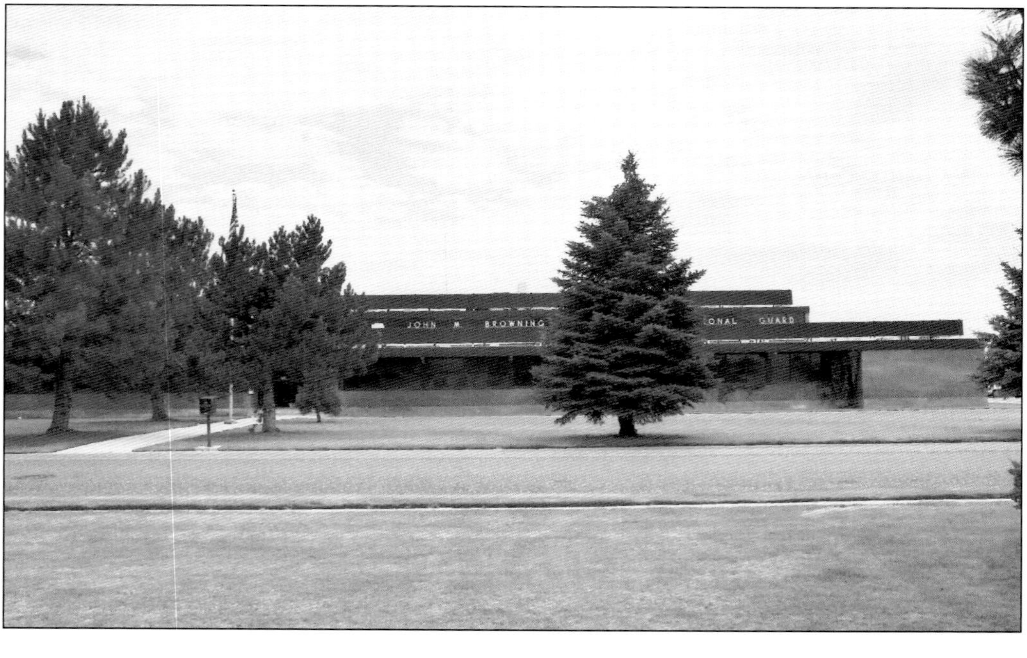

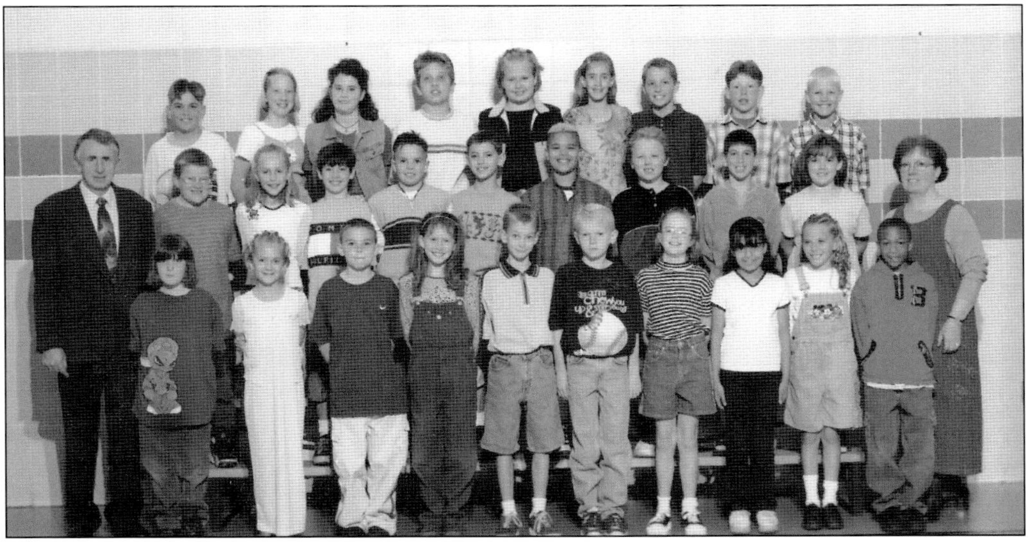

This is Janet Bailey's 1998–1999 fourth-grade class picture at Uintah Elementary. Pictured are, from left to right, (first row) Rachael Hughey, Julia Gibson, Mark Harris, Heather Olsen, Shad Bybee, Shay Underwood, Heidi Bybee, Cherish Martinez, Angela Stander, and Anthony Law; (second row) Principal Robert Wood, Troy Leininger, Nicole Bullard, Chris Shenefelt, Joshua Goff, James McCaskey, Jordan Lacey, C.J. Allen, Steven Christensen, Natalie Kimber, and teacher Janet Bailey; (third row) Joseph Pringle, Amy Kendell, Brittany Deges, Kurtis Coles, Porsche Bartholomew, Natalie Johnson, Von Bergen, Alec Stanczyk, and Tyson Land. (Courtesy Uintah Elementary.)

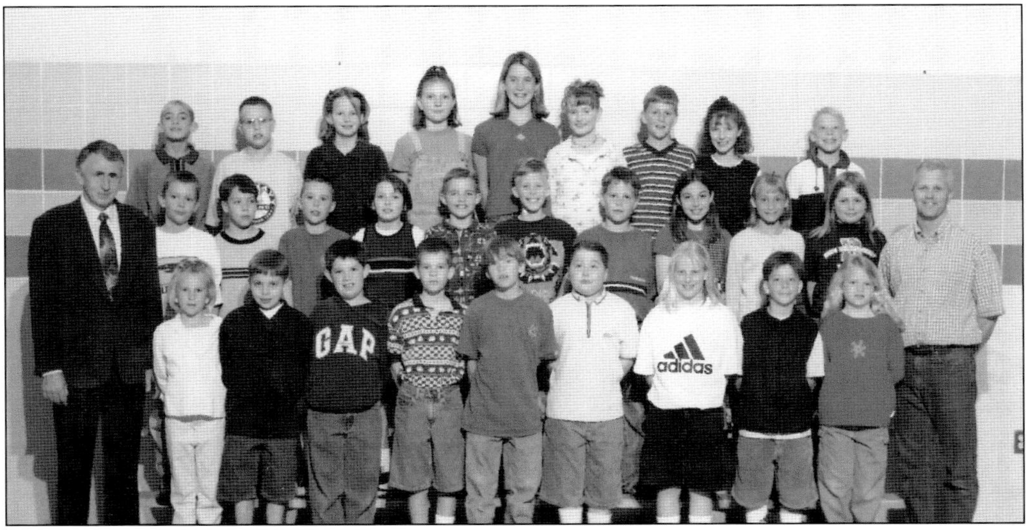

This is Kim Squires's 1998–1999 fourth-grade class picture at Uintah Elementary. Pictured are, from left to right, (first row) Jordan Muir, Alan Bishop, Brad Aven, Austin Burton, Omar Budge, Zach Howell, Halie Gundersen, Andy Pappas, and Ashli Gleed; (second row) Principal Robert Wood, Garrett Phillips, Kevin Proctor, Tyson Jorgensen, Jessica Wallace, Reyden Egbert, Joseph Holdaway, Layne Nelson, Shona Tondreau, Heather Cashmore, Karlee Covington, and teacher Kim Squires; (third row) John Christiansen, Zach Lyon, Cecelia Udy, Elizabeth Van Uitert, Kaci Cameron, Brittany Jaynes, Brian Galm, Jennica Vaughan, and Bryant Hall. (Courtesy Uintah Elementary.)

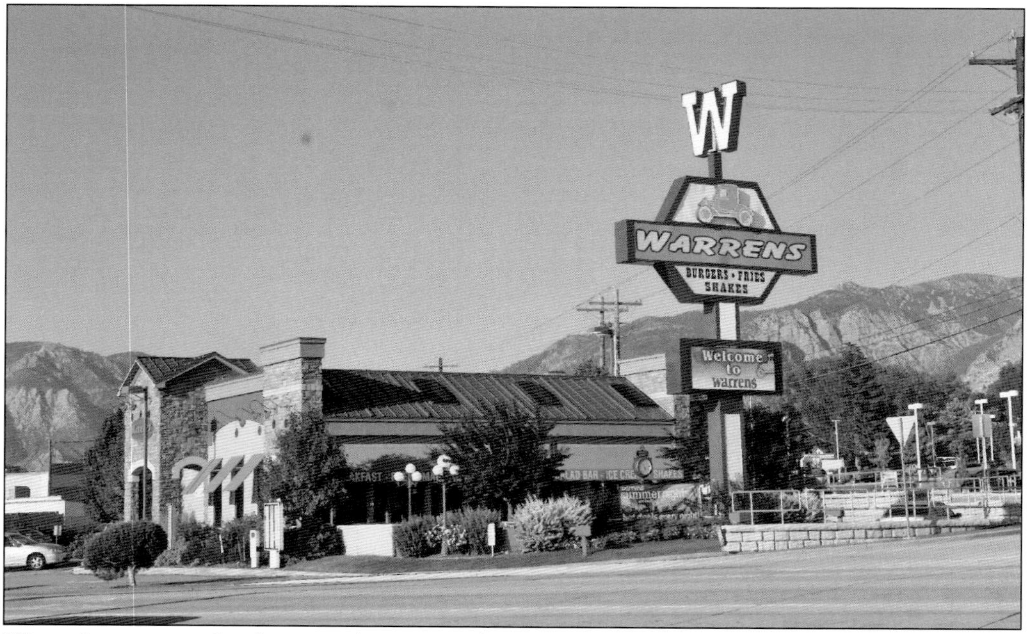

Warren's restaurant has been on the corner where Wall Avenue, Riverdale Road, and 40th Street meet for decades. Started by Doug Warren in the 1950s, then sold to Keith Combe in the 1960s, it has been the home of the Mount Ogden Burger and other popular fast food. In 2003, Kirk Dean purchased Warren's from the Combe family and has kept the traditions alive. (Courtesy Nicholas Porter.)

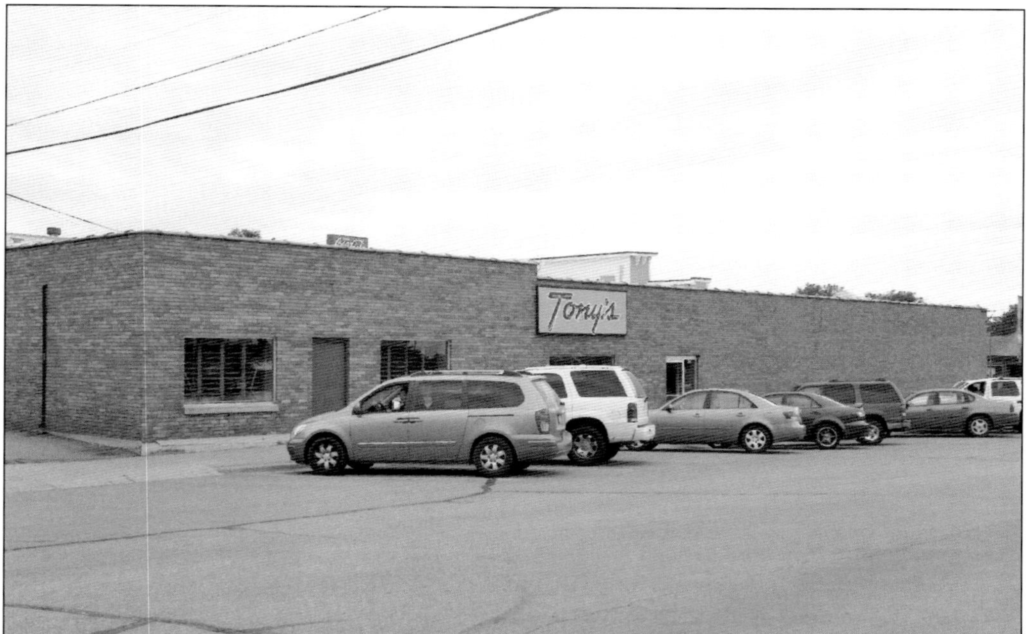

Tony L. Toscan started Tony's Pizza in 1975 at 403 39th Street. This is a recent photograph, but the building would look the same in one taken 20 or more years ago. It is safe to assume that every person in South Ogden has tasted a Tony's pizza, either inside the restaurant or one delivered from a youth fundraiser in the neighborhood. (Courtesy Sherri Porter.)

Seven

2000s

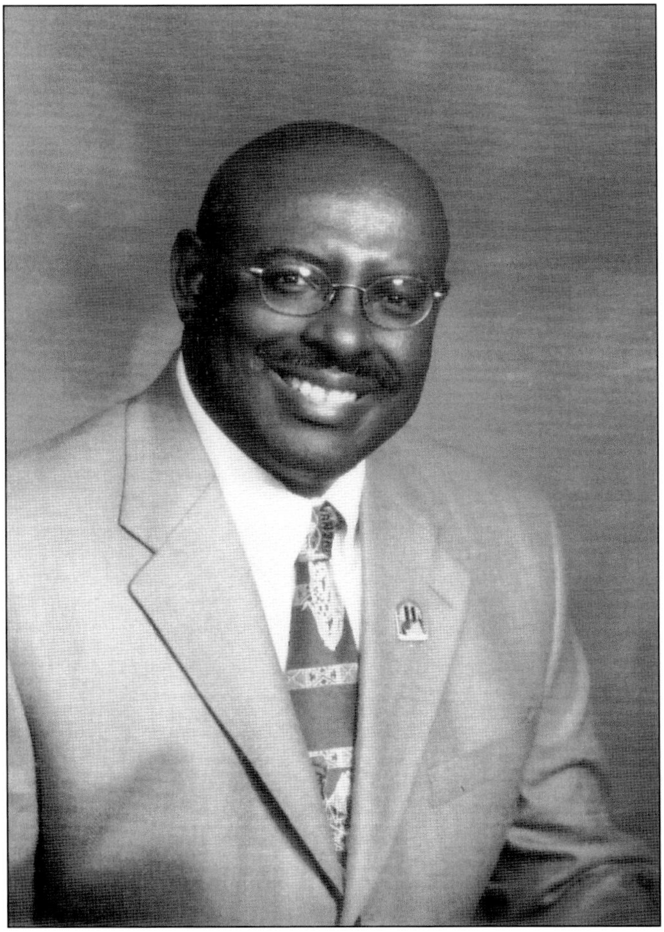

George Garwood was mayor of South Ogden from 2000 to 2009. When Garwood received the most votes on election night 2001, he became the first African American mayor in Utah's history, with a winning margin of 2,010 votes to 776. Garwood served for 10 years on the council before becoming mayor. After his two terms as mayor ended, he left elected public service. In January 2011, Garwood began singing with the Mormon Tabernacle Choir.

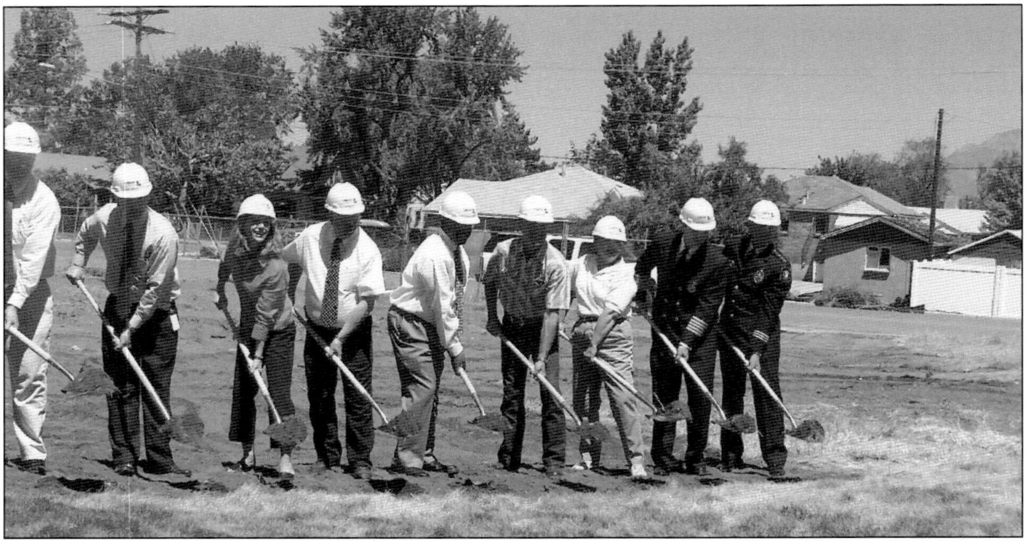

The ground-breaking ceremony for construction of the new city hall was on June 2, 2004. Pictured are, from left to right, city manager J. Scott Darrington, Councilmember Jon Bradley, Councilmember Shannan Sebahar, Councilmember James Minster, Mayor George Garwood, Councilmember Alma Richins, Councilmember Vickie Mattson, fire chief David Powers, and police chief Val Shupe.

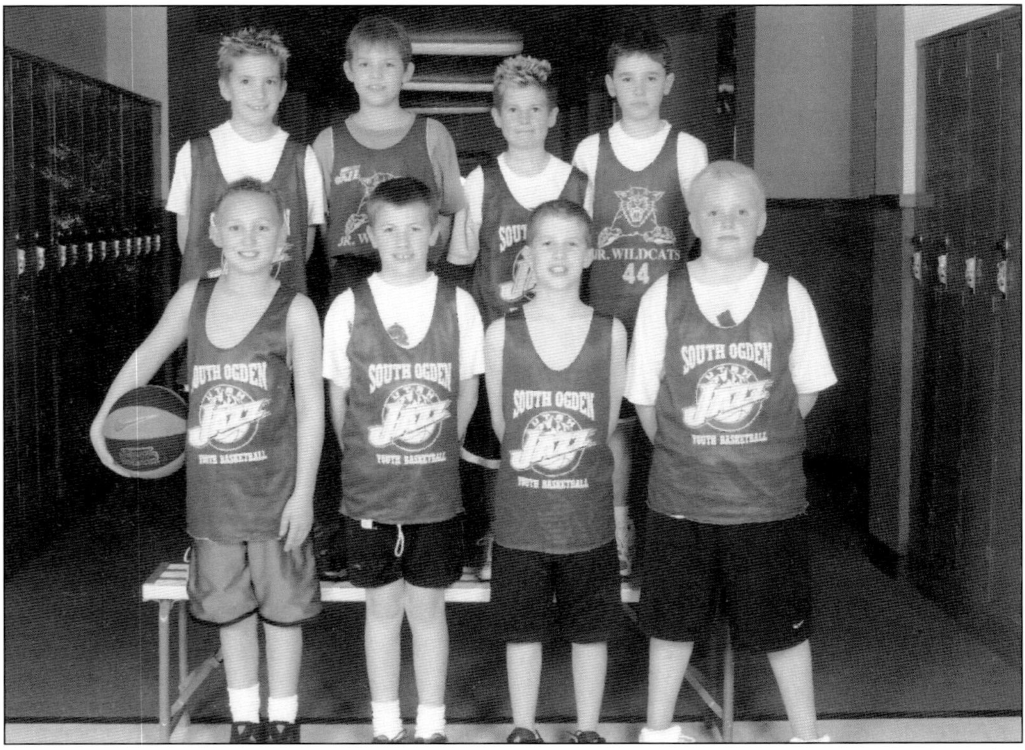

The Junior Jazz basketball team is pictured in January 2003 in the hallway of the old South Ogden Junior High School. The players all attended MarLon Hills Elementary. They are, from left to right, (first row) Carson Smith, Nicholas Porter, C.J. West, and Evan Parker; (second row) Austin Baker, Adam Sorensen, Nick Toller, and Boston Schroeder.

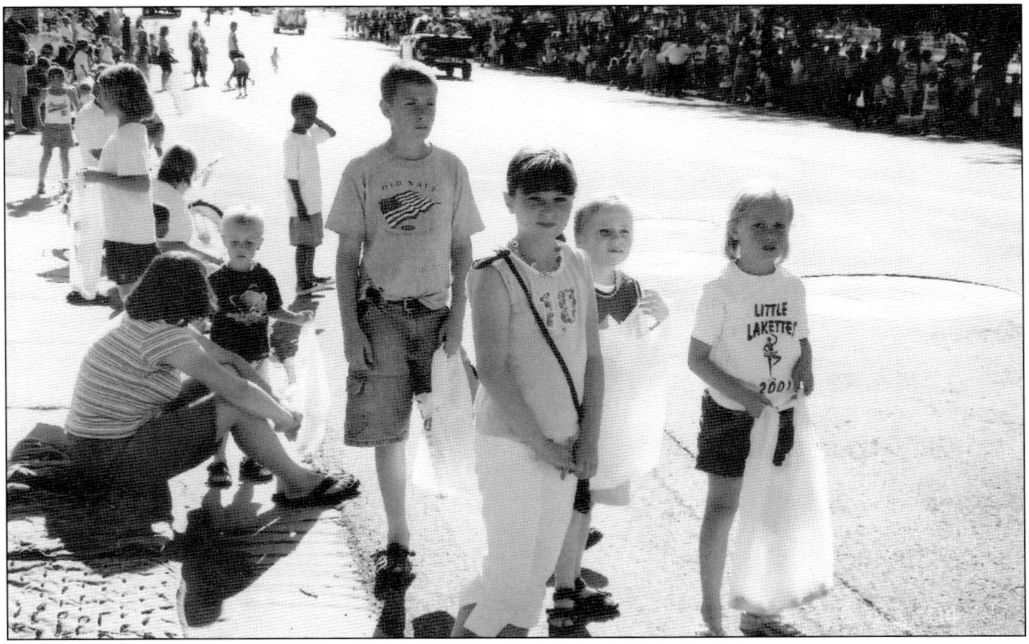

Kids on 40th Street, with grocery bags at the ready, wait impatiently for the parade to arrive on June 23, 2004. The bags are to gather the large amounts of candy still thrown from entries in the South Ogden Days Parade. In the foreground are, from left to right, Cortney Porter (with bag, facing left), Sherri Porter (sitting), Spencer Porter (in gutter), Nicholas Porter, Hailey Beesley, Rochelle Porter, and Brooklyn Porter. (Courtesy Glade Porter.)

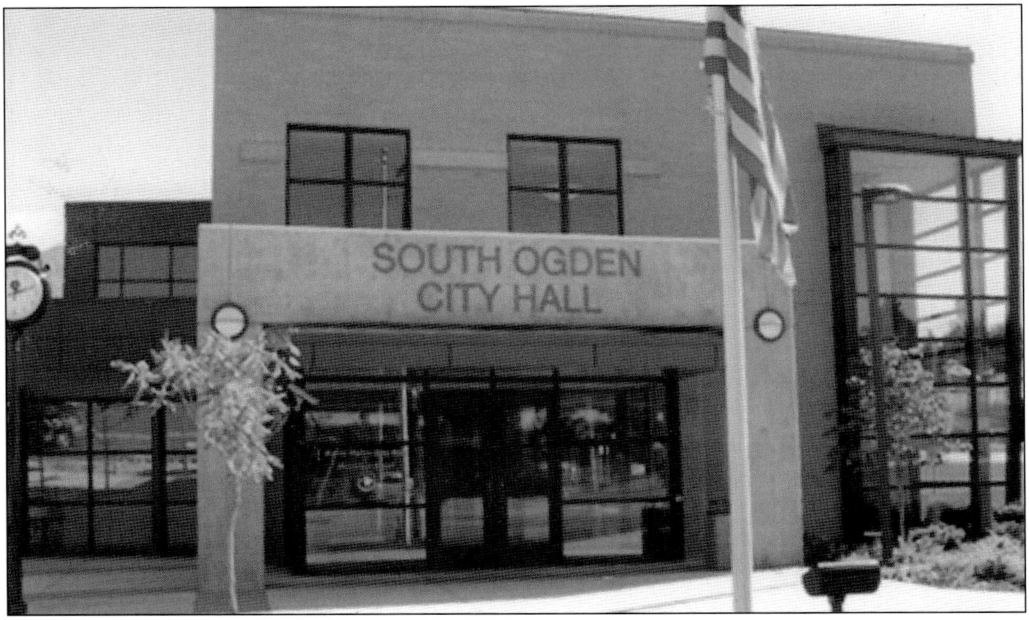

This is the current South Ogden City Hall, the fourth in the city's history. It was dedicated July 6, 2005, on the 69th anniversary of the city's incorporation. Mayor at the time was George Garwood Jr., with Councilmembers Alma E. Richins, James F. Minster, Vickie Mattson, John W. Bradley, and Shannon Sebahar. J. Scott Darrington was the city manager. JRCA Architects designed the building, and the general contractor was Layton Construction.

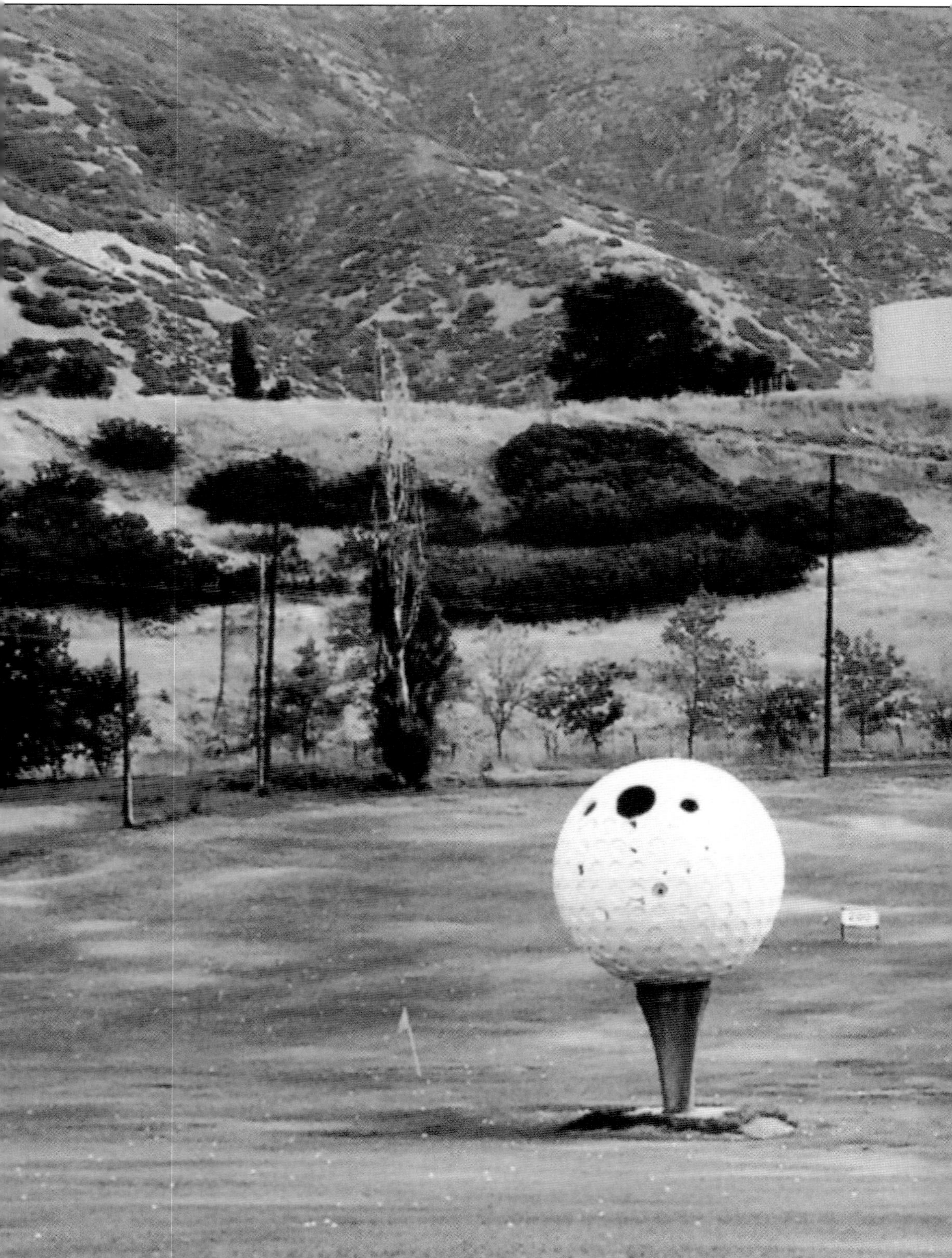

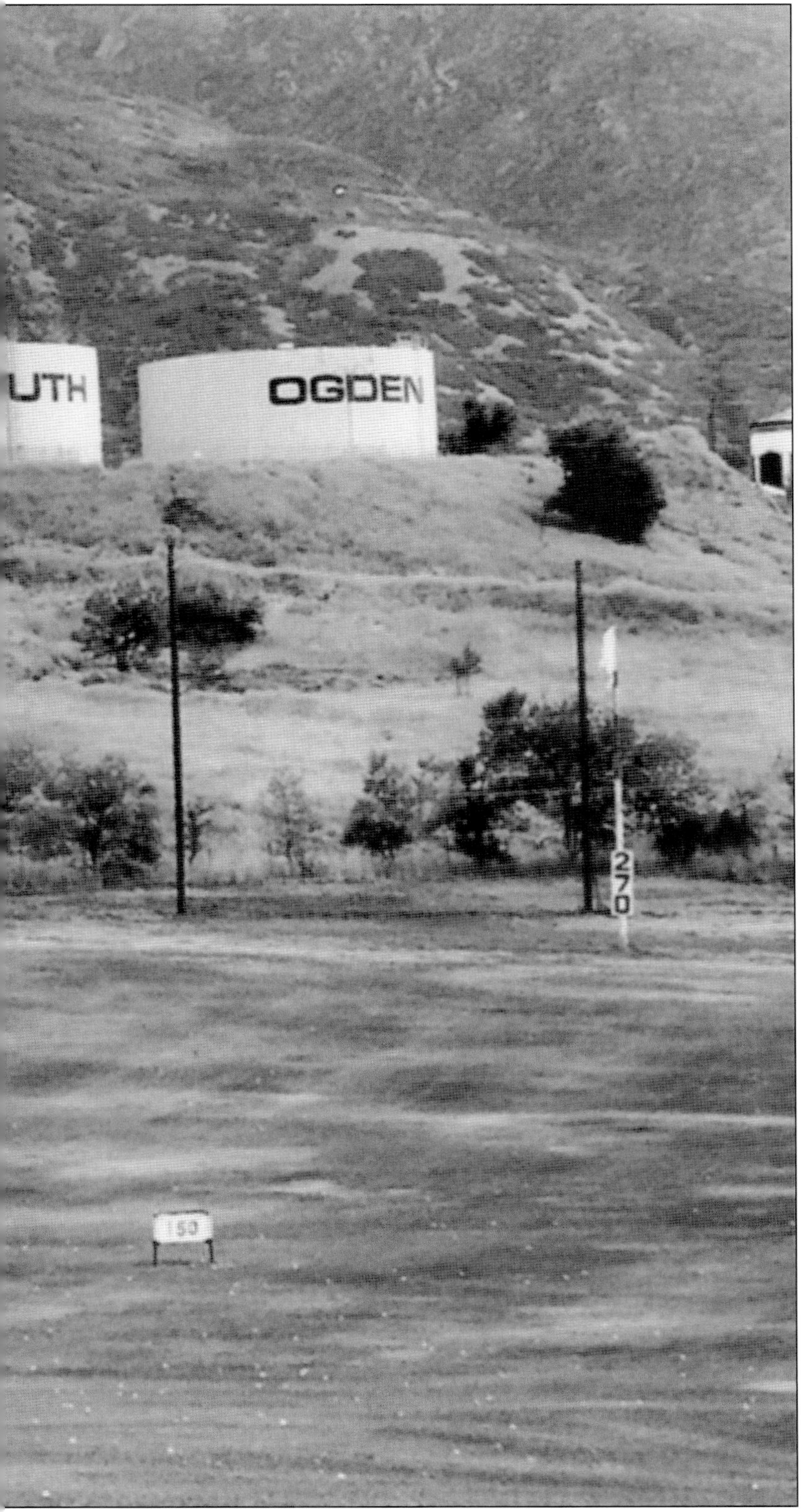

This is the giant golf ball and tee in the middle of the driving range at Golf City. This iconic symbol stood for decades and, because of its visibility from Harrison Boulevard, was known to everyone in the top of Utah. The summer of 2006 was the last season for the Golf City Family Fun Center and the end of an era in South Ogden entertainment, as the property was sold to housing developers. The days of trying to hit the ball into one of the holes in the giant ball and win a prize were gone. Youth learning how to play golf on the small course and losing their balls in the water on No. 9 were over, and family outings and date nights to play mini-golf ended. (Courtesy Jodi Gale.)

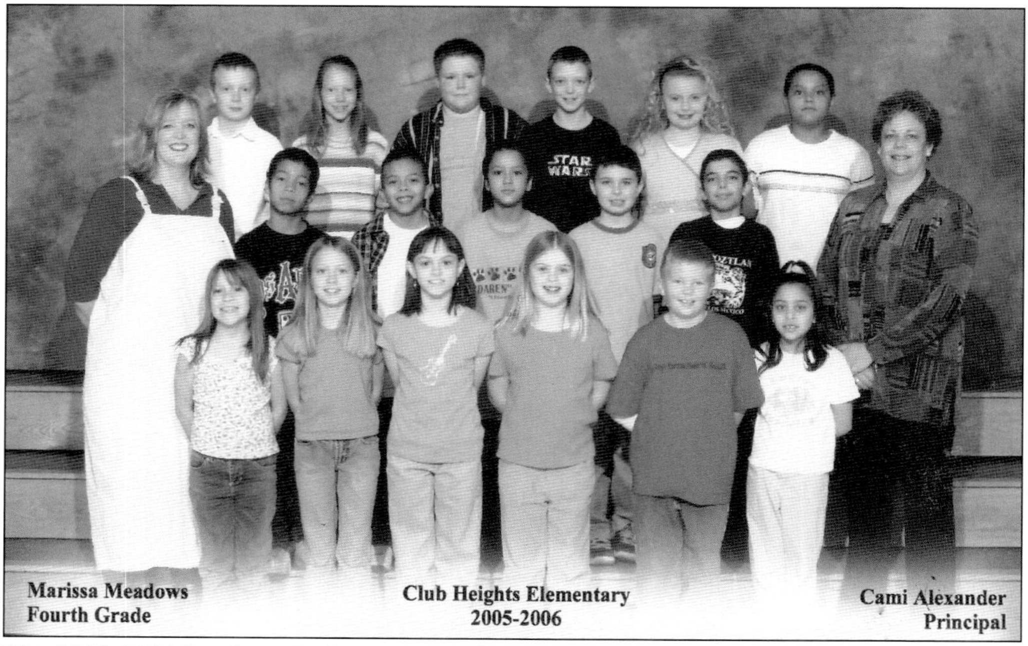

This 2005–2006 fourth-grade class picture is from Club Heights Elementary. From left to right are (first row) Eucharistia Strickling, Amy Butts, Faith Gudgell, Jessica Swanson, Joshua MacCarthy, and Emily Bowers; (second row) teacher Marissa Meadows, Juan Lopez, Marco Gomez, Kevin DeJesus, Devin Shinney, Erik Graham, and Principal Cami Alexander; (third row) Eric Cottle, Kaitlynn Meiners, Ryan Garner, William Palmer, Kylee Frost, and Victor Dominguez. (Courtesy Angie MacCarthy.)

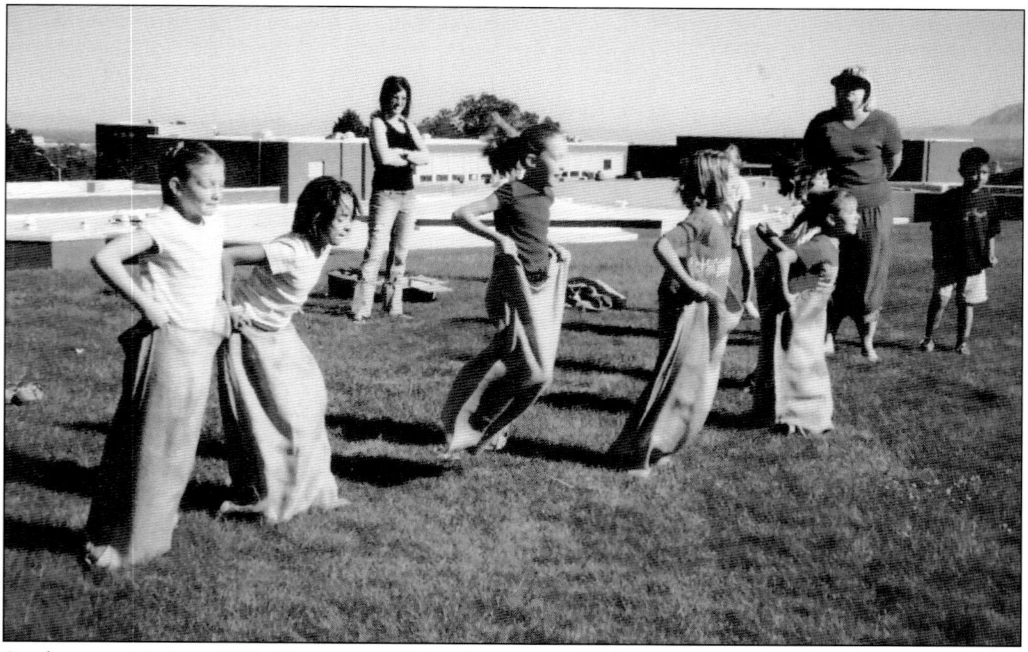

Students at MarLon Hills Elementary School participate in a sack race during field day, May 2005. From left to right are Abby Toller, Hadley Payan, Stephanie Shaw (arms folded in background), Alyssa DeFisher, Cortney Porter, unidentified, Jennie Atagi, and Noah Atagi. (Courtesy Sherri Porter.)

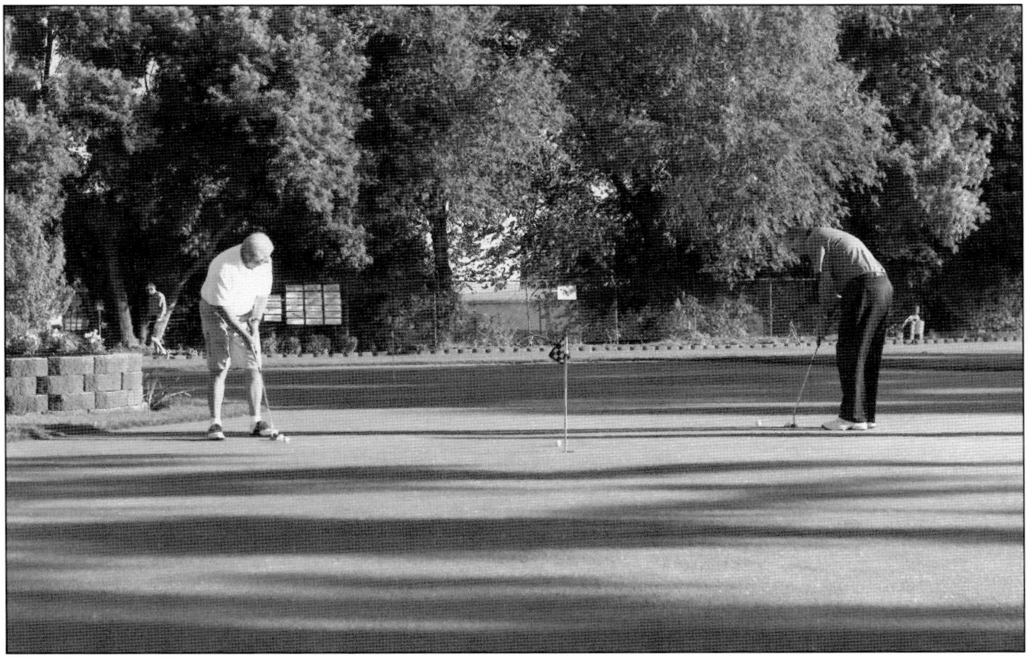

Participants practice their putts before the 2006 South Ogden Days golf tournament at Schneiter's Riverside Golf Course. Golfers are K. Ray Gottfredson (left) and Robert Dunn, longtime residents and ecclesiastical leaders in South Ogden. (Courtesy Scott Sumner.)

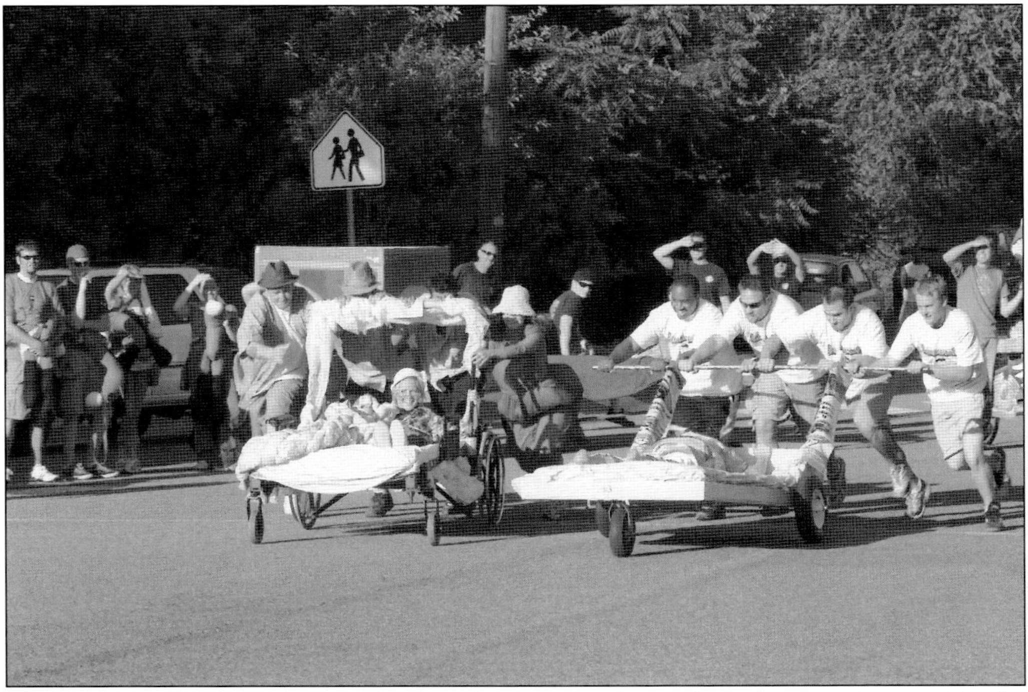

Two teams compete in a bed race down 39th Street during South Ogden Days, June 2006. The competitions were held right after the Wednesday evening parade. Teams of five (four pushing and one holding on the bed for dear life), representing businesses or a department in the city, compete for a new mattress and bragging rights. Team Costco is on the right. (Courtesy Scott Sumner.)

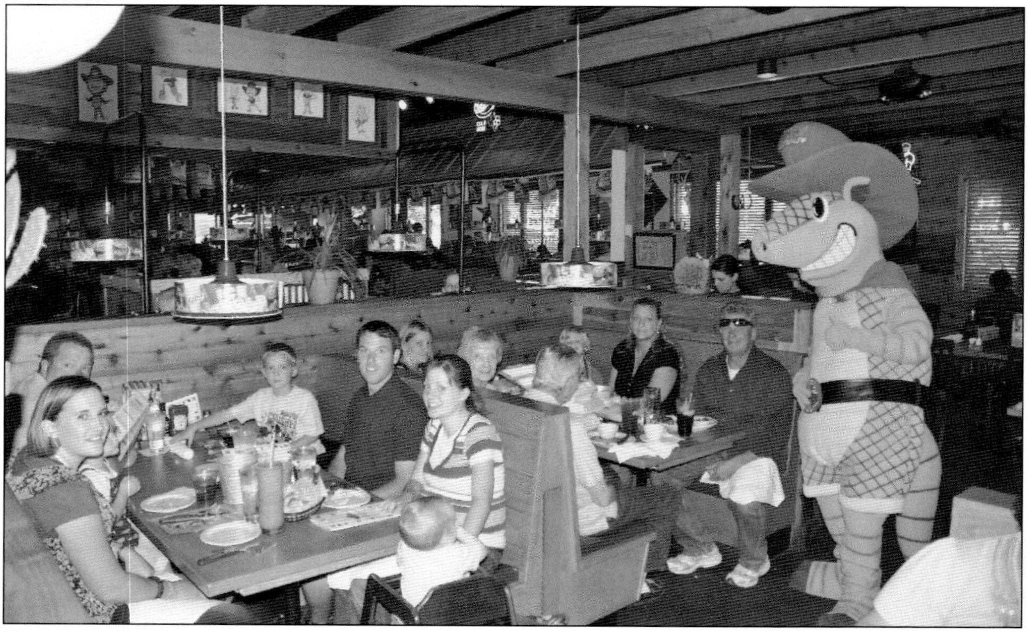

Texas Roadhouse opened May 28, 2007, at 3969 Wall Avenue in South Ogden. From the beginning, they have gotten involved in the community and contribute to many city events. Pictured inside the restaurant are, from left to right, the Walkers—Janelle, Teagan, Brandon, Brickman, Landon, Timorie, and Lawson; (right booth) the Tidwells—Charles, Ruth, Bailey, Drent, Audrey, Trent, and Andy Armadillo. (Courtesy Nicholas Porter.)

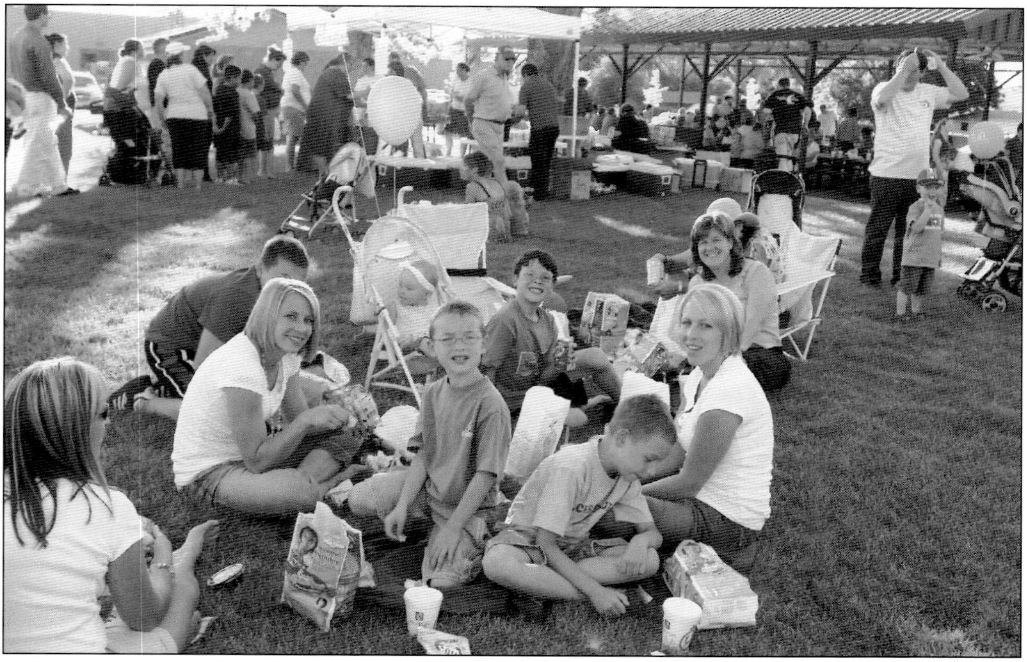

A family enjoys the Picnic in the Park, June 20, 2007. After the Wednesday night South Ogden Days Parade ends at 40th Street Park, local vendors supply dinner in the park. It is a great time to relax, socialize with neighbors and friends, or walk over to 39th Street and check out the bed races. (Courtesy Scott Sumner.)

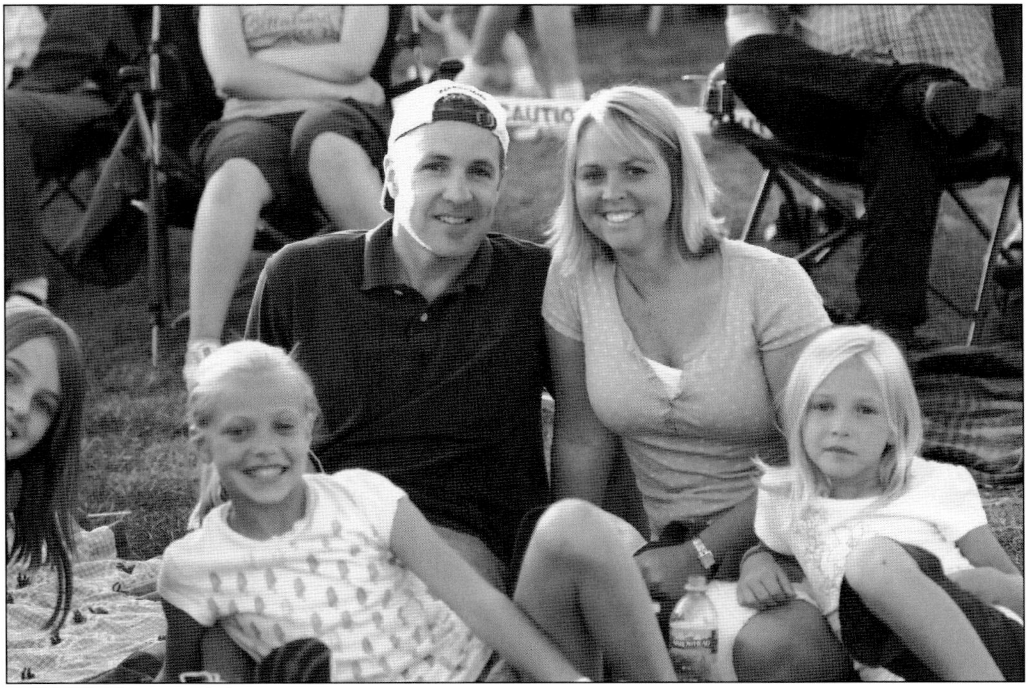

The Lane family relaxes on the grass of Friendship Park waiting for the Joe Diffie concert to begin, June 23, 2007. From left to right are Sadie, Mitch, Bridgette, and Jessica. The concert and following fireworks show are the culminating events of South Ogden Days. (Courtesy Scott Sumner.)

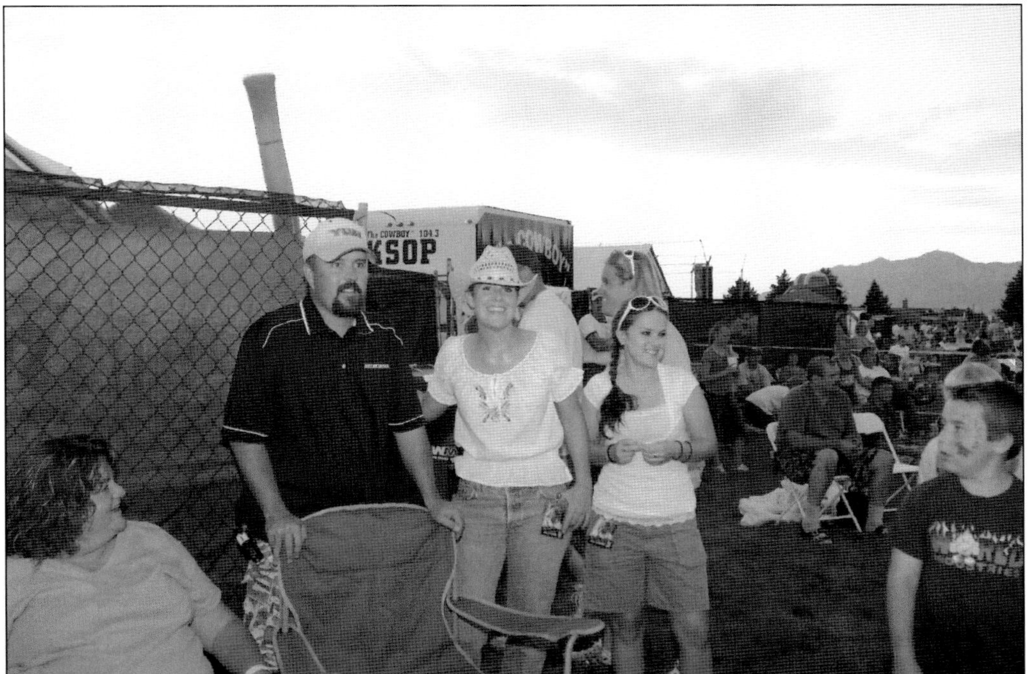

Holly Kenison, city treasurer; Shane Douglas, assistant public works director; Christy McBride, special events coordinator; and Amy DeSaul await the start of the concert in this June 23, 2007, photograph. (Courtesy Scott Sumner.)

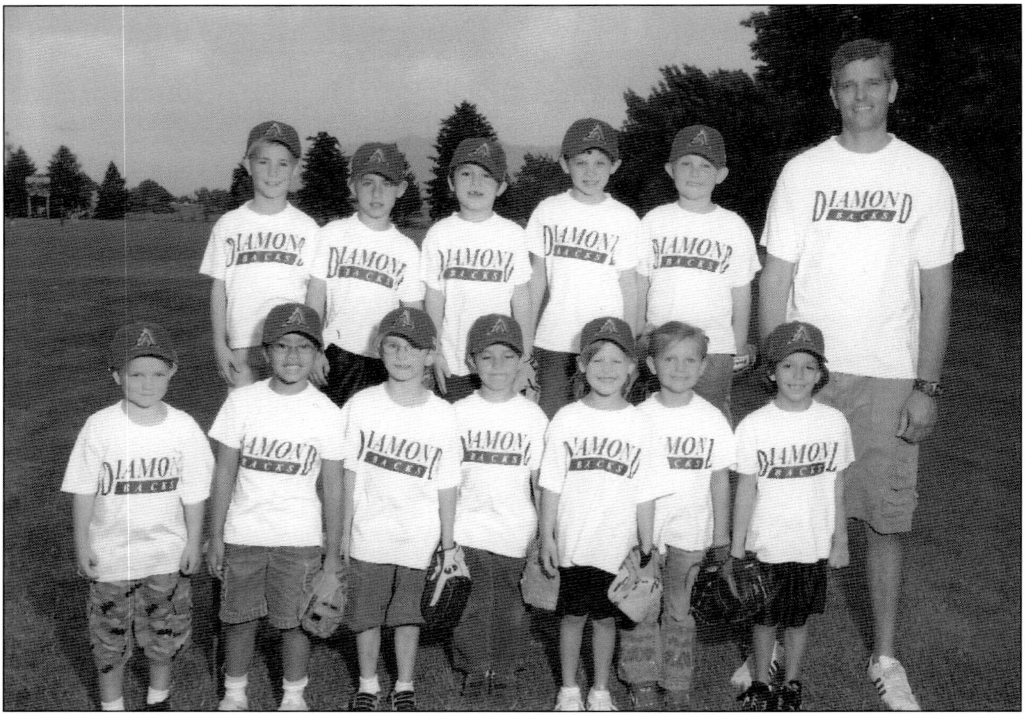

Six-and-seven-year-old kids make up the 2007 South Ogden Diamondbacks recreation baseball team. The players are, from left to right, (first row) Gabe Smith, unidentified, Spencer Hildebrand, Joseph Cramer, unidentified, Sydnee Smith, and Cambree Hassell; (second row) Spencer Porter, Kaleb Stanger, Alex Piaget, two unidentified, and Guy Hassell. (Courtesy Tot Shots.)

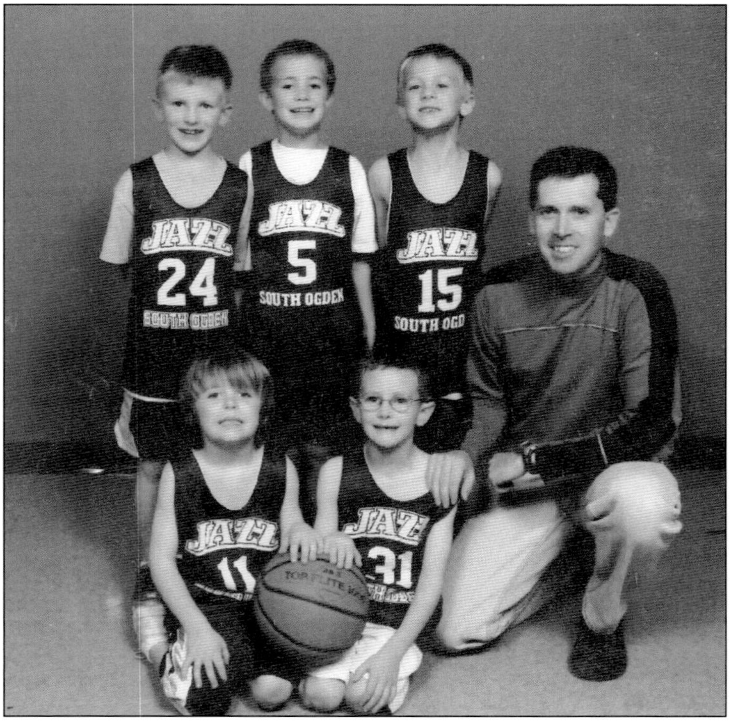

A Junior Jazz basketball team poses during the 2007 season. From left to right are (first row) Ryker Jensen, Spencer Hildebrand, and coach Travis Hildebrand; (second row) Joseph Cloward, Spencer Porter, and Wesley Castlemain. Junior Jazz is offered to boys and girls by the South Ogden City recreation department. Games were played at the original South Ogden Junior High School, South Weber Recreation Center, and the Browning Armory. (Courtesy K&S Photography.)

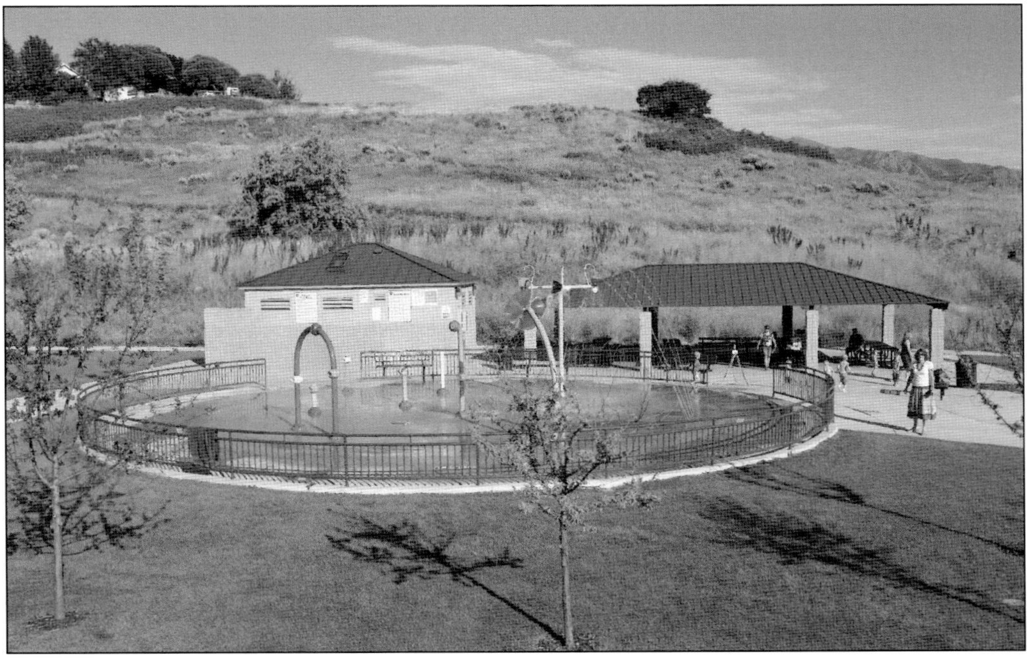

Above, the South Ogden Splash Pad opened Memorial Day 2008 and has been a gathering place for local kids every sunny day since. An August 2009 survey even showed people visited from at least seven other cities and two other counties during a three-day testing period. The park sits in a beautiful setting between the Ogden Athletic Club and the Nature Park on 5850 South. Below, this August 2011 photograph shows, from left to right, Lindsay Strickland (adult), Bobby Strickland, Grace Strickland, Mia Sugimoto, Driggs Petersen, Gates Petersen, and Erik Warren. (Both, courtesy Nicholas Porter.)

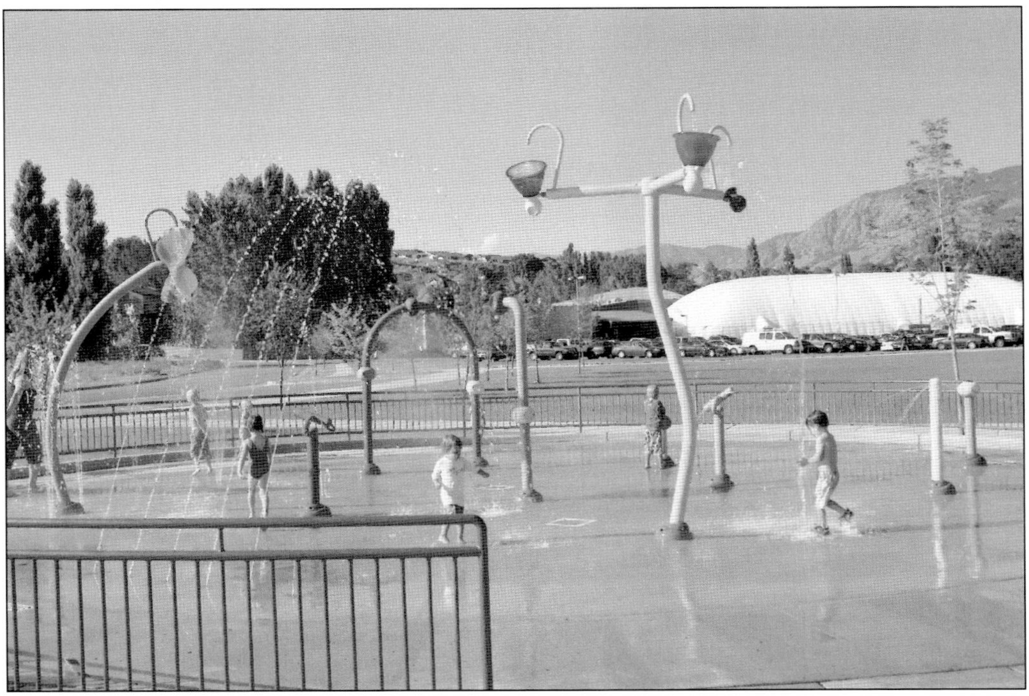

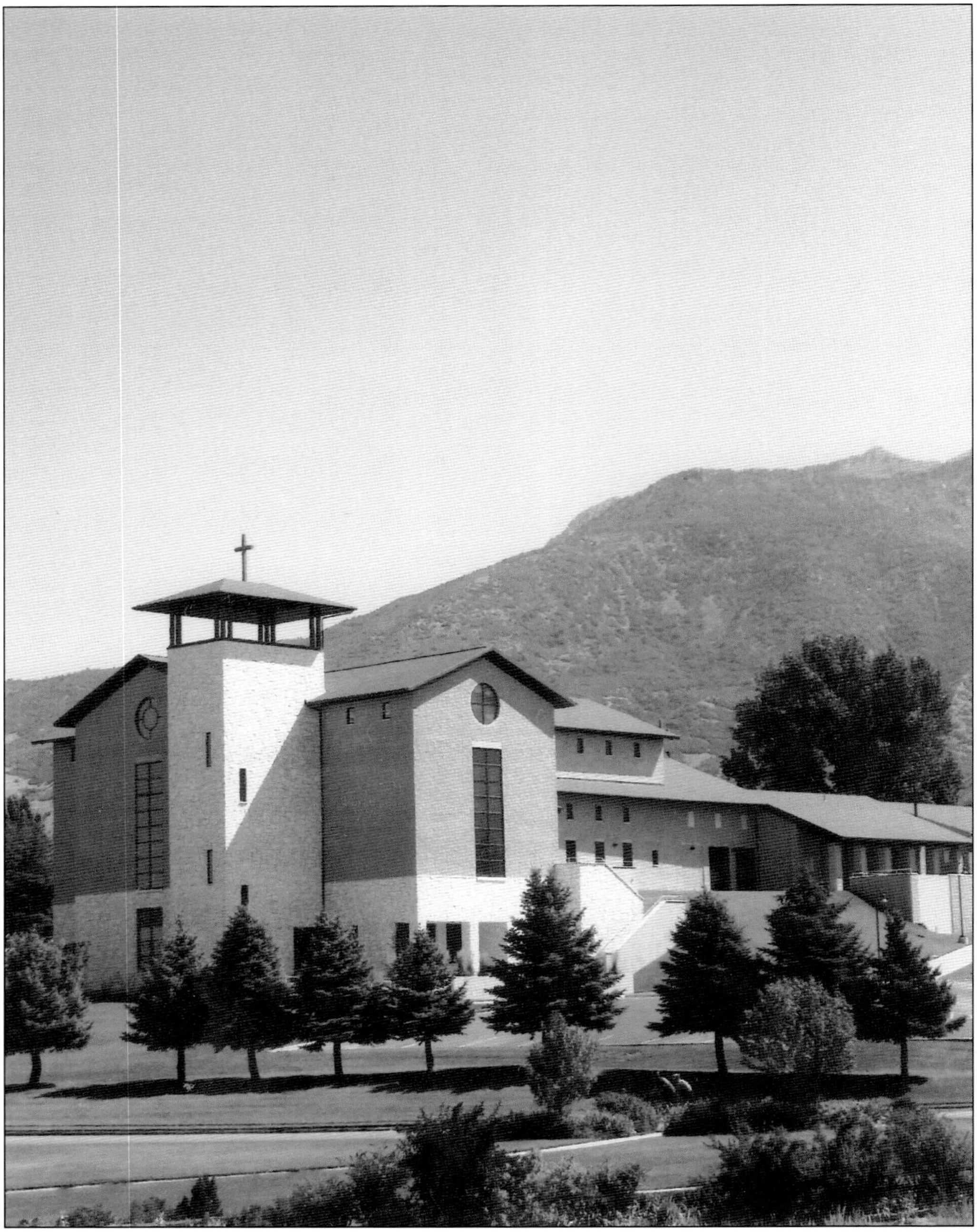

Holy Family Catholic Parish in South Ogden is located at 1100 East 5550 South. This modern building sits on an eight-acre campus with well-landscaped grounds and great views of the city and Mount Ogden. Holy Family Parish began in August 1979, when founding bishop, Joseph Lennox Federal, and founding pastor, Msgr. George Davich, began masses at the Country Club Theater on Washington Boulevard. After holding mass at the theater, Bonneville High School, and the Alamo Storage Center for a couple of years, Bishop William Weigand dedicated church buildings on the current property in May 1981. The current edifice, the one in this photograph, was dedicated on October 21, 2008, by Bishop John C. Wester. Fr. Patrick Elliot, the current pastor, was appointed in 2005 by Bishop George H. Niederauer. (Courtesy Holy Family Catholic Church.)

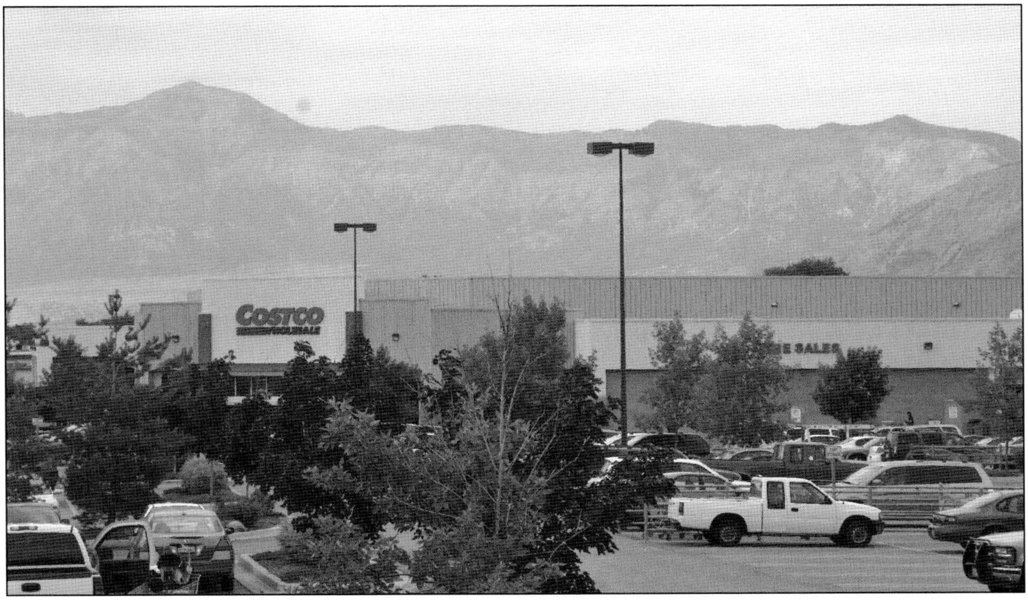

This is a 2011 photograph of Costco Wholesale. Costco opened to the public on November 18, 2003, at 36th Street and Wall Avenue. The building is 136,000 square feet and employs 205 people. There are over 39,000 card-carrying members in the surrounding area. For decades, this site was home to Kmart and a row of smaller business, like Andy's Chuckwagon. (Courtesy Sherri Porter.)

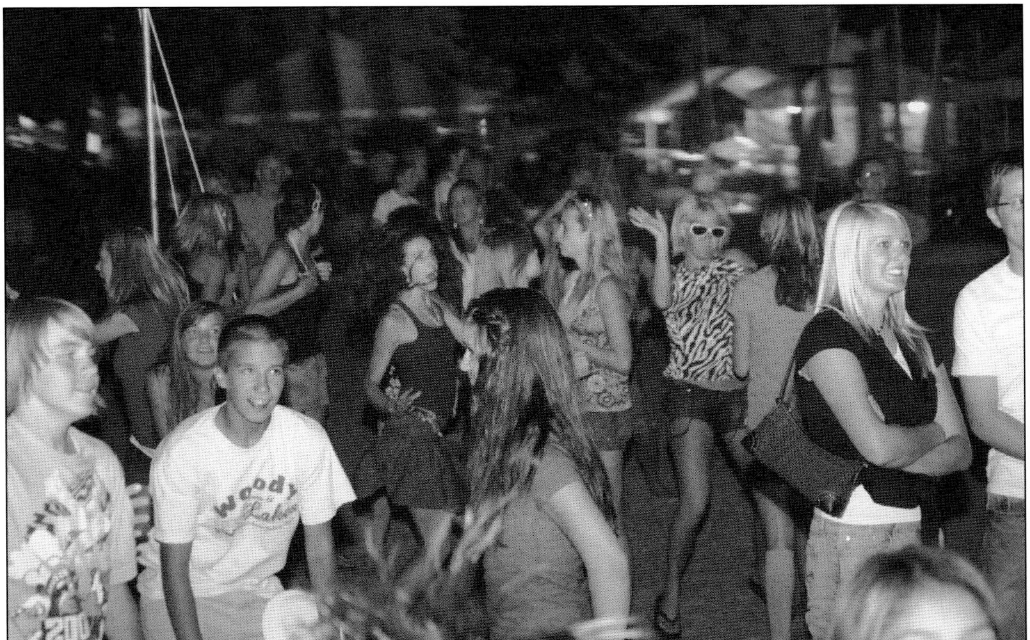

Area youth enjoy the South Ogden Days Teen Dance in 2008. It is not an annual event, but the teen dance and karaoke night were a success on this June night at Friendship Park. Kids from South Ogden Junior High, T.H. Bell Junior High, and Bonneville High School participated. (Courtesy Scott Sumner.)

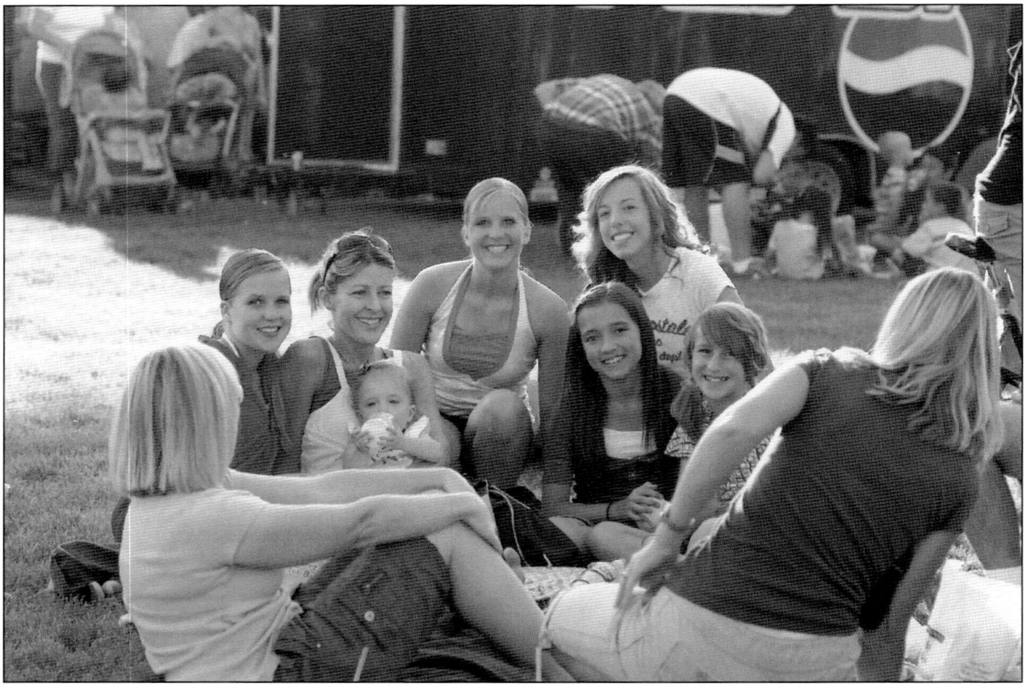

Families congregate in 40th Street Park after the 2008 South Ogden Days Parade and enjoy the Picnic in the Park. Above are, from left to right, (facing the camera) Morgan Jacobs, Tonya Jacobs, baby ?, Taylor Jacobs, Courtney Jacobs, Erin Ulibarri, and unidentified. Below are, from left to right, Spencer Porter, Sherri Porter, Stockton Porter (facing away from camera), Russell Porter, Nicholas Porter, and Cortney Porter. (Both, courtesy Scott Sumner.)

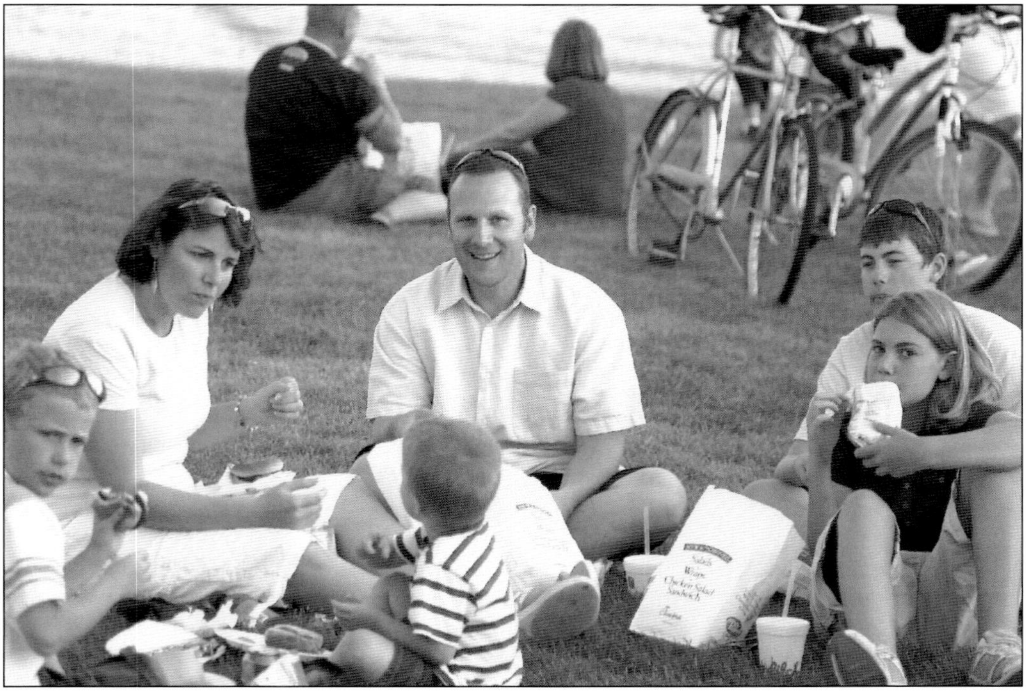

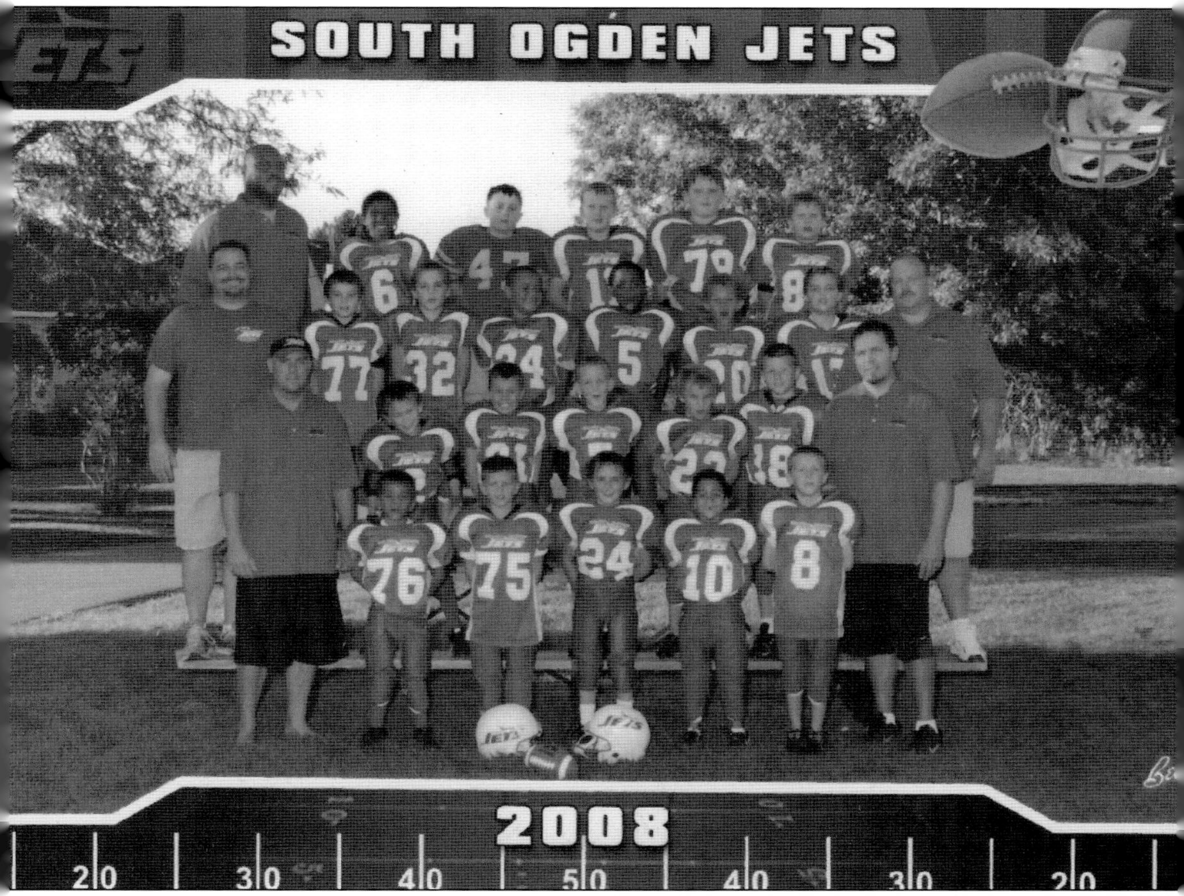

The South Ogden Jets Junior Mites football team is pictured in 2008. Recreation programs have always been, and continue to be, a big part of the South Ogden community. Since the mid-1990s, all South Ogden teams have been named the Jets, a connection to the actual jets from Hill Air Force Base that consistently fly over Friendship Park during practices and games. Pictured are, from left to right, (first row) coach Doug Ney, Brecken Benard, Dax Pedersen, ? Mills, ? Huemiller, Caden Smith, and coach Cody Pedersen; (second row) Dylan Wayment, Josh Russo, Garrett Smith, Colton Hill, and Leland Mundy; (third row) coach Jason Buckway, ? Ketts, Hunter Buckway, Brennan Green, Kaden Spens, Breven Perkins, unidentified, and coach Wayne Smith; (fourth row) coach Eddie Green, Breven Benard, ? Fitzgerald, Porter Cochran, Austin Miller, and ? Blocker. (Photograph by Bell Photography; courtesy South Ogden City.)

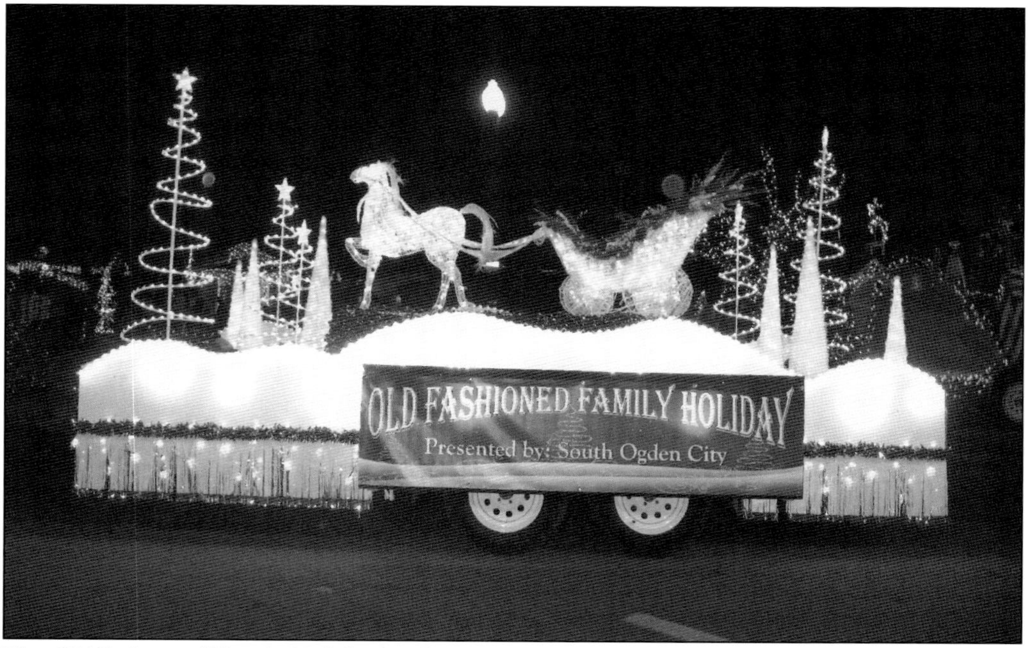

The Old Fashioned Family Holiday has been an annual event since its 2004 beginning. Above, a lit South Ogden float was entered into a local parade. Councilmember Vickie Mattson is credited with first mentioning the city sponsor an outdoor event at Christmastime. During the evening, there is a countdown for the mayor to "light the tree" and Santa comes to take free photographs with the kids—and some adults. Free chili and hot chocolate are served by the Boy Scouts and the Youth City Council and bonfires surround the bowery. Throughout the evening, choirs from the local elementary schools sing and perform (below). (Both, courtesy Christy McBride.)

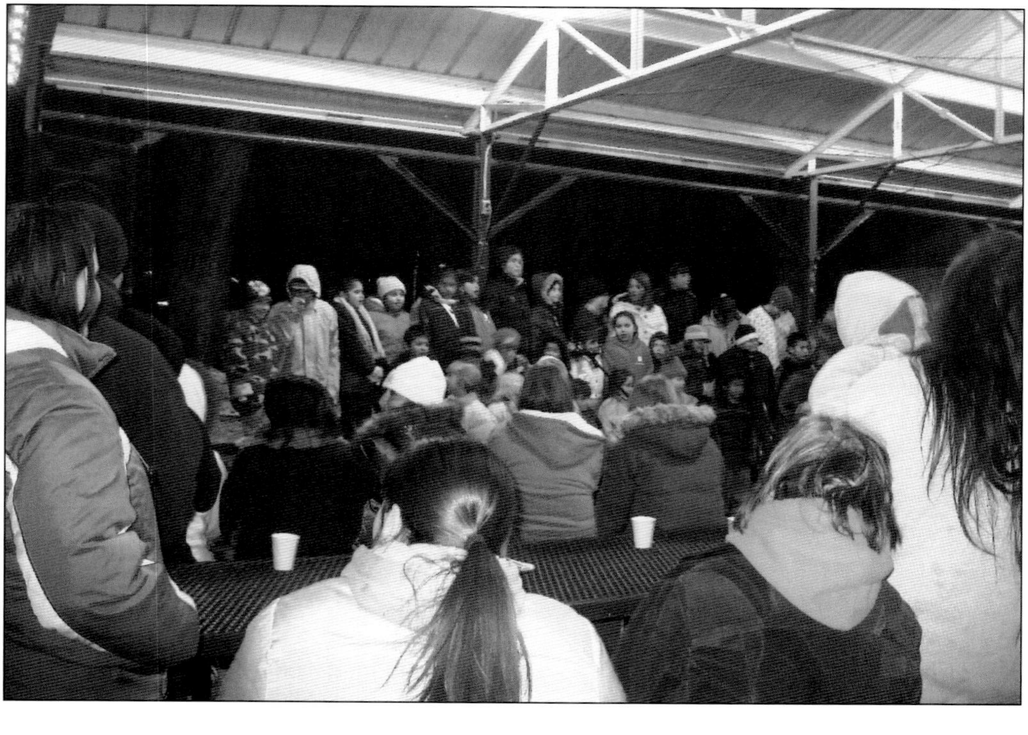

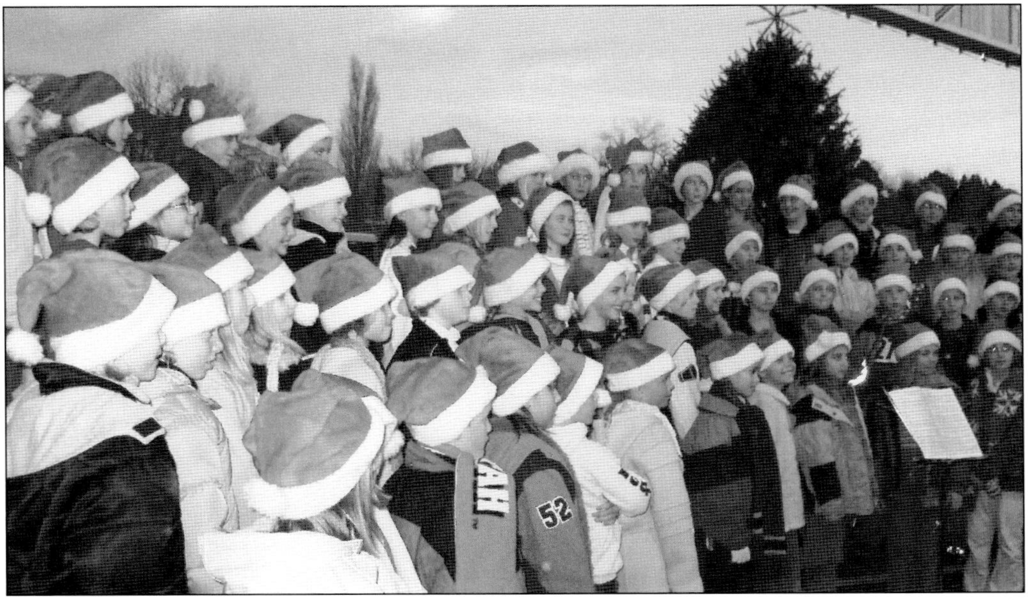

The Old Fashioned Family Holiday is pictured in December 2008. The annual activity is held on the second Saturday in December at the 40th Street Park bowery. Above and below, local elementary students sing Christmas and winter song throughout the evening. The night also includes an "angel tree" and the Warm Hearts/Warm Hands program, where residents who attend bring new hats, gloves, and scarves to be given to charity. In 2011, one hundred fifty new winter hats, scarves, and gloves were donated to those in need. (Both, courtesy Christy McBride.)

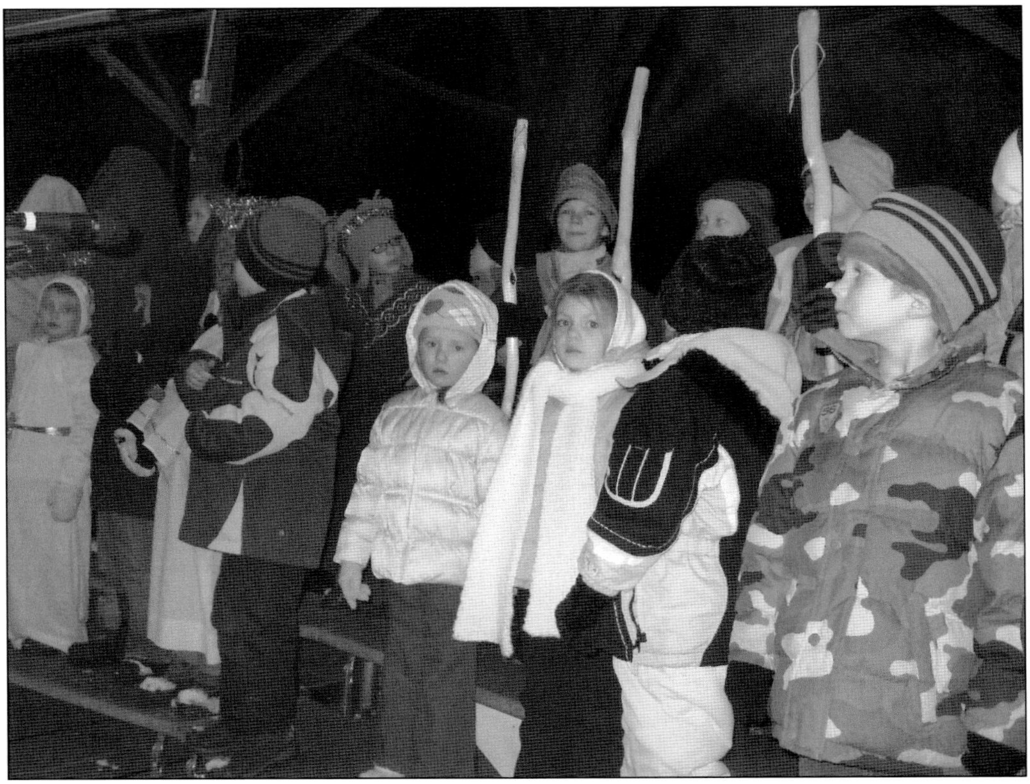

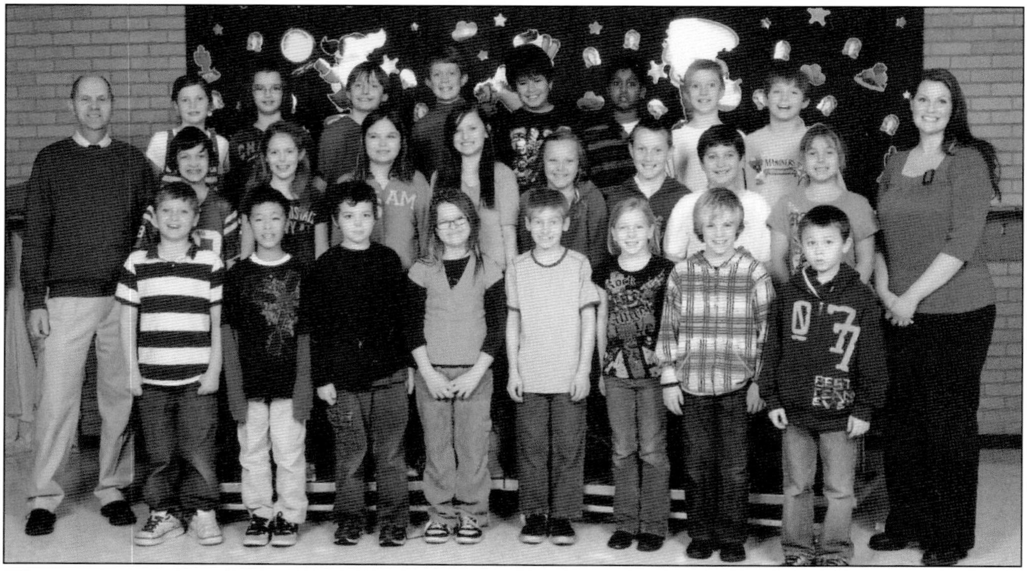

This is a 2009–2010 fourth-grade class picture at H. Guy Child Elementary School. Pictured are, from left to right, (first row) Dax Loftus, Li Lao, Darren Ladrew, Alex Emmons, Caleb Nelson, Delaney Burton, Colton Hill, and Dylan Wayment; (second row) Principal Blake Hadley, McKade Maw, Alyssa Hunter, Mylee Parkinson, Taitum Wangsgard, Kylee Garrett, Cameron Tucker, David Acord, Cheyenne Anderson, and teacher Marie Christensen; (third row) Meghan Wold, Maddison McCullough, Jaden Kane, Brian Dyer, Mitchell Harvey, Aashish Gottipati, Connor Hatch, and Dylan Sandberg. (Courtesy H. Guy Child Elementary.)

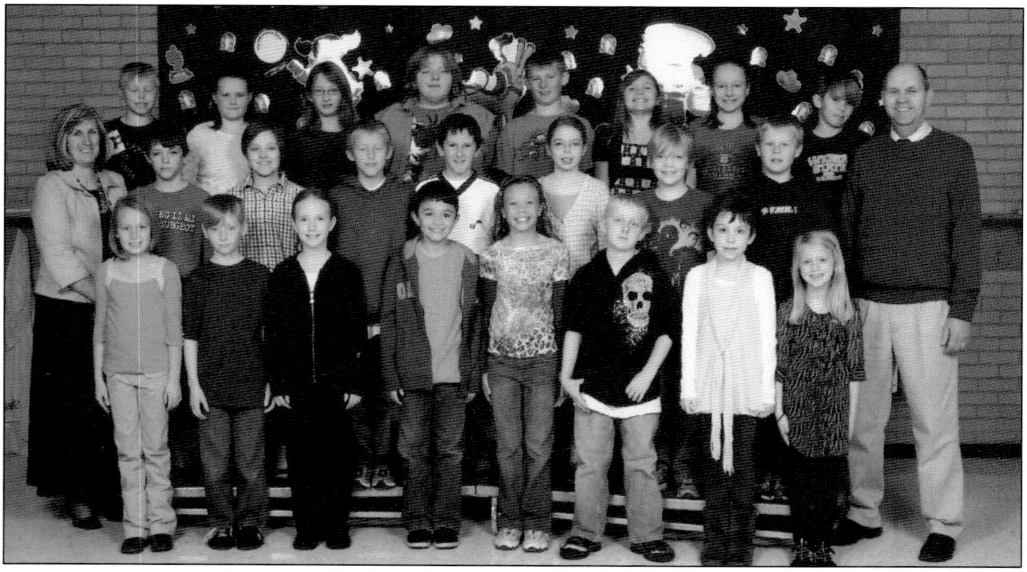

This is a 2009–2010 fourth-grade class picture at H. Guy Child Elementary School. Pictured are, from left to right, (first row) Jessica Hatch, Connor Gibson, Rebecca Ryan, Joseph Gonzalez, Maya Draney, Matt Story, Shaylee Price, and Jasmine Brown; (second row) Lori Brown, Gunner Orton, Seth Swanke, Caleb Sorenson, Isaac MacFarlane, Ashley Beckwith, Ivan Rice, Nathan Davis, and Principal Blake Hadley; (third row) Kyle Palmer, Courtni Carter, Amity Howell, Austin Tolman, Kaleb Gurr, Kayla Foschia, Joey Wheatley, and Carson Morris. (Courtesy H. Guy Child Elementary.)

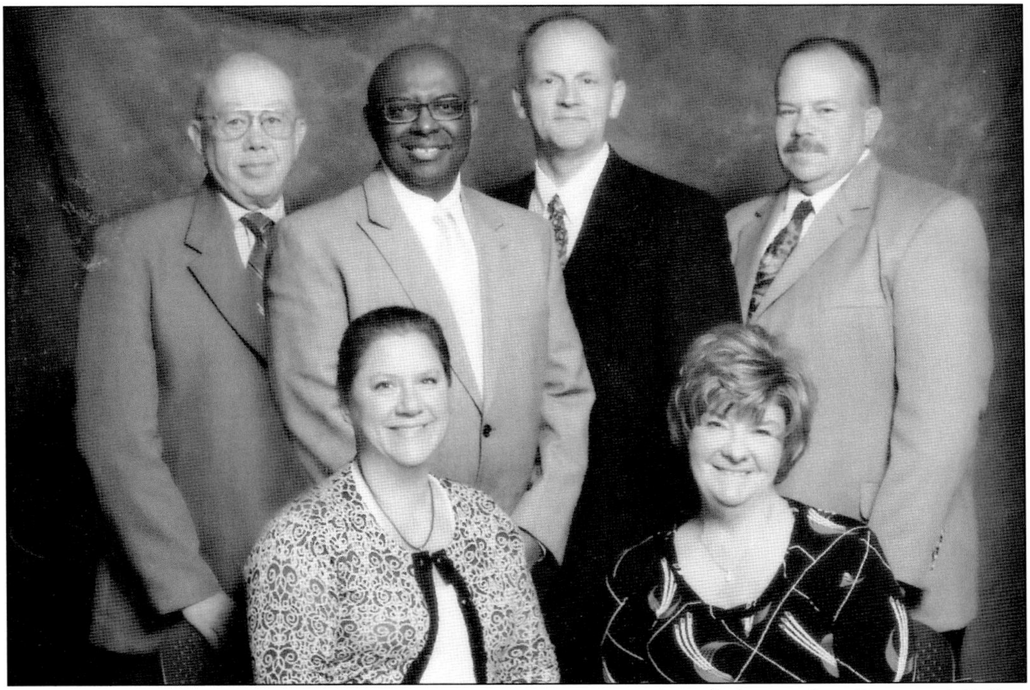

South Ogden City's elected officials from 2008 to 2009 are, from left to right, (first row) Sallee Orr and Vickie Mattson; (second row) James F. Minster, Mayor George Garwood, John Bradley, and Wayne Smith.

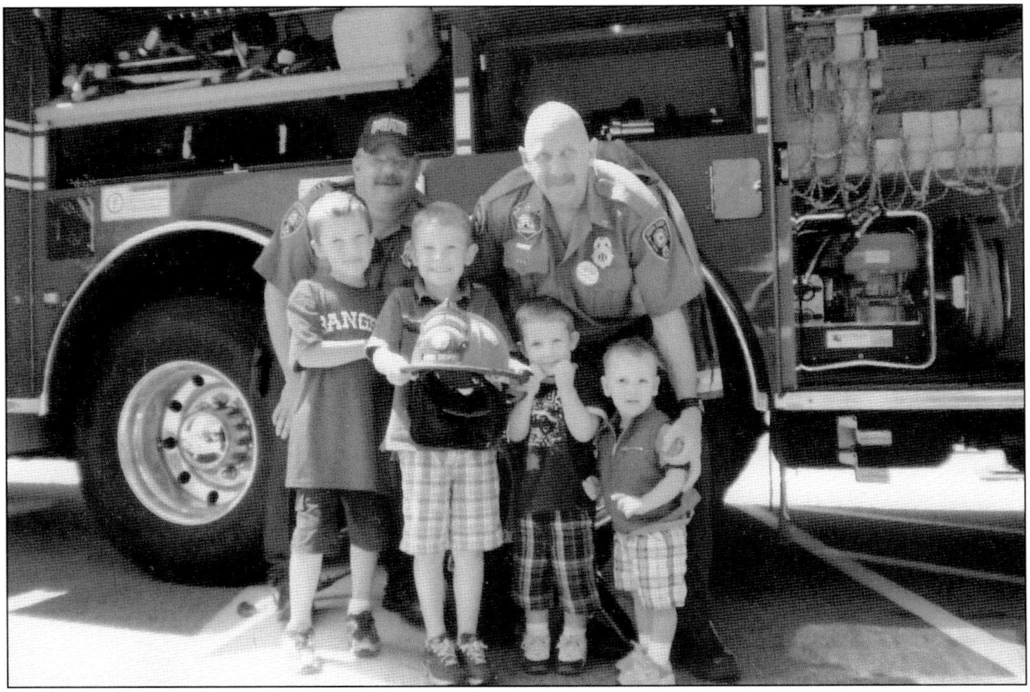

This 2009 photograph is from the Safety Fair, held in the Costco parking lot. Engineer Scott Myers (left) and Capt. Bill Stoddard (right) of the South Ogden Fire Department pose with four local boys and potential firefighters.

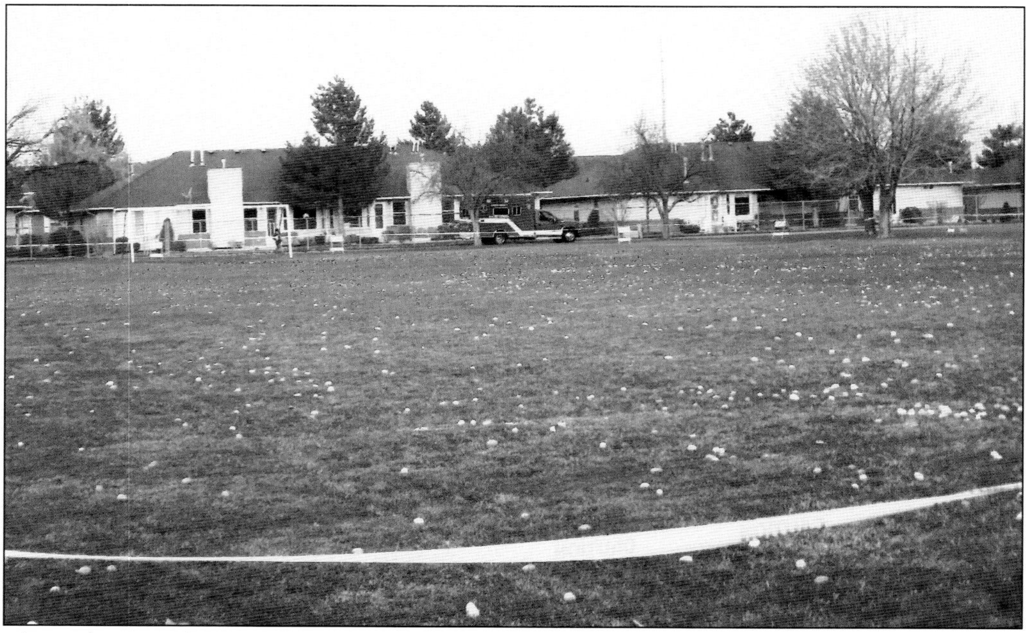

These photographs are of the 2009 South Ogden Easter Egg Hunt. Above, a section of grass full of eggs at Friendship Park is taped off until the fire engine sounds the start alarm at 9:00 a.m. sharp. The annual event is the Saturday morning before Easter and over 2,000 area youth show up to get treats and take their picture with the Easter Bunny. Below, kids head to the west to fill their baskets. What took so long to prepare for is over in no time at all.

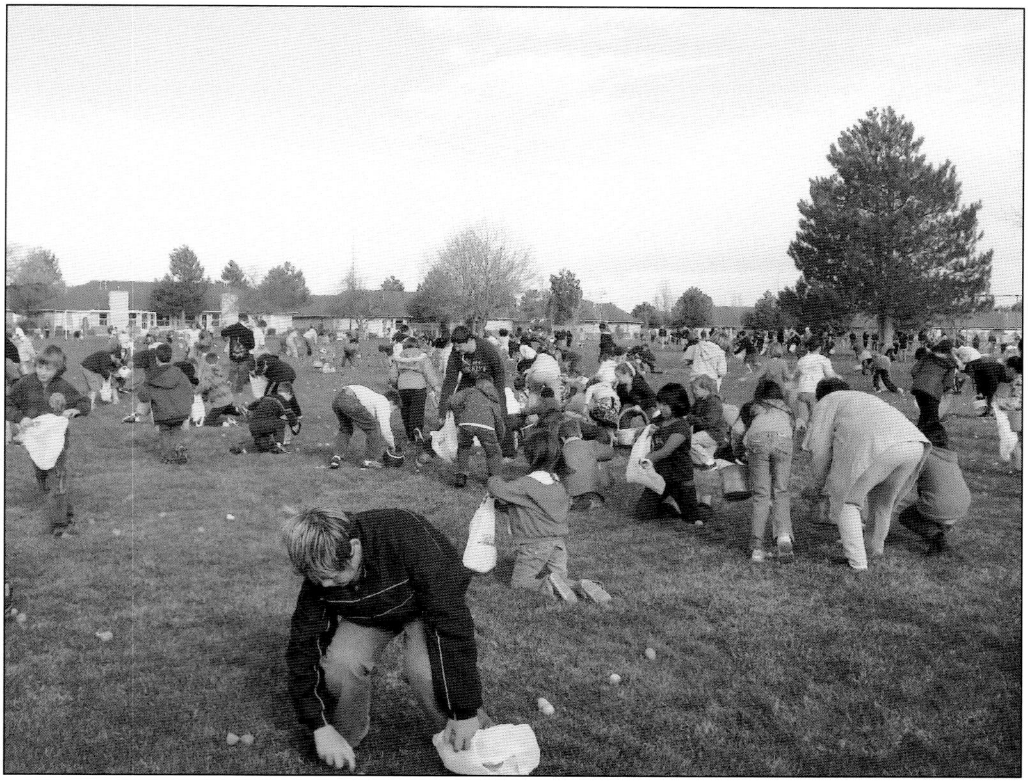

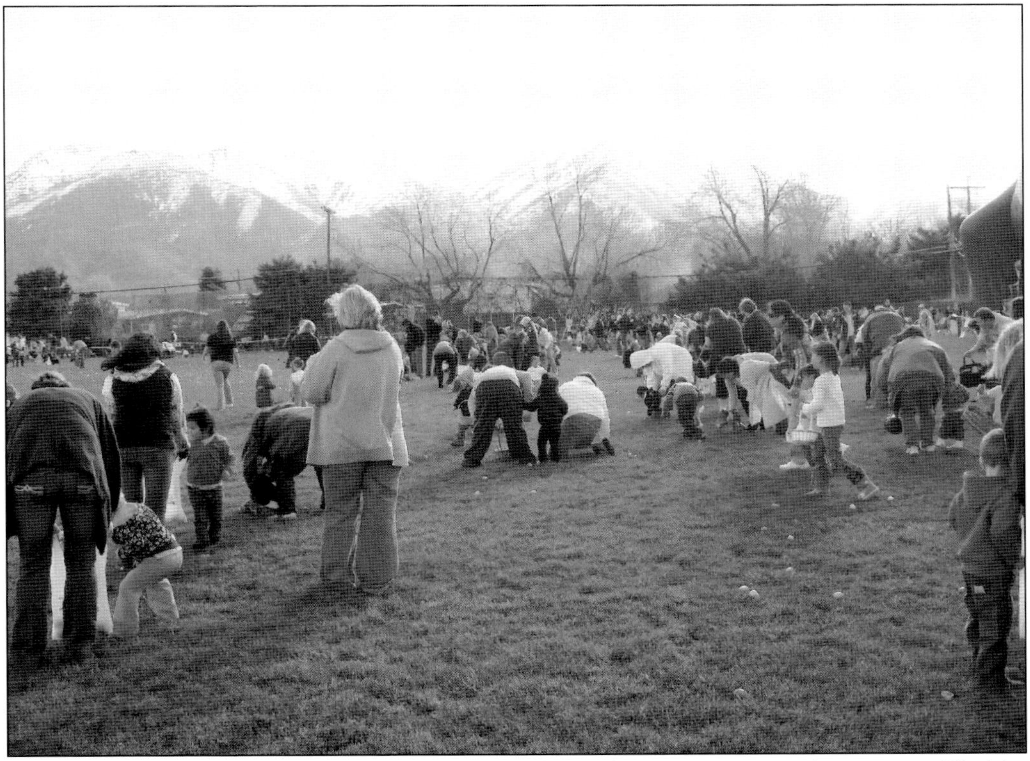

The Easter egg hunt each year at Friendship Park involves over 20,000 plastic eggs, filled by volunteers in the weeks preceding the event. The eggs are placed throughout the park by city employees and the Youth City Council. Above, kids head east to clear the field of anything colored. Below, Scott Darrington and Mayor George Garwood oversee the event and try to stay warm. Earlier in the city's history, the Easter egg hunt took place at Club Heights Park and was sponsored by the Kiwanis Club. When the club left, the city made sure it still took place.

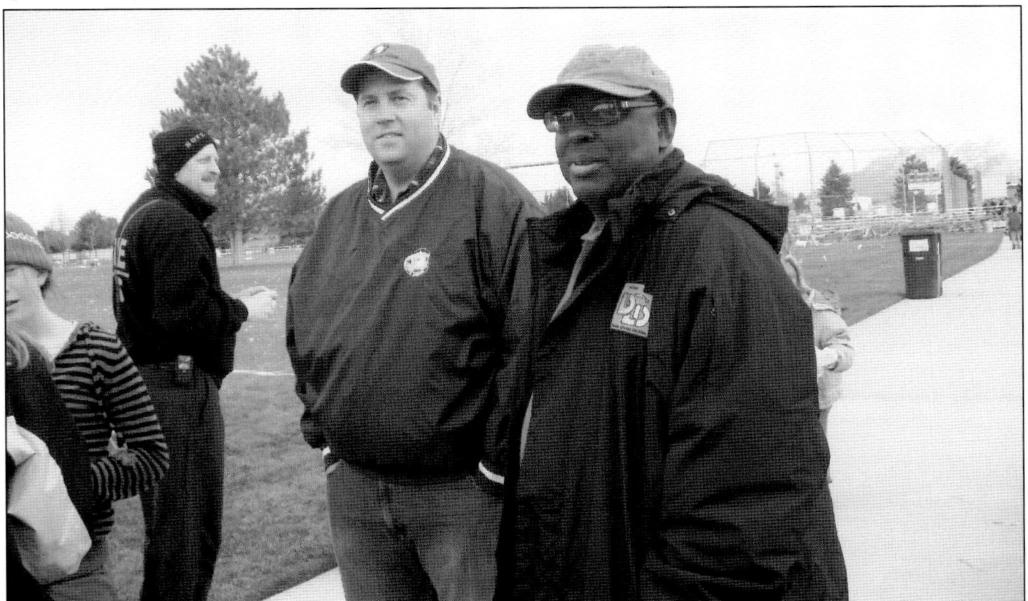

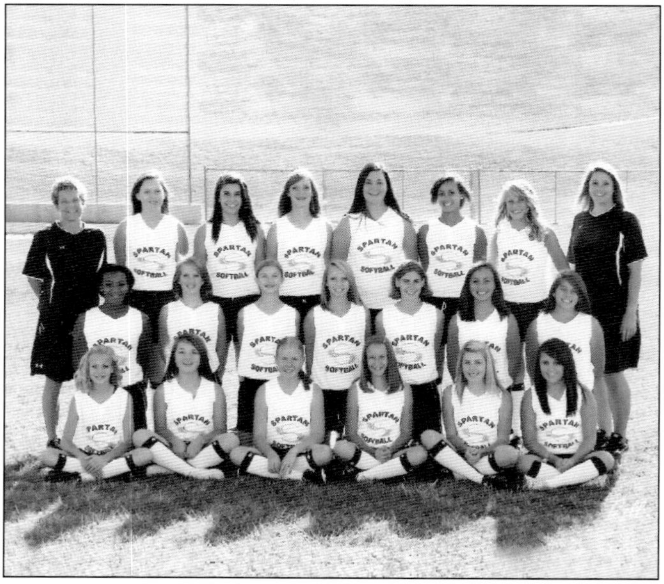

The 2009 South Ogden Junior High School softball team is, from left to right, (first row) Sadie Lane, Haylee Sotomayor, Natalie Porter, Lexie Haas, Morgan Kenney, and Marlo Vigil; (second row) Taylor Mickles, Shayla Smith, Kayla Eilertson, Maren McDaniel, Cortney Porter, Emilee Tafuna'I, and Jaden Juergens; (third row) coach Chris Earnest, Alex Sorrell, Jamie Garner, Abby Toller, Kalyn Sotomayor, Tavia Young, Lexie Stratford, and coach Kerry Taylor. (Photograph by Bell Photography; courtesy Cortney Porter.)

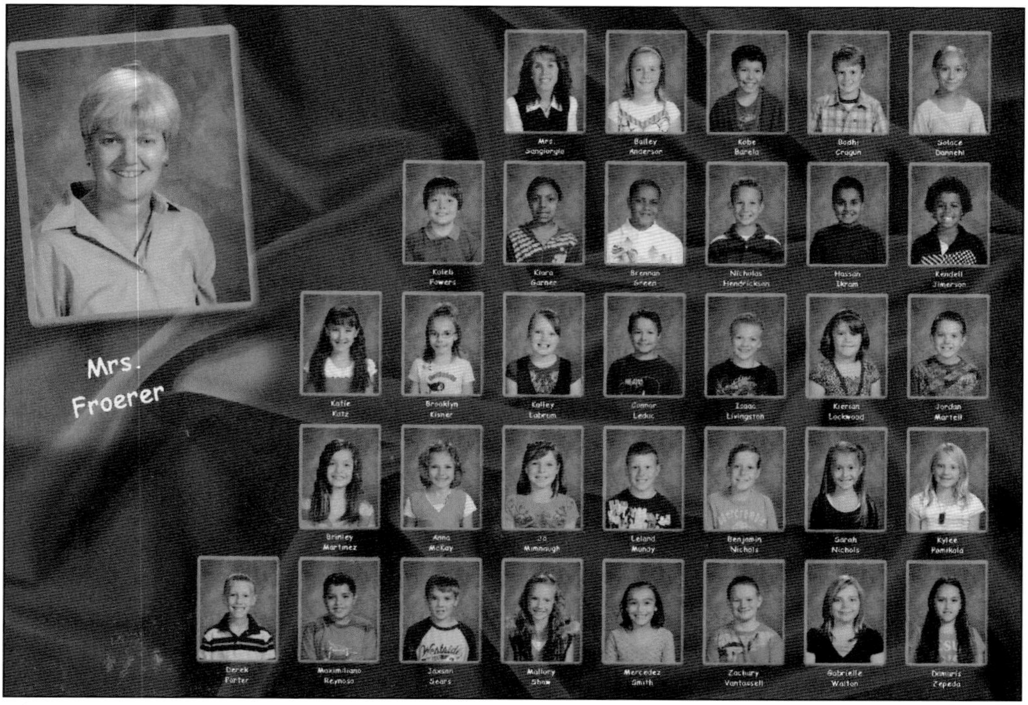

This is Maren Froerer's 2009–2010 fourth-grade class at MarLon Hills Elementary School. From left to right are (first row) Principal Darlene Sangiorgio, Bailey Anderson, Kobe Barela, Bodhi Cragun, and Dolace Dannehl; (second row) Kaleb Fowers, Kiara Garner, Brennan Green, Nicholas Hendrickson, Hassan Ikram, and Kendell Jimerson; (third row) Katie Katz, Brooklyn Kisner, Kalley Labrum, Connor Leduc, Isaac Livingston, Kierian Lockwood, and Jordan Martell; (fourth row) Brinley Martinez, Anna McKay, Jo Mimnaugh, Leland Mundy, Benjamin Nichols, Sarah Nichols and Kylee Pomikala; (fifth row) Derek Porter, Maximiliano Reynoso, Jaxson Sears, Mallory Shaw, Mercedes Smith, Zachary Vantassell, Gabrielle Walton, and Damaris Zepeda. (Courtesy MarLon Hills Elementary.)

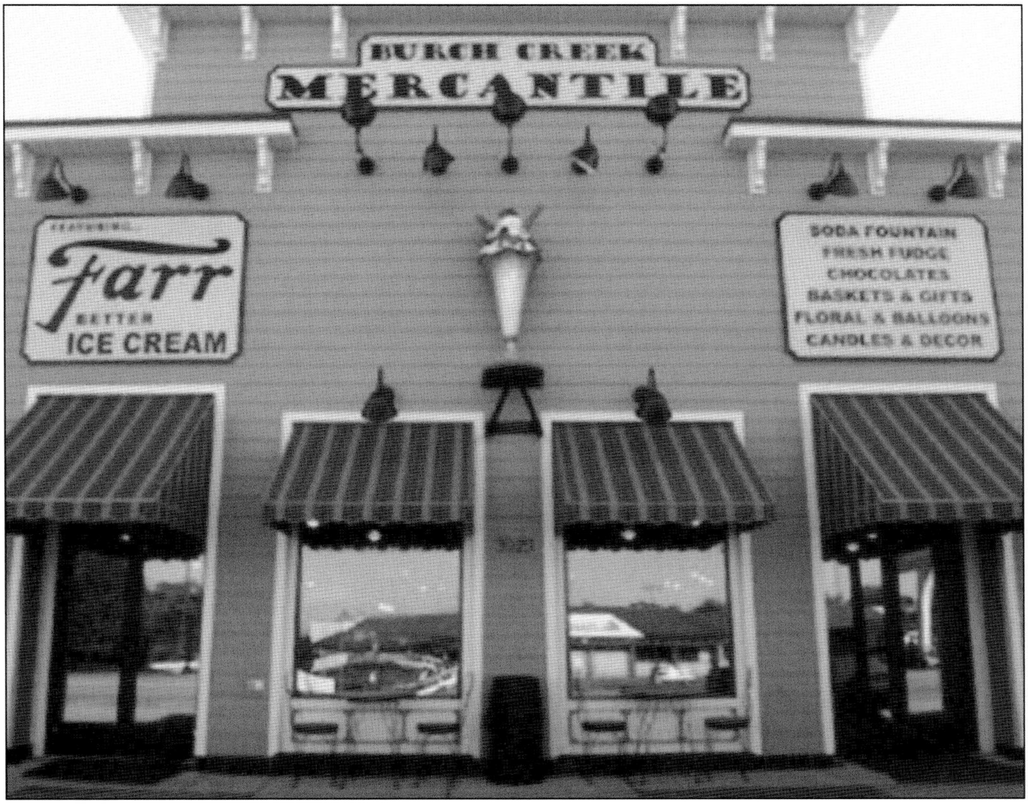

Burch Creek Mercantile at 3920 Washington Boulevard was established in 2009. This old-looking but very new store (above) has revitalized the historic downtown area and has become a gathering place for the locals. Owned and operated by South Ogden resident Robert Higgs, it contains a fully working vintage 1912 soda fountain (below) and over 70 flavors of Farr's ice cream. The store also makes its own fudge and sells flowers and balloons along with many handmade crafts and gifts. The decor and the music inside the shop feel like an earlier period in the city's history. Higgs actually lives in a fully restored 1914 Victorian home, and he allowed the public to tour it during the 1936 In the Park festivities associated with the 75th anniversary. (Both, courtesy Robert Higgs.)

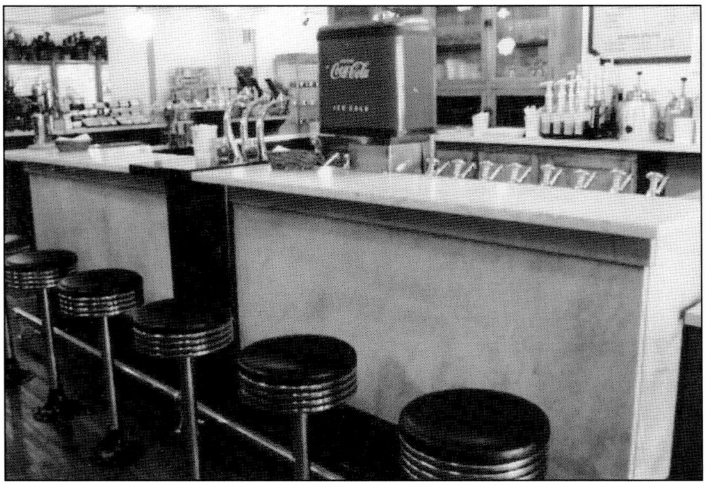

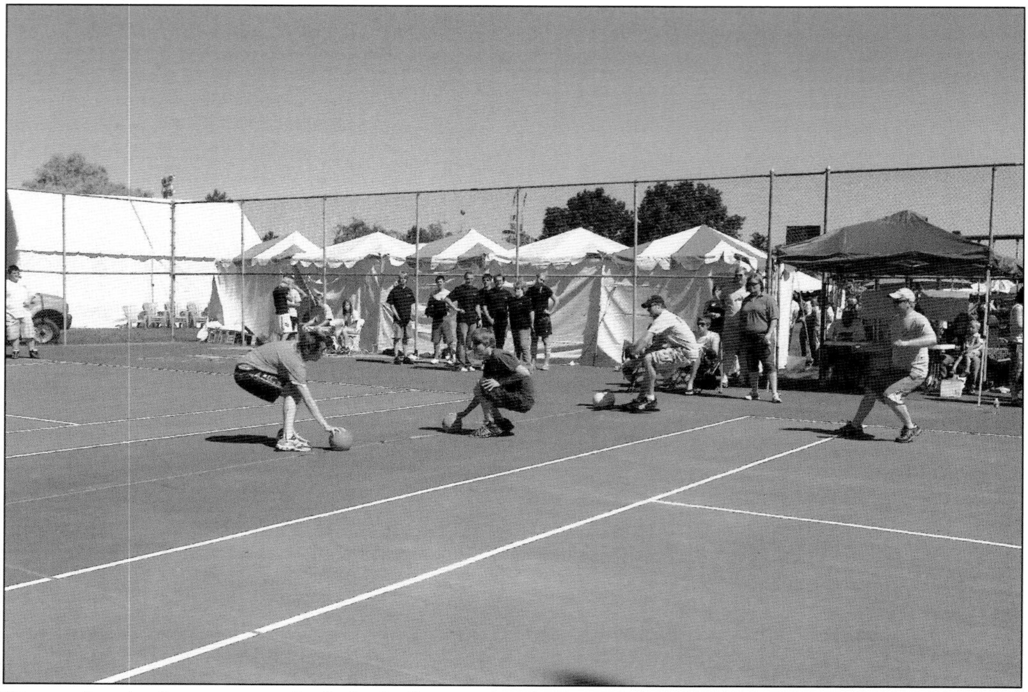

Pictured is the beginning of a dodgeball game on the tennis courts of Friendship Park, June 2009. Although not an annual event, dodgeball tournaments have been held periodically during the week of South Ogden Days. Recreation supervisor Julianna Silvester can be seen in the background officiating. (Courtesy Scott Sumner.)

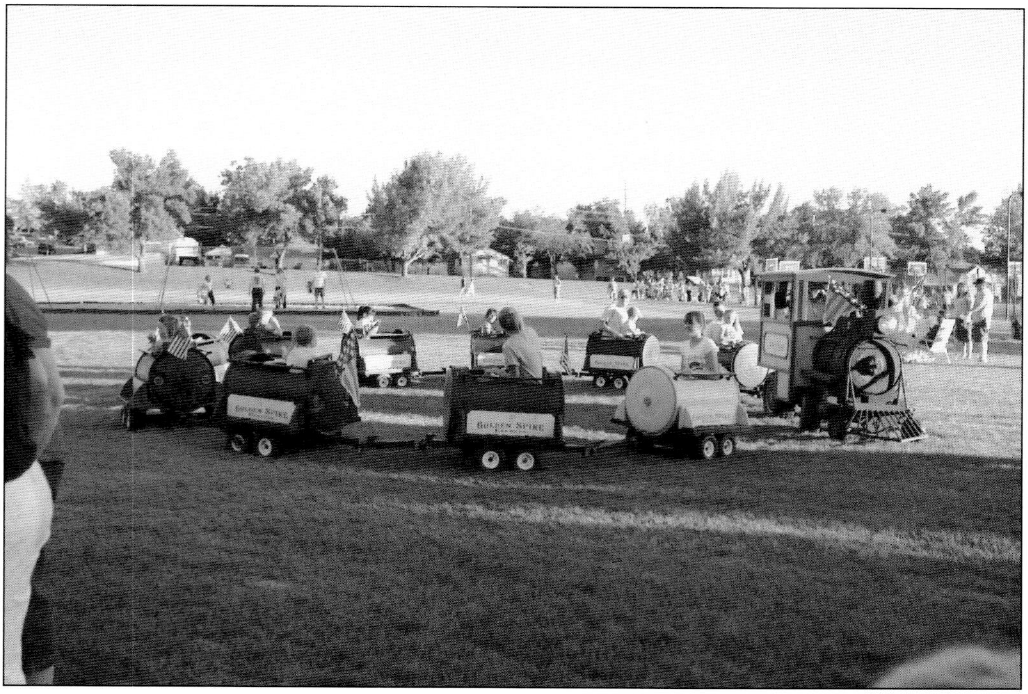

The Golden Spike Train gives kids rides around 40th Street Park after the South Ogden Days Parade in June 2009. (Courtesy Scott Sumner.)

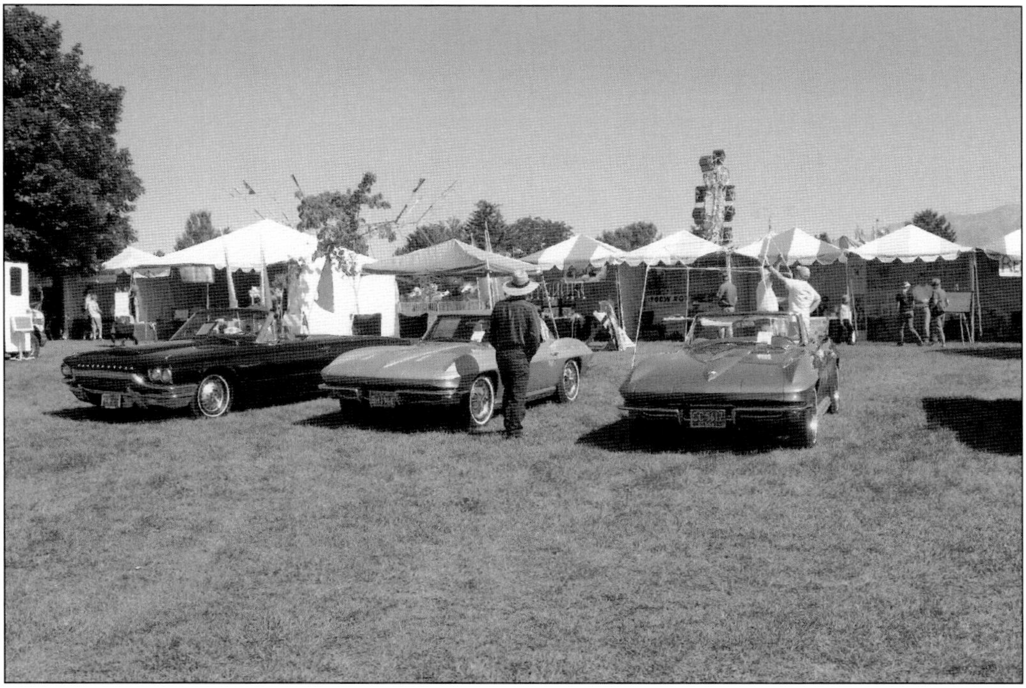

Car shows have been a tradition of the South Ogden Day festivities. These Corvettes, parked at Friendship Park for the show, are just some of many vintage and new cars on display each year. (Courtesy Scott Sumner.)

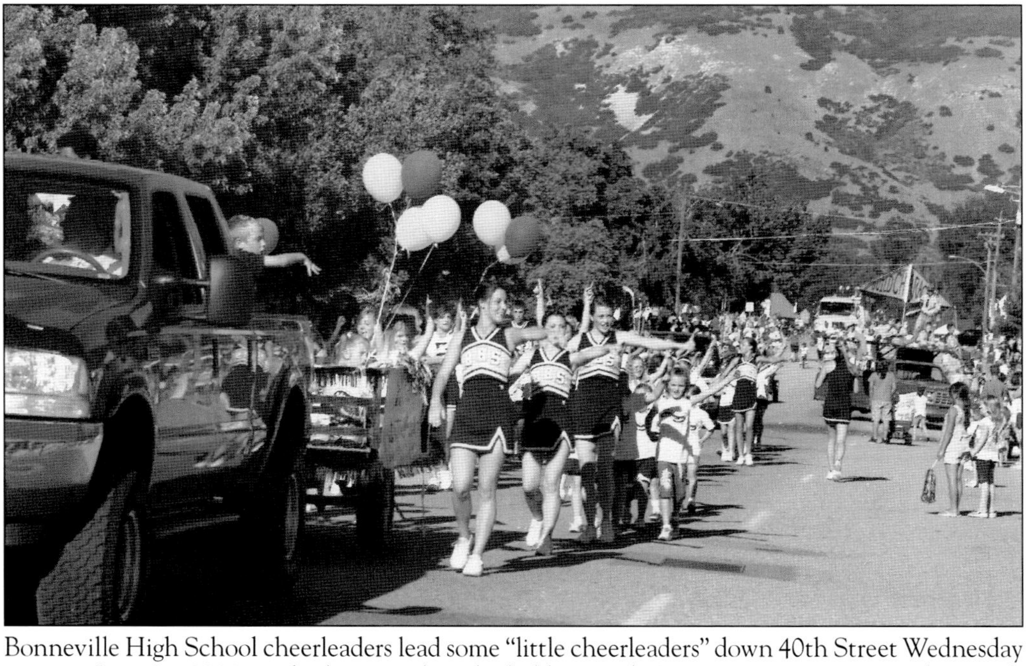

Bonneville High School cheerleaders lead some "little cheerleaders" down 40th Street Wednesday evening June 24, 2009, in the last parade to be held on 40th Street. Starting in 2010, the South Ogden Days Parade was moved to the Saturday morning of South Ogden Days, and the parade route began at the new South Ogden Junior High School and travelled around the south end of the city. (Courtesy Scott Sumner.)

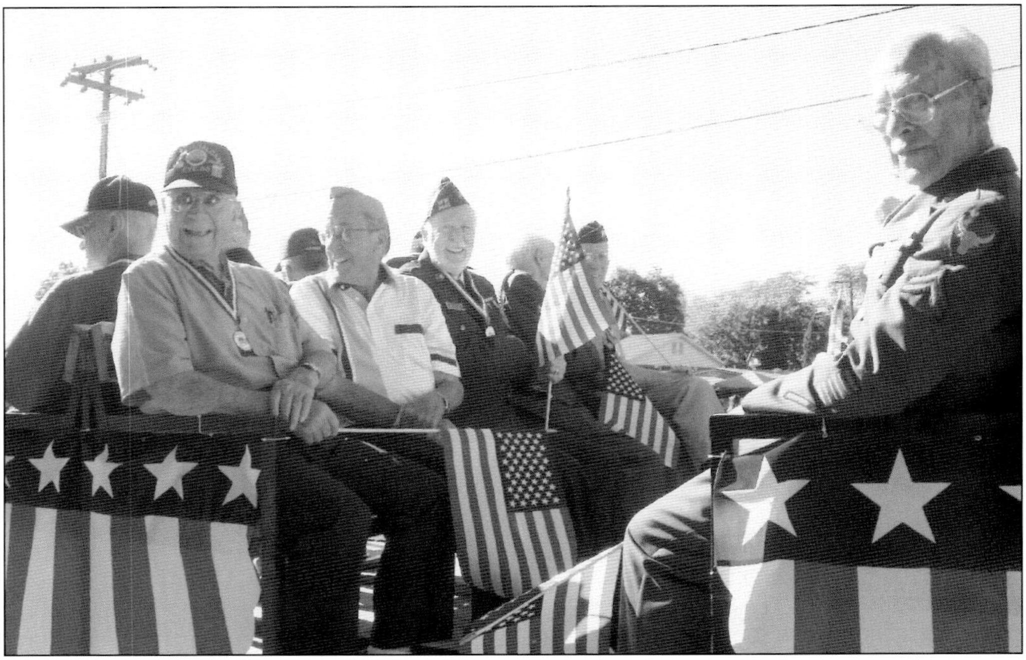

The military veterans of the city were asked to be the grand marshals of the 2009 South Ogden Days Parade (above). After the 2009 parade, during the picnic in the park, the veterans met for a special ceremony by the war memorials in 40th Street Park. Below are, from left to right, C. William Gilman, Grant C. Hogan, and unidentified. The veterans were given a commemorative medal that night and were treated to a private concert. The Utah Symphony musicians, along with the East Street Band led by South Ogden's own C.J. Sontoro, played patriotic music for the vets. (Both, courtesy Scott Sumner.)

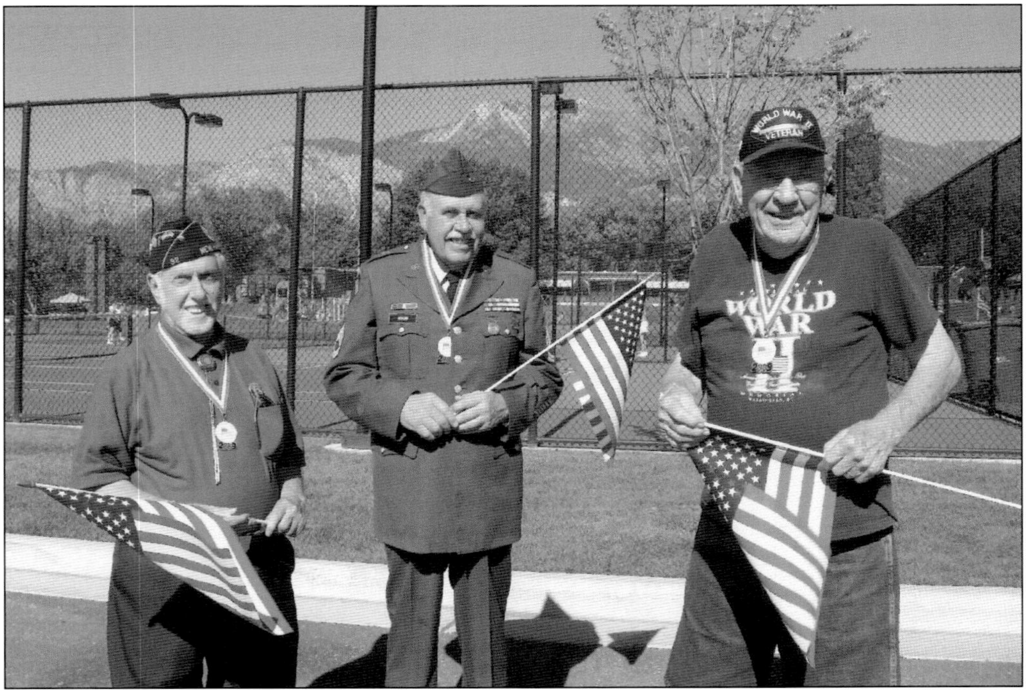

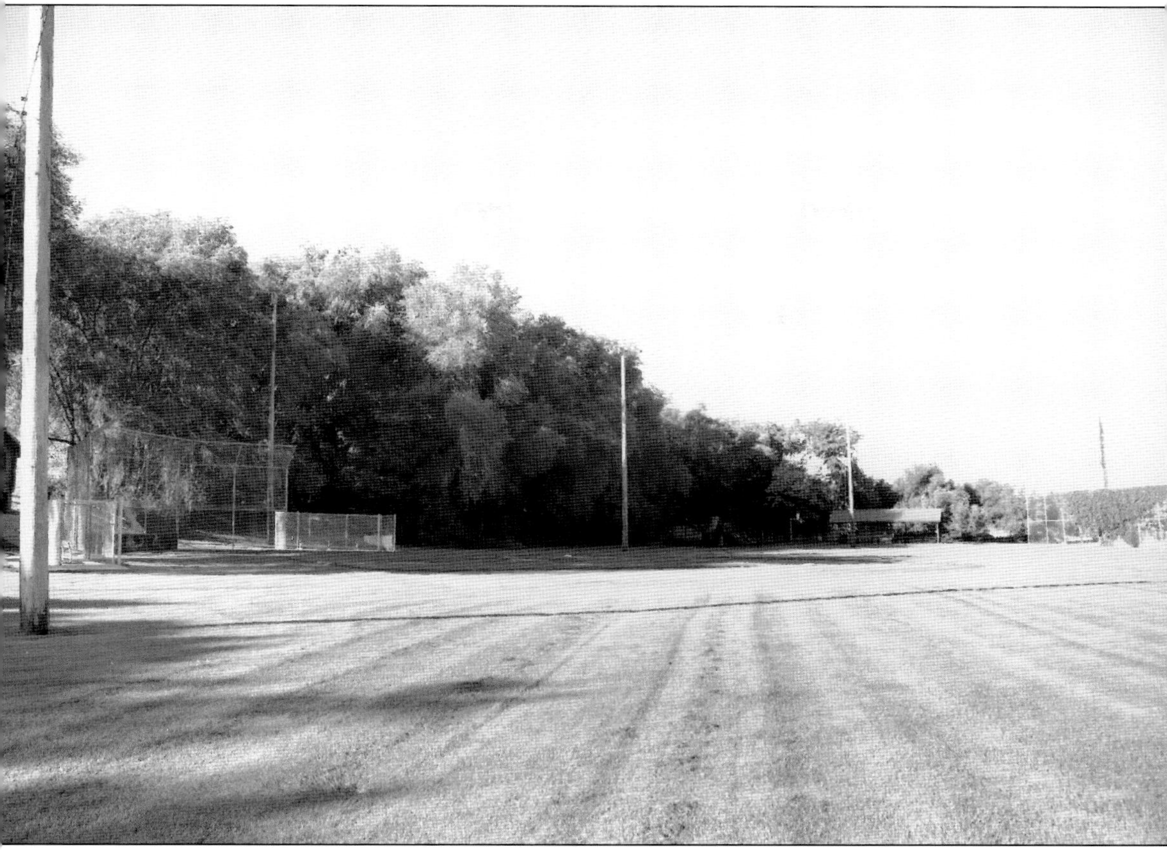

This is a recent photograph of the baseball field at Club Heights Park, 4100 South Palmer Drive. The land for the park was conveyed to the city by the Weber County School Board decades ago. The name of the park and the school on the south end are derived from the Kiwanis Club building that was located just southwest of the current bowery. Earlier in the city's history, the park was called South Ogden Kiwanis Park and was used for LDS Church softball games. The close but very high outfield fence was a great challenge. The park is still used for recreation baseball and flag football, and the kids love to play there because it is a place to play "under the lights." In recent years, an off-leash dog area has been added where the Kiwanis building used to stand. (Courtesy Russell Porter.)

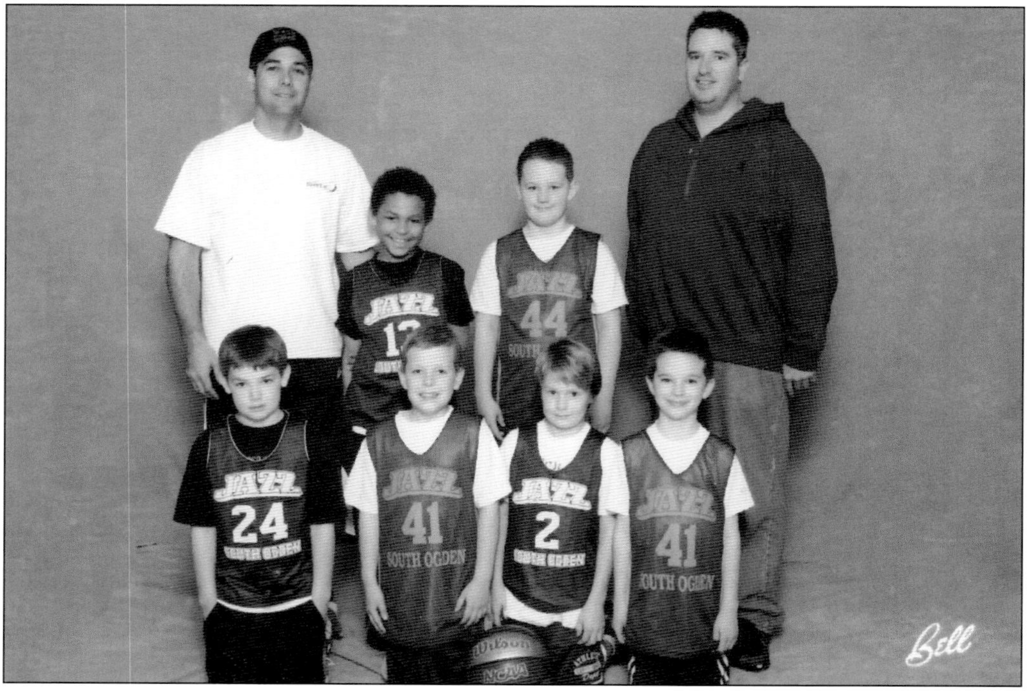

A 2009 Junior Jazz basketball team are, from left to right, (first row) Jaxson Sears, Ben Nicholls, Bodhi Cragun, and Parker Beesley; (second row) coach Blake Sears, Hampton Bouwhuis, Zack VanTassell, and coach Aaron Beesley. (Photograph by Bell Photography; courtesy Stacie Sears.)

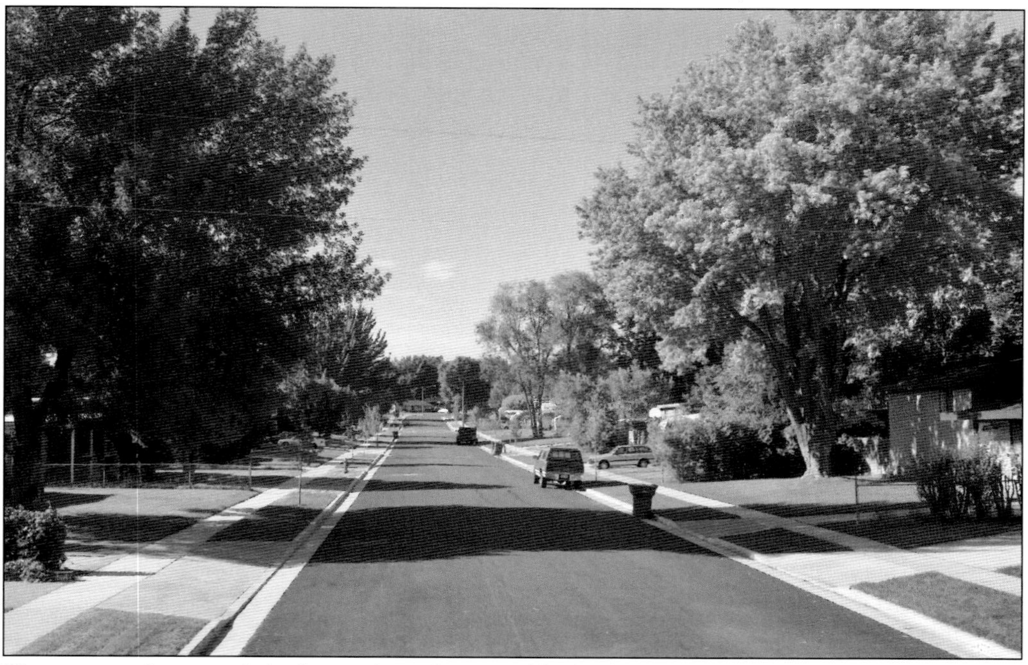

This recent photograph looks south at the 4200 block of 850 East. This street was the site of a Community Development Block Grant (CDBG). Federal and city money was used to install new water lines; inspect sewer lines; rebuild the road; install new curbs, gutters, and sidewalks; and landscape. (Courtesy Russell Porter.)

Eight

2010s

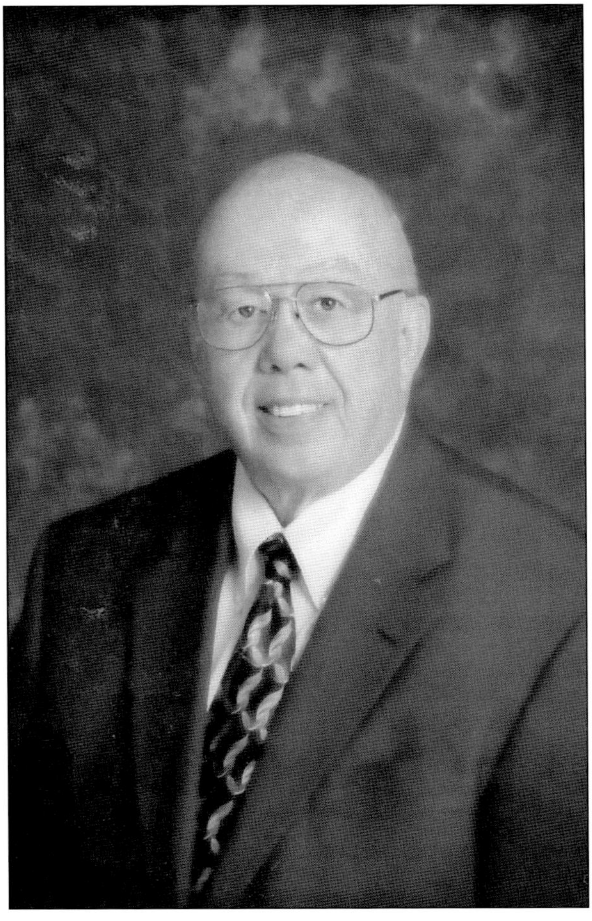

James F. Minster is the current mayor of South Ogden. Mayor Minster was elected in 2010 after spending eight years on the city council. Minster has lived in the city for 66 years. He has been involved in the Boy Scouts of America throughout his life and is a former South Ogden police officer and fire chief.

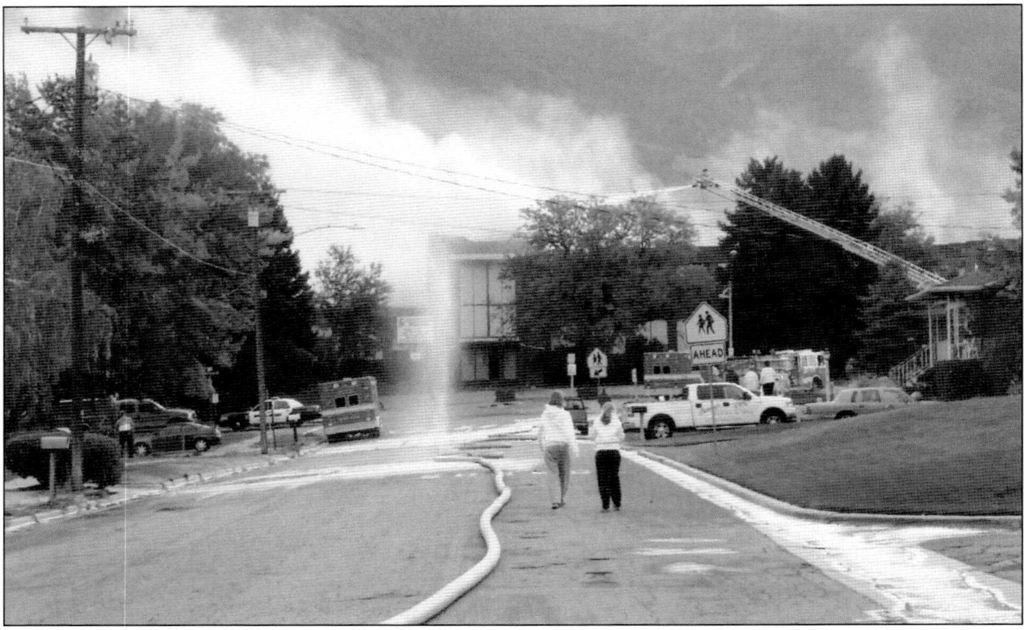

In the early morning hours of October 23, 2010, fire broke out in the old South Ogden Junior High School, 4300 Madison Avenue. The school was no longer being used and was scheduled for demolition. Over 40 firefighters from three different jurisdictions worked on site for many hours, putting water on the building until later that same afternoon. Fortunately, no one was injured in the fire. Eventually four juveniles were charged with reckless burning in the incident. Above, Cortney Porter (left) and Brooklyn Porter walk alongside a fire hose stretching up 43rd Street on their way to get a better view. Below, the South Ogden Fire Department's ladder truck No. 81 puts water on the structure from above. (Above, courtesy Sherri Porter; below, courtesy David Labbe.)

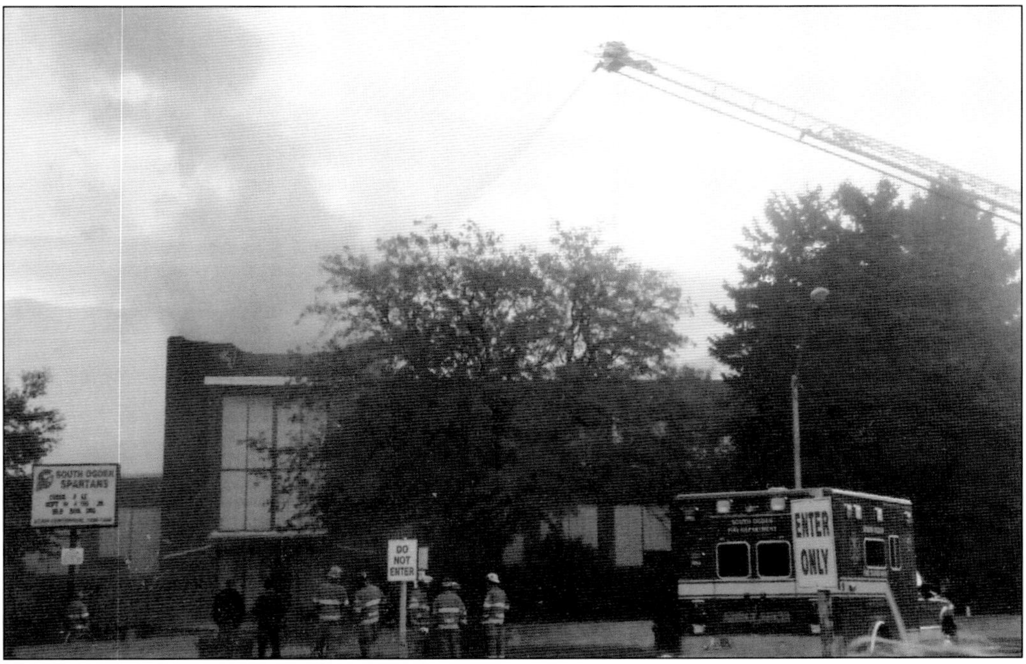

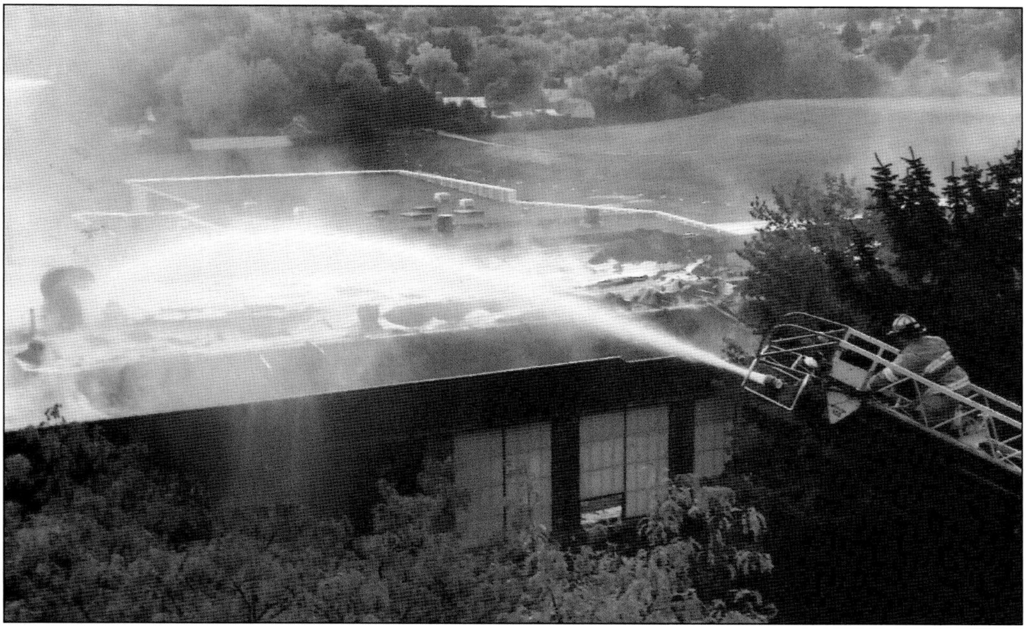

Above is an aerial photograph of a firefighter on an extended ladder truck putting water onto the roof of the empty South Ogden Junior High School. Smoke and steam rise above the school during this October 23, 2010, blaze. Below is aerial photograph of the damage to the roof and upper floor of the two-story structure. The school had been unoccupied for just five months. After the investigation, the school was demolished. Demolition workers were interrupted so often by locals wanting a brick from their old school that they dumped a large pile of bricks in the parking lot so sentimentalists could take one; the pile did not last long. The area is now a dirt field, with district officials planning to landscape the area and eventually build a new elementary school on the site. (Both, courtesy David Labbe.)

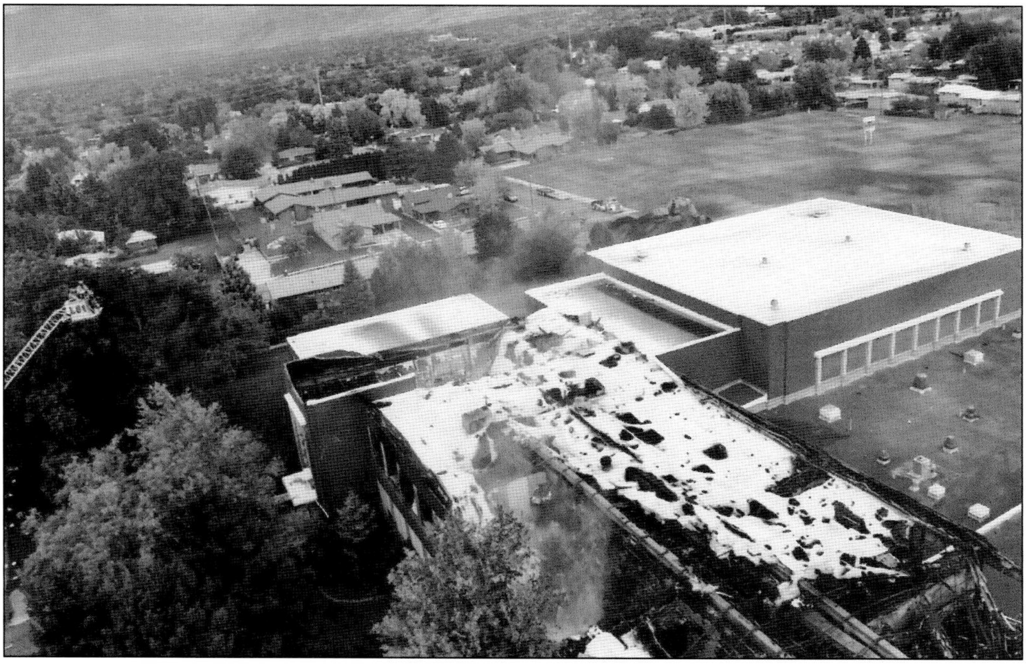

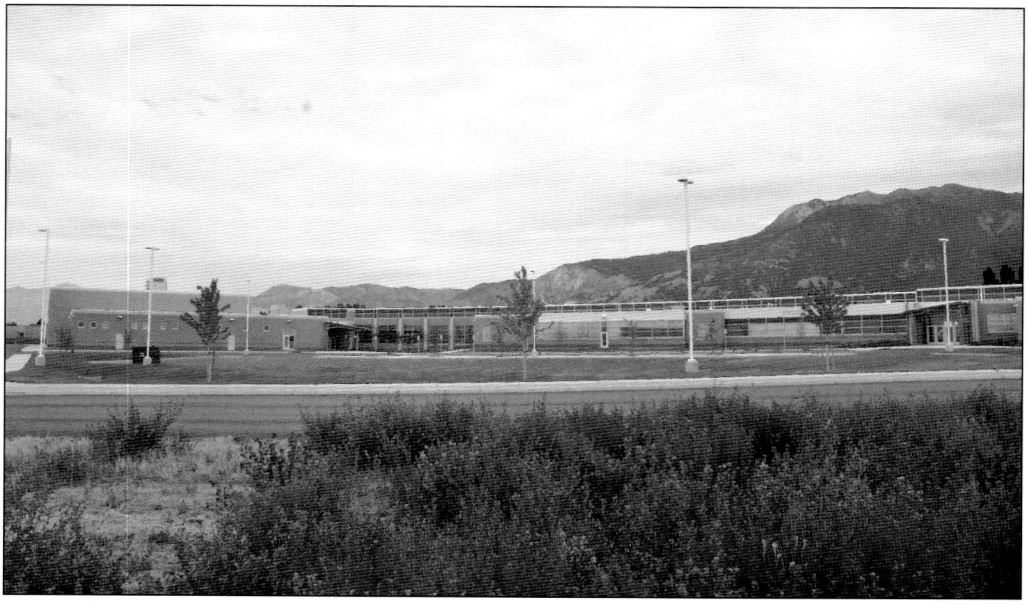

Pictured is the new South Ogden Junior High School. The new home of the Spartans was built two miles south of the original junior high school, at 650 East 5700 South. The school opened to 850 students in August 2010 with Don Tanner as principal, Chad Marriott as assistant principal, and a staff of 75. The school, part of the Weber County School District, boasts a proud tradition of choir, band, performing arts, visual arts, academics, and athletics. The school was built with two full-sized gymnasiums in a joint effort with South Ogden City. The city paid $2 million for the added expense of a second gym so the recreation programs could use the facility in the evenings and on weekends for basketball, volleyball, and dodgeball. Below is the inside of the gym facility. (Both, courtesy Scott Sumner.)

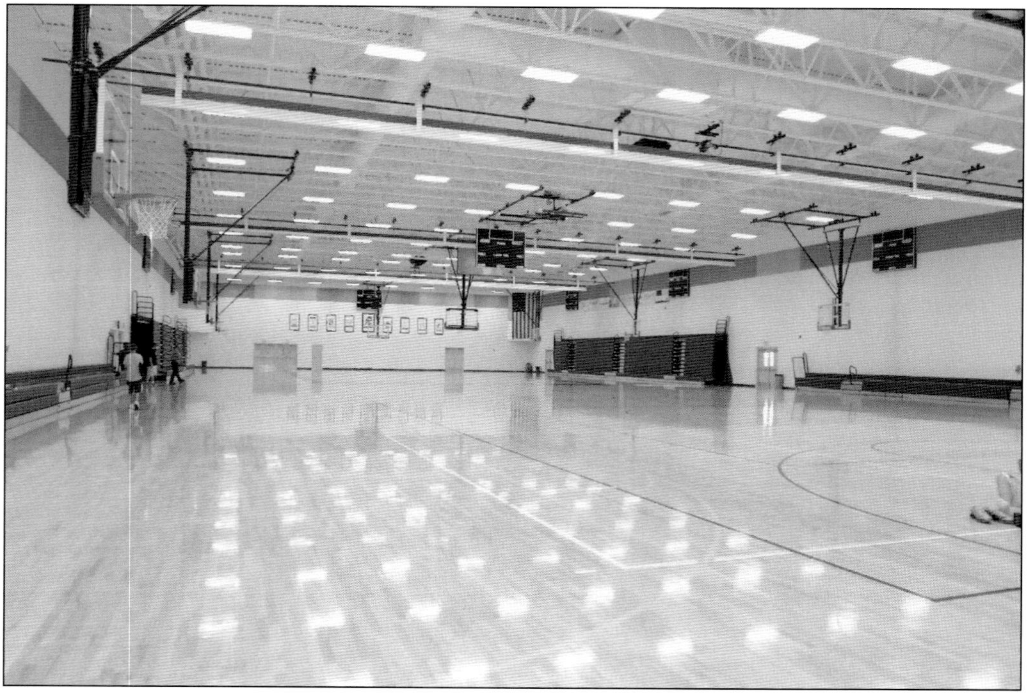

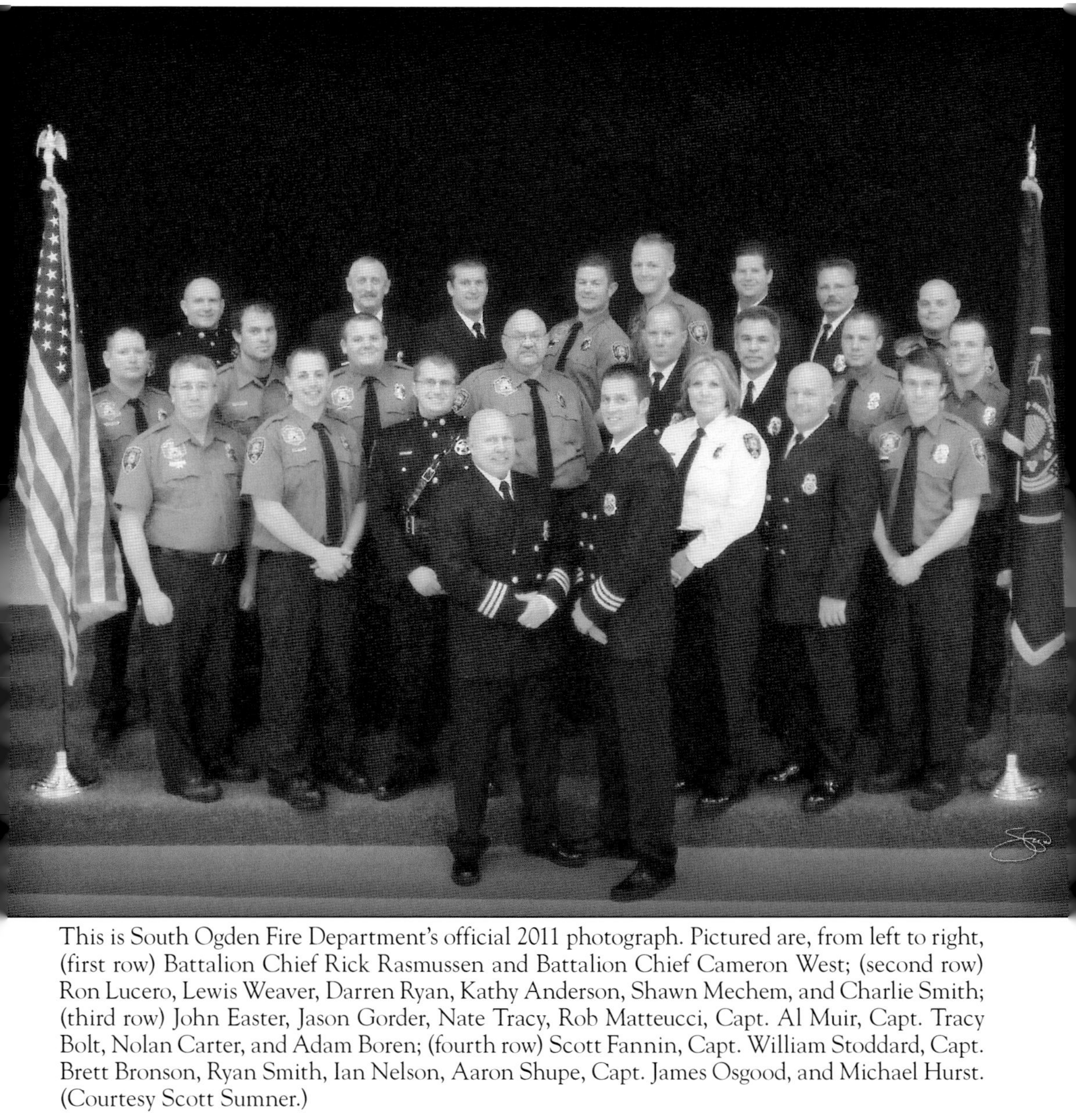

This is South Ogden Fire Department's official 2011 photograph. Pictured are, from left to right, (first row) Battalion Chief Rick Rasmussen and Battalion Chief Cameron West; (second row) Ron Lucero, Lewis Weaver, Darren Ryan, Kathy Anderson, Shawn Mechem, and Charlie Smith; (third row) John Easter, Jason Gorder, Nate Tracy, Rob Matteucci, Capt. Al Muir, Capt. Tracy Bolt, Nolan Carter, and Adam Boren; (fourth row) Scott Fannin, Capt. William Stoddard, Capt. Brett Bronson, Ryan Smith, Ian Nelson, Aaron Shupe, Capt. James Osgood, and Michael Hurst. (Courtesy Scott Sumner.)

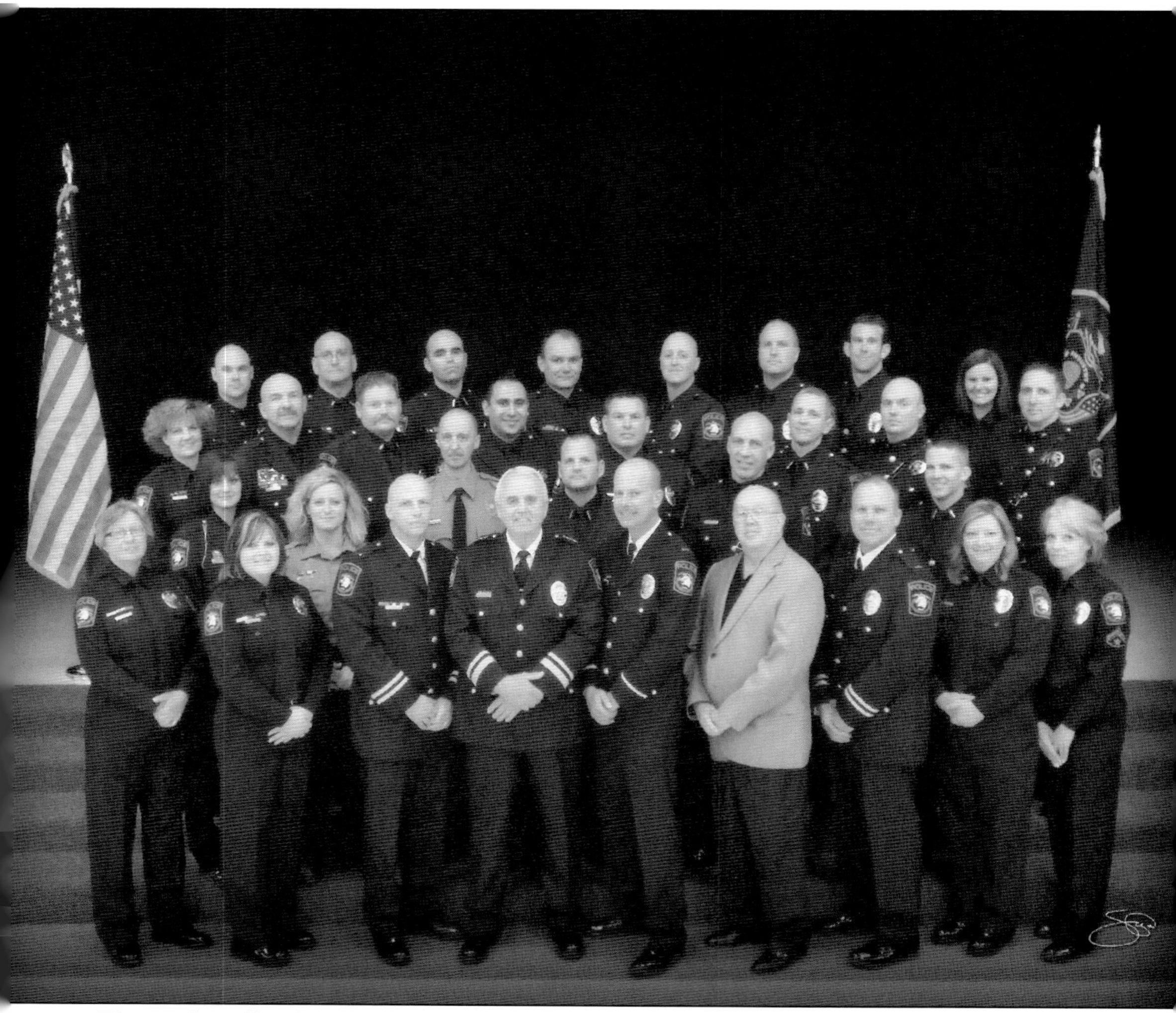

This is the official 2011 photograph of South Ogden Department of Public Safety. They are, from left to right, (first row) Kaye Jones, Cindee Poulsen, Lt. Jeff Nelson, Chief Val Shupe, Lt. Darin Parke, Mayor James Minster, Lt. Dwight Ruth, Jackie Butters, and Karen Disney; (second row) Lisa Dalton, Kim Busby, Mitch Jones, Matthew Thompson, Sgt. David Labbe, and Cortney Roskelley; (third row) Janette Kirkland, Ron VanBeekum, Sgt. Todd Hardman, Gerardo Vazquez, Brian Schultz, Bryan Hough, Michael McNeely, and Shawn Read; (fourth row) Randy Thomason, Sgt. Wilford DeHart, Ryan Bailey, Dan Buttars, Jeff Dingman, Greg Dingman, Sgt. Trent Olsen, and Marci Edwards. (Courtesy Scott Sumner.)

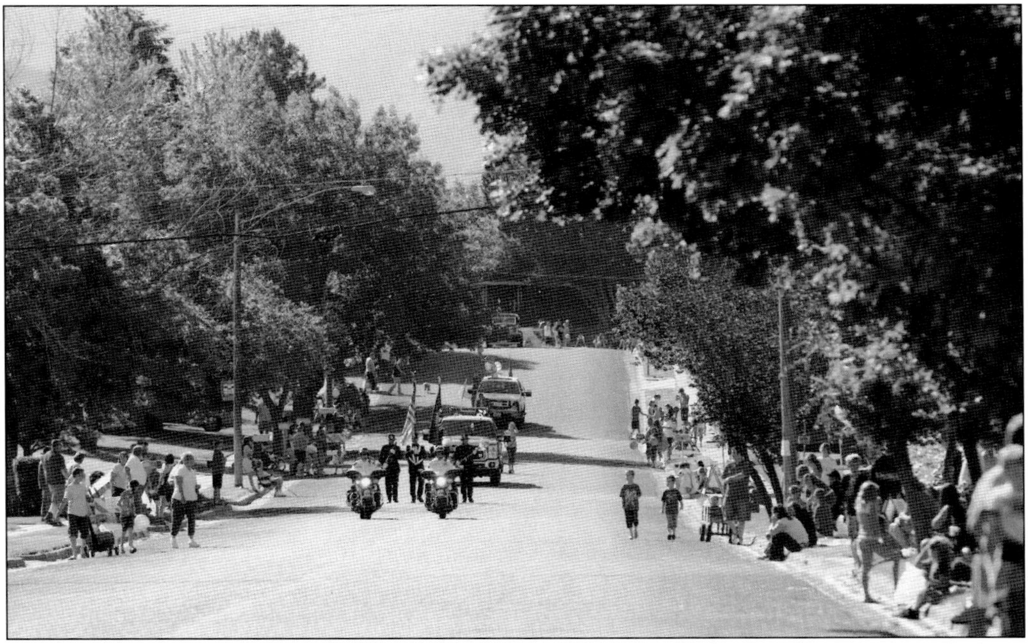

This is the first South Ogden Days Parade at its new location. This June 2010 view is looking east on 5300 South as the parade nears. This was also the first Saturday morning parade after decades of an evening procession. Local residents were happy to have the route closer, but those who had traditionally enjoyed the parade in their neighborhood were disappointed by the change. (Courtesy Scott Sumner.)

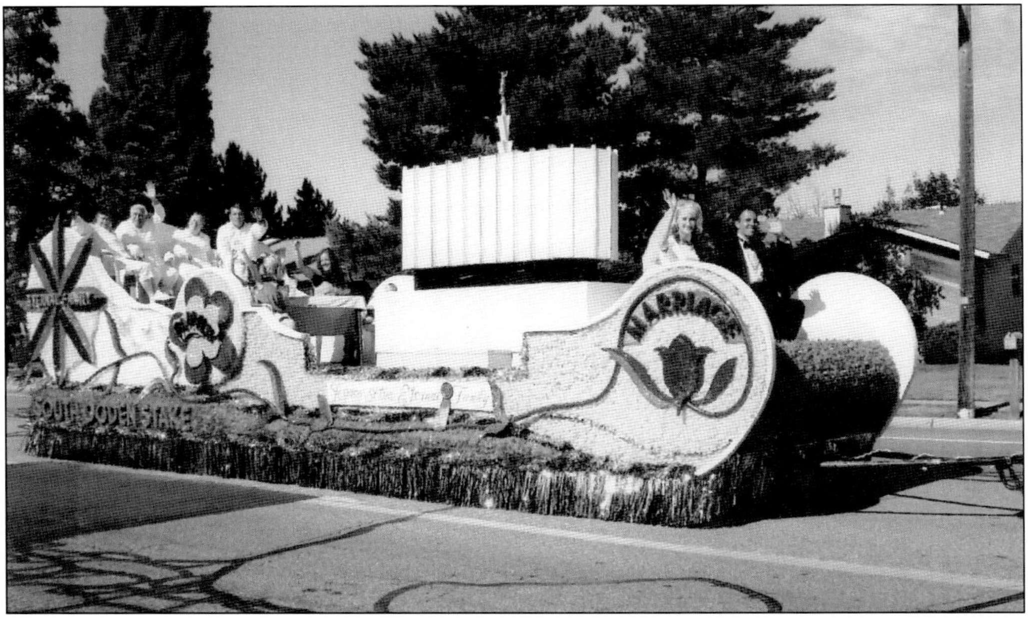

This float was built by the South Ogden Stake of the Church of Jesus Christ of Latter-day Saints for the 2010 parade season. The float, titled "Legacy of the Eternal Family," won ribbons in the South Ogden Days Parade, Pioneer Day Parade in Ogden City, and Peach Days in Brigham City. The float was built by the volunteer labor of Manuel Cypers, Joe Holmes, Paul Powell, and Ed Wygal. (Courtesy Manuel Cypers.)

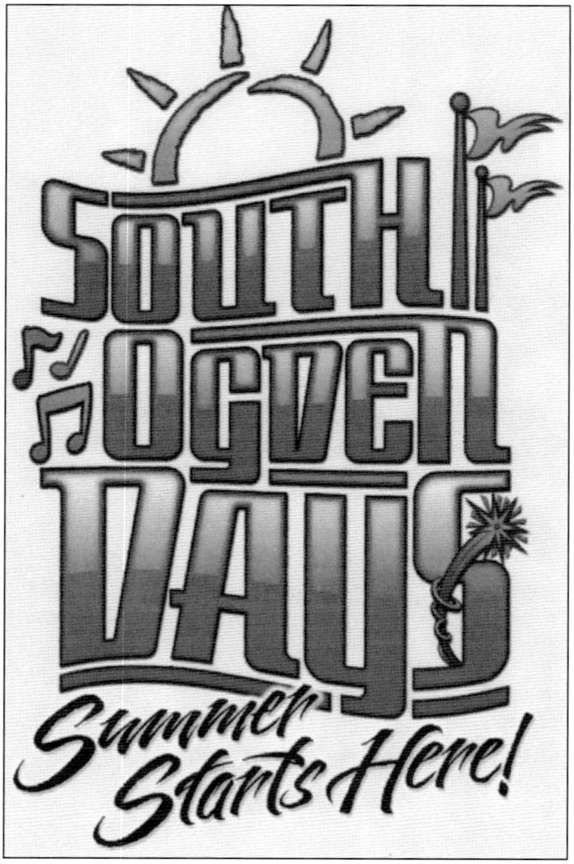

The South Ogden Days activities in June have been going on since 1999. Since then, the following events have taken place (some have occurred annually without missing a year): golf tournament, three-on-three basketball tournament, baby contest, art show, photograph contest, Picnic in the Park, bed races, mud volleyball, dodgeball, parade, carnival, teen dance, karaoke, fireman's breakfast, car and motorcycle shows, eating contests, vendors, carnival, concerts, local entertainment, and fireworks. At left, the logo created by Gabe Pencock debuted in 2006 and has been used ever since. Below, one of the more popular events, the three-on-three basketball tournament, is held at 40th Street Park in this 2010 photograph. (Both, courtesy Scott Sumner.)

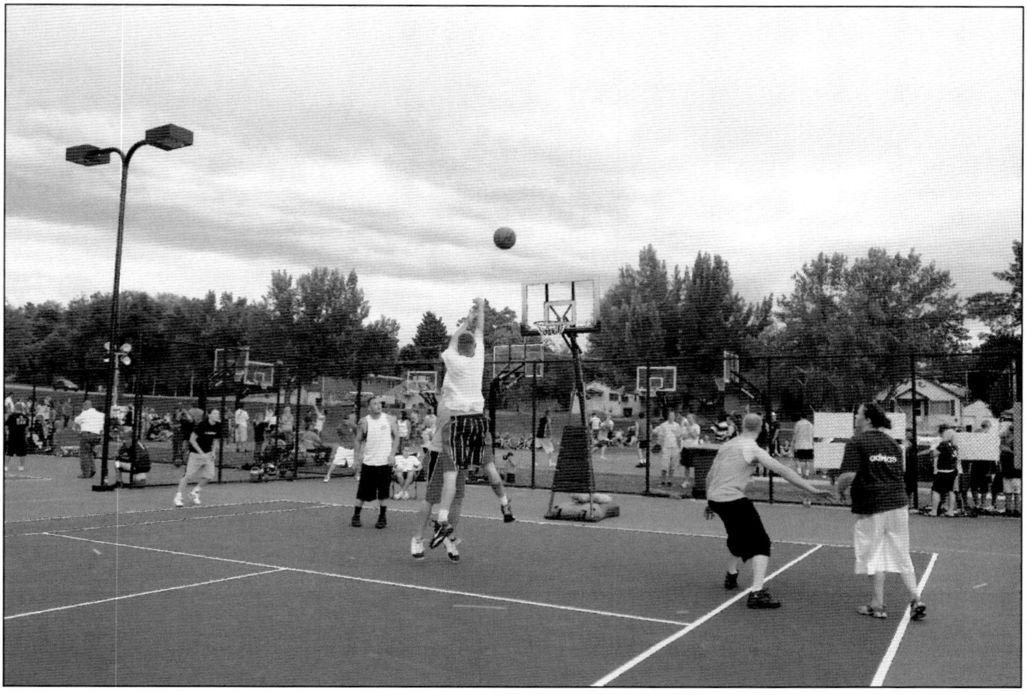

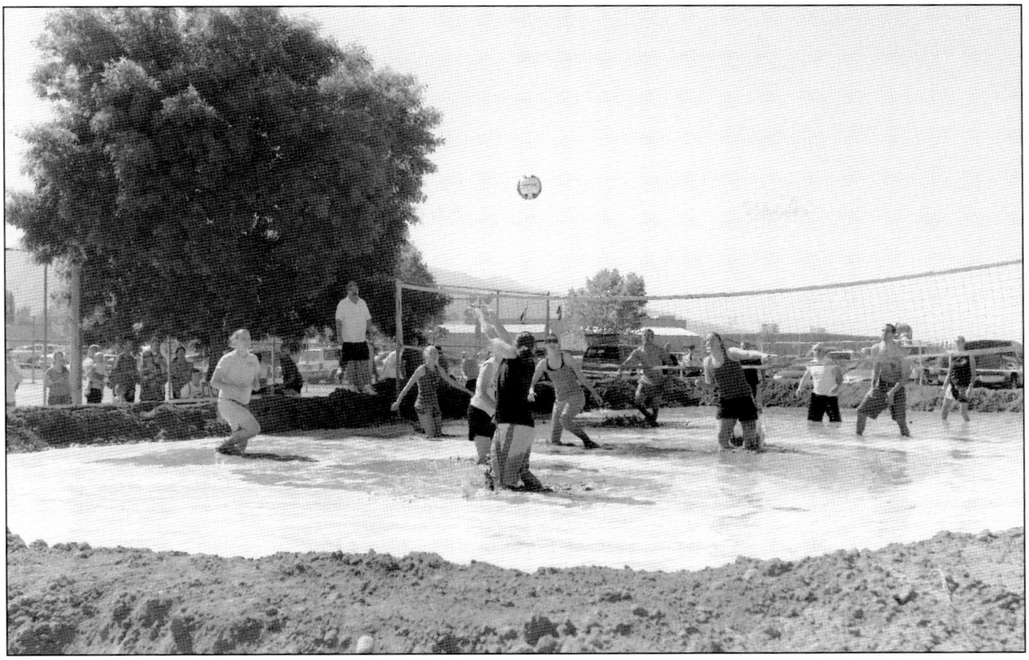

The mud volleyball tournament is one of the most anticipated events of South Ogden Days. Held annually at Friendship Park, the tournament draws teams from within and outside the city. This action photograph is a girls' team versus a coed team. Win or lose, everyone gets muddy. John West, assistant recreation director, is officiating. (Courtesy Scott Sumner.)

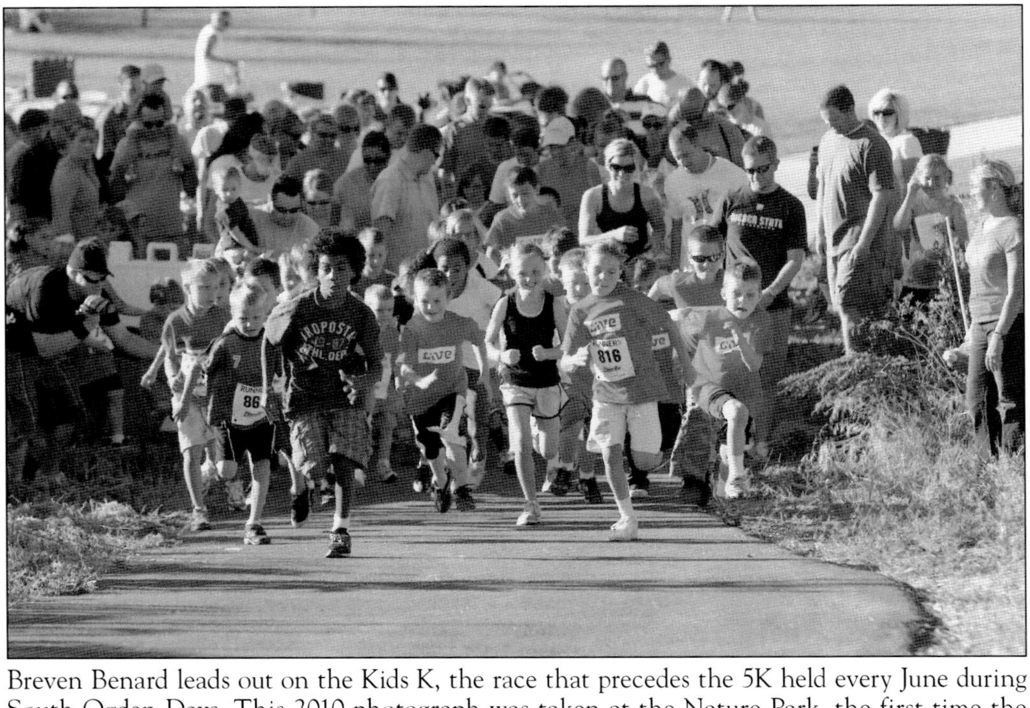

Breven Benard leads out on the Kids K, the race that precedes the 5K held every June during South Ogden Days. This 2010 photograph was taken at the Nature Park, the first time the race was held there. In previous years, the race was held in the streets around Friendship Park. (Courtesy Scott Sumner.)

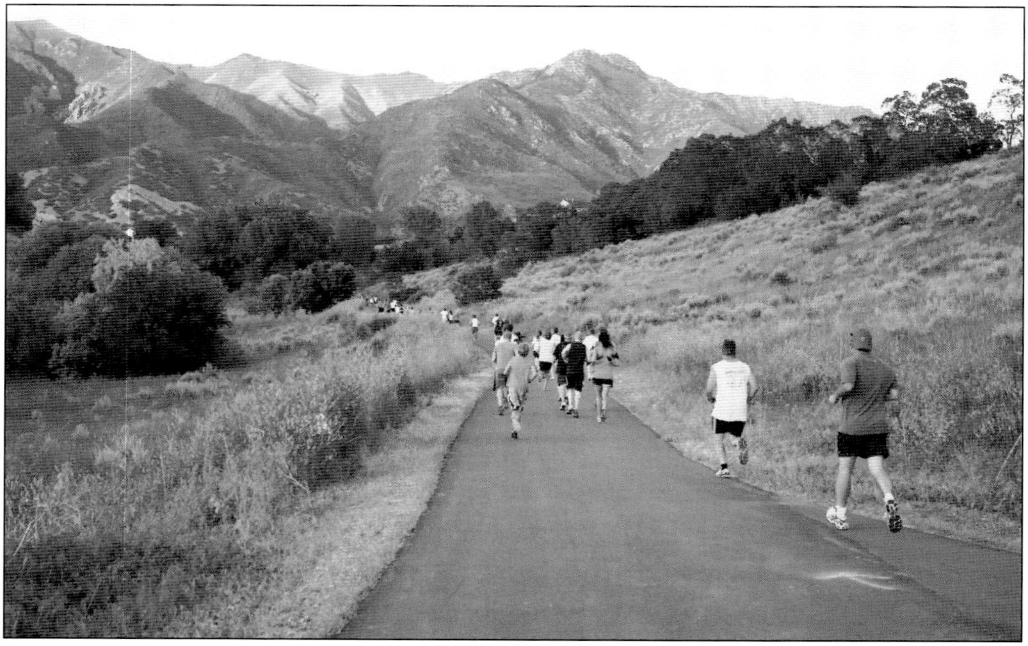

These 2010 photographs show the South Ogden Days 5K, held at the Nature Park. The race is held in the evening, usually on the Thursday of the week of activities. There are over 500 runners that participate annually in the city's 5K. The South Ogden Nature Park opened on the south end of the city in the fall of 2007. It is approximately 50 acres and contains a one-mile loop walking path that has three entry points into it from the surrounding neighborhoods. The area has fabulous views, and the path surrounds a marshy area full of wildlife and birds. Above, runners head east on a downhill slope with the Wasatch Mountains in the background. Below, participants head toward the finish line, including Jeannie Petersen, runner 734. (Both, courtesy Scott Sumner.)

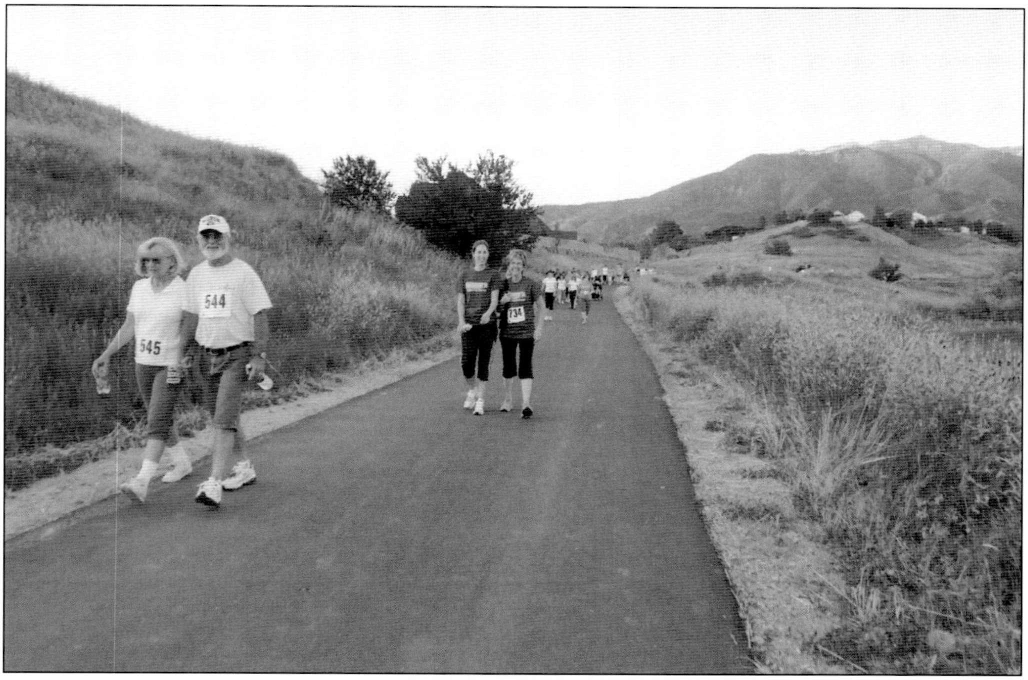

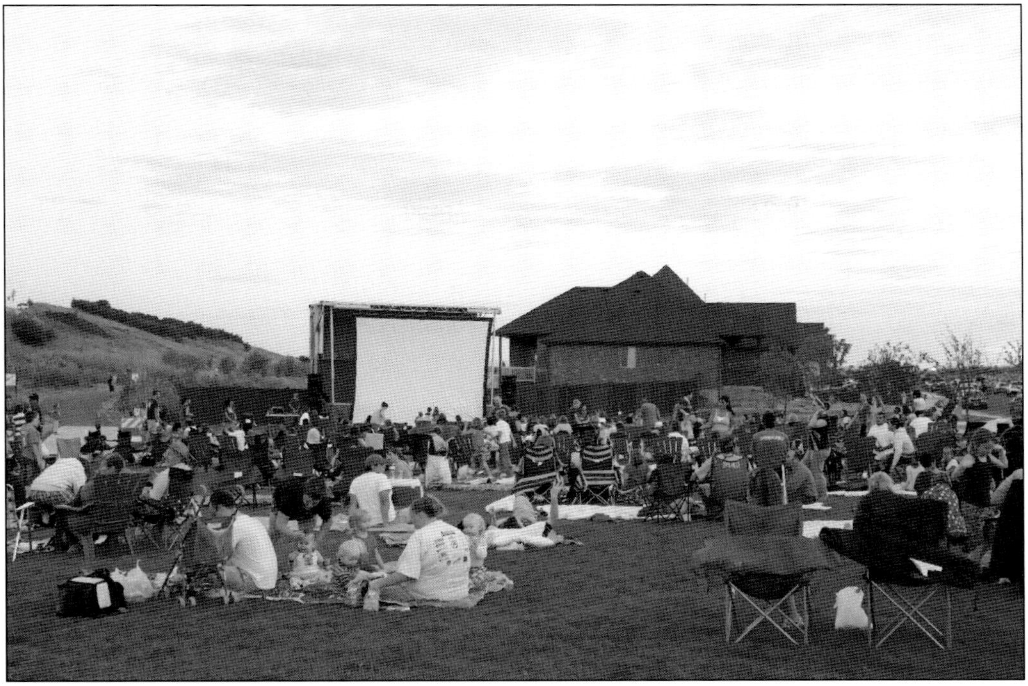

Families get ready for the Movie in the Park, another South Ogden Days tradition, above. Previously held in Friendship Park, this 2010 showing was held in the Nature Park later in the evening after the Kids K and 5K. Sponsored by Mountain Ridge Assistant Living in South Ogden, locals get to enjoy a family-friendly movie complete with free popcorn. Below, residents on blankets and chairs prepare for the movie. Looking at the camera are, from left to right, Tony Hanebrink (waving), Diana Hanebrink, and Lauren Bailey. (Both, courtesy Scott Sumner.)

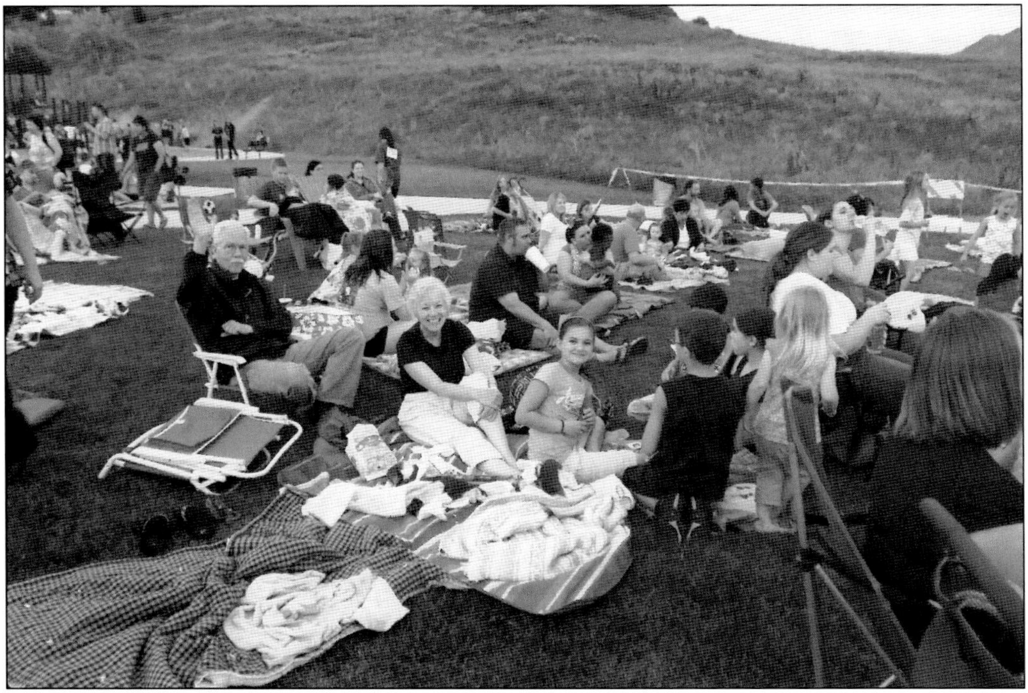

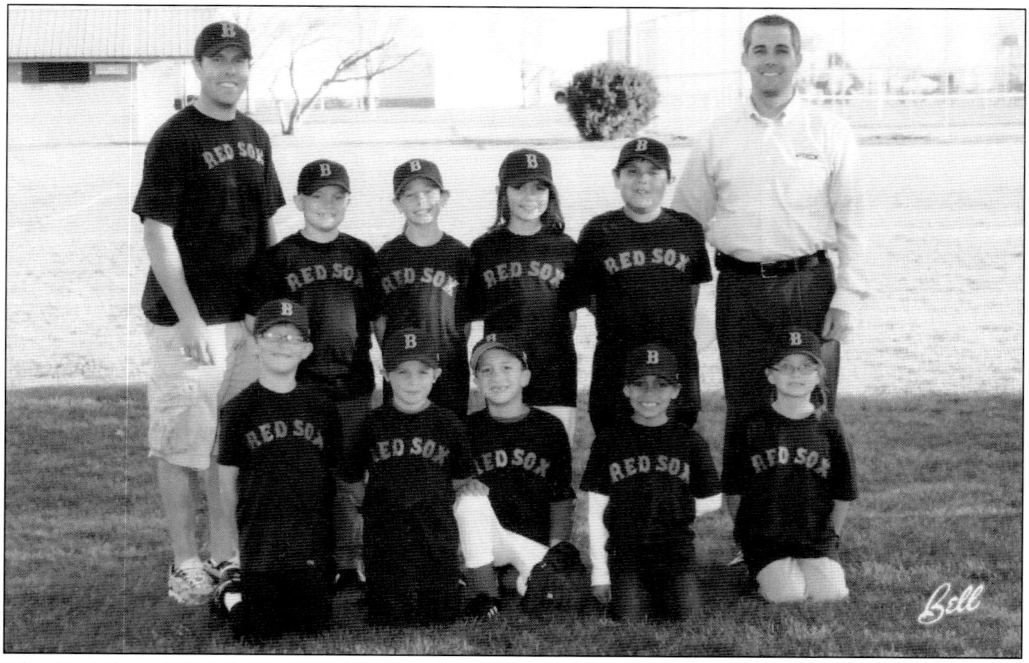

The Red Sox of South Ogden City Recreation baseball are photographed in 2010. The team is, from left to right, (first row) unidentified, Cory Stettler, ? Afuvai, Taijania Galvez, and Sierra Smith; (second row) coach Brian Hassell, Luke Walton, Bailey Hassell, Aspen Sears, Xavier Garcia, and coach Blake Sears. (Photograph by Bell Photography; courtesy Stacie Sears.)

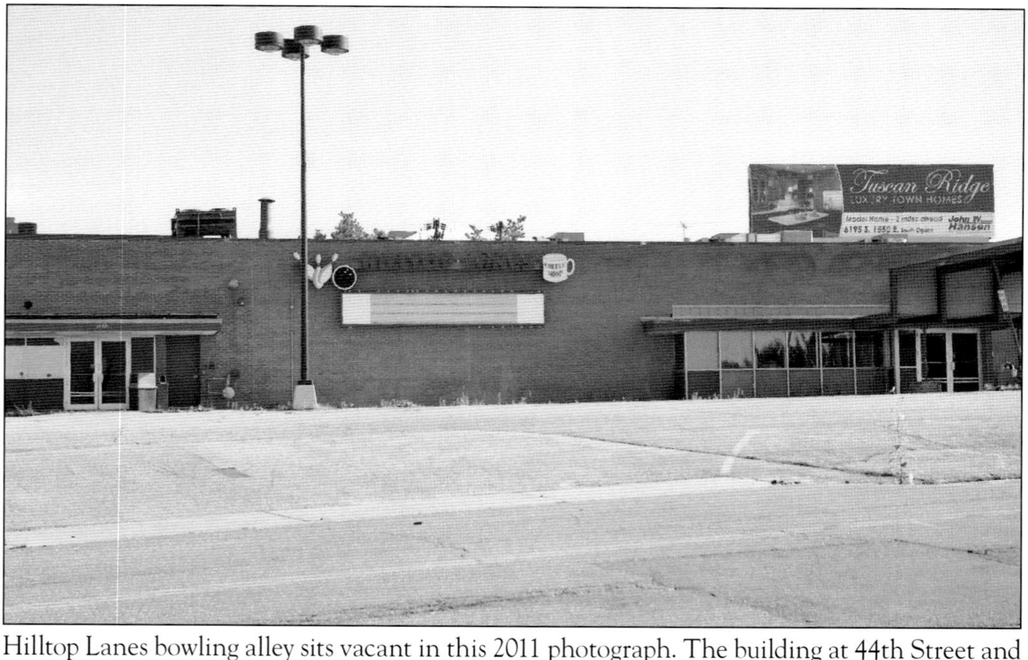

Hilltop Lanes bowling alley sits vacant in this 2011 photograph. The building at 44th Street and Washington Boulevard has been empty for years. From the 1970s to the early 1990s, Hilltop was a major meeting place to bowl, play pool, or eat at the grill. Many residents, especially teenagers, loved that it was open 24 hours a day, and police cars from South Ogden, Riverdale, and Washington Terrace were generally in the parking lot. (Courtesy Sherri Porter.)

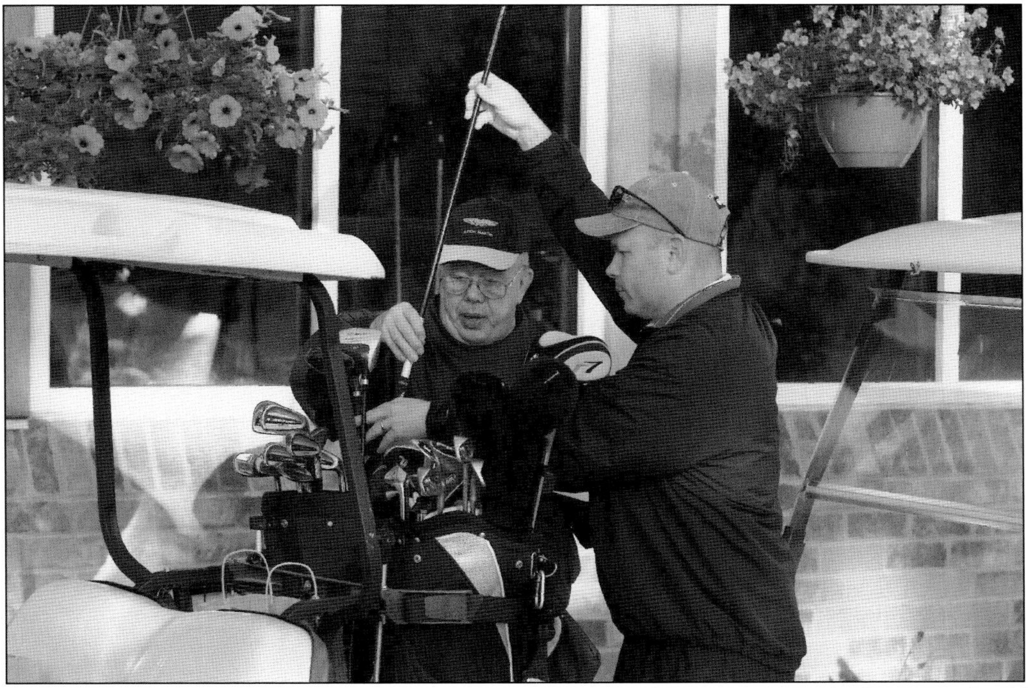

The week of events for South Ogden Days kicks off Monday morning with the annual golf tournament, held at Schneiter's Riverside Golf Course in Riverdale. These June 20, 2011, photographs show (above) Mayor James F. Minster (left) and city manager Matthew Dixon getting their clubs ready for the round. Below are, from left to right, Jason Brennan; Tim Zampedri; public works, parks, and recreation director Jon Andersen; and unidentified posing on one of the greens in 2009. (Both, courtesy Scott Sumner.)

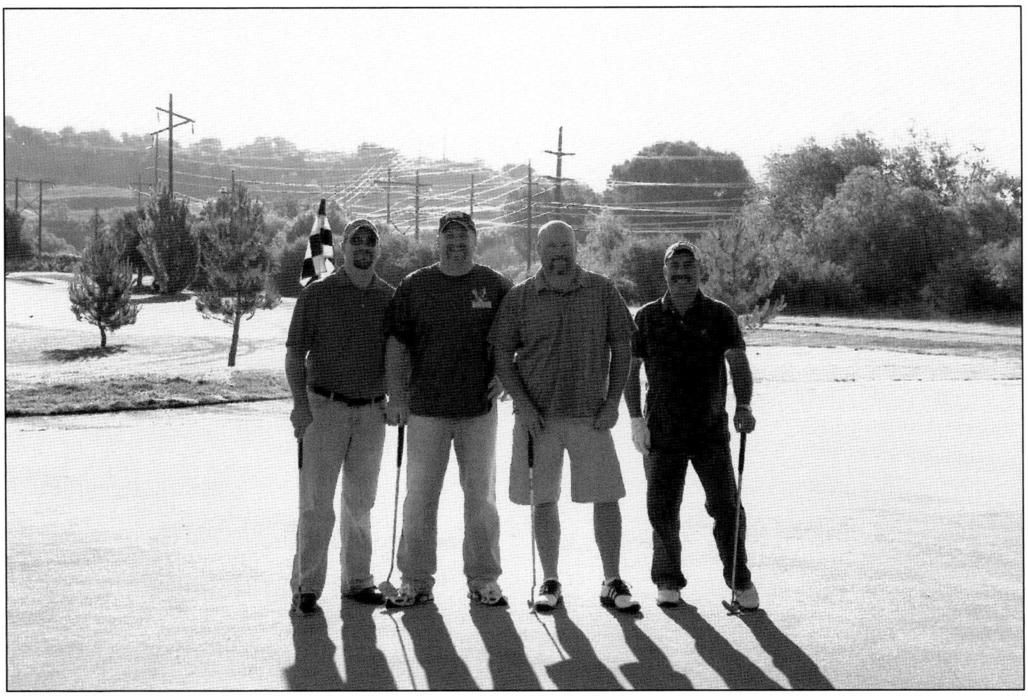

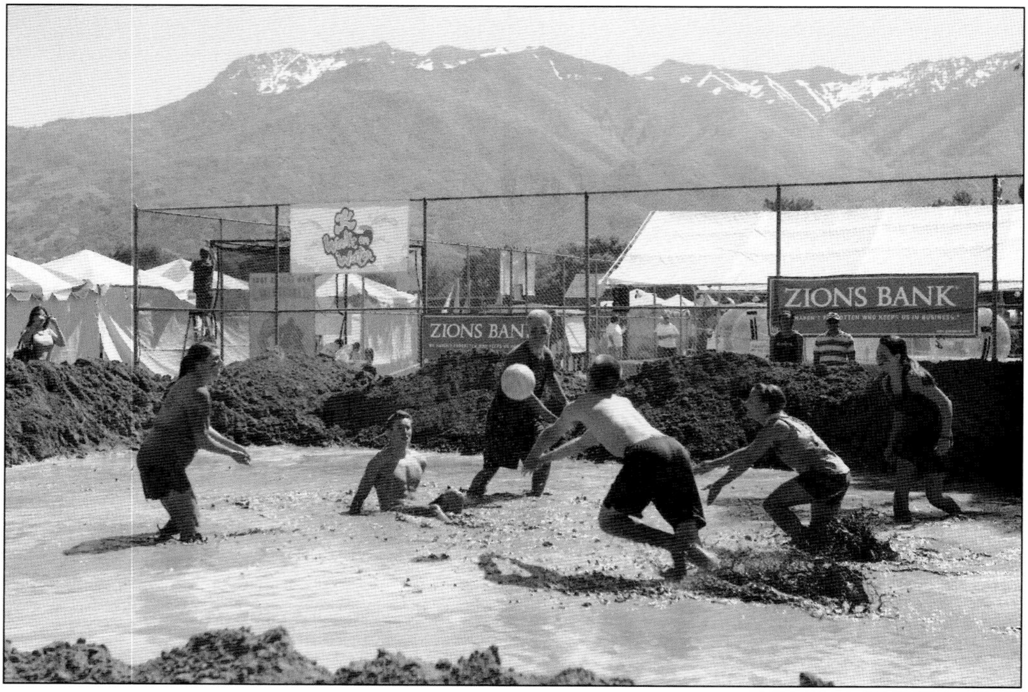

Mud volleyball tournament action is pictured in June 2011 at Friendship Park. Above, Connor Cross dives for a ball while his teammates watch. There were 36 total volleyball teams entered in the tournament. Note the amount of snow still on the mountains for late June. Spring 2011 was a very snowy, rainy, and colder than usual time. Below, the team poses after one of their games. They are, from left to right, Jamie Shaw, Connor Cross, Kelsi Quigley, Ryan Banner, Shelby Cravens, and Ryan Anderson. (Both, courtesy Scott Sumner.)

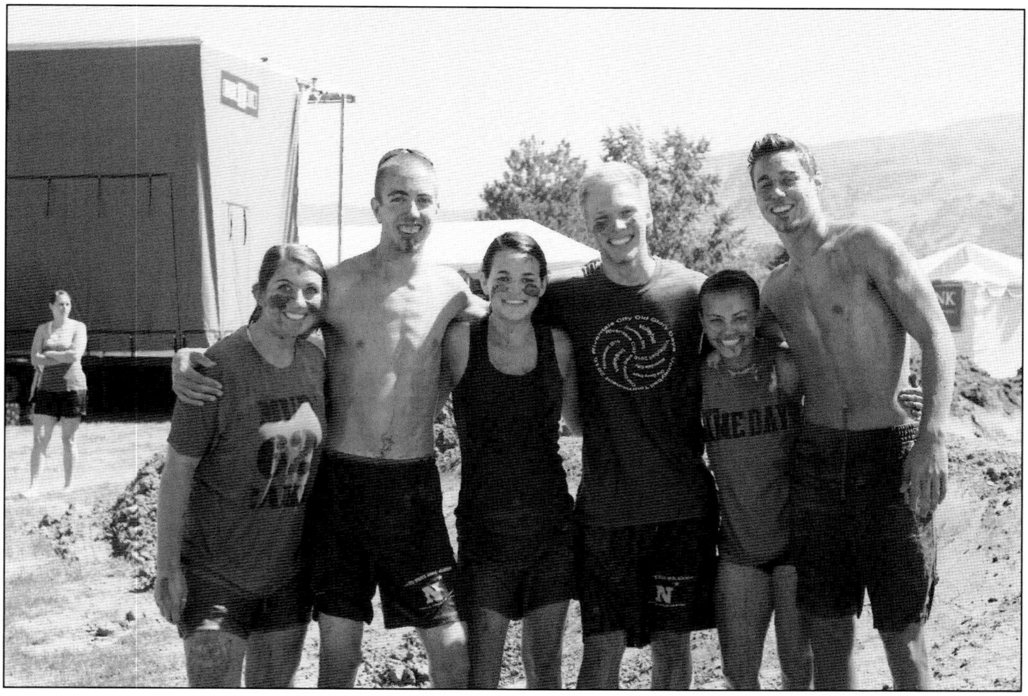

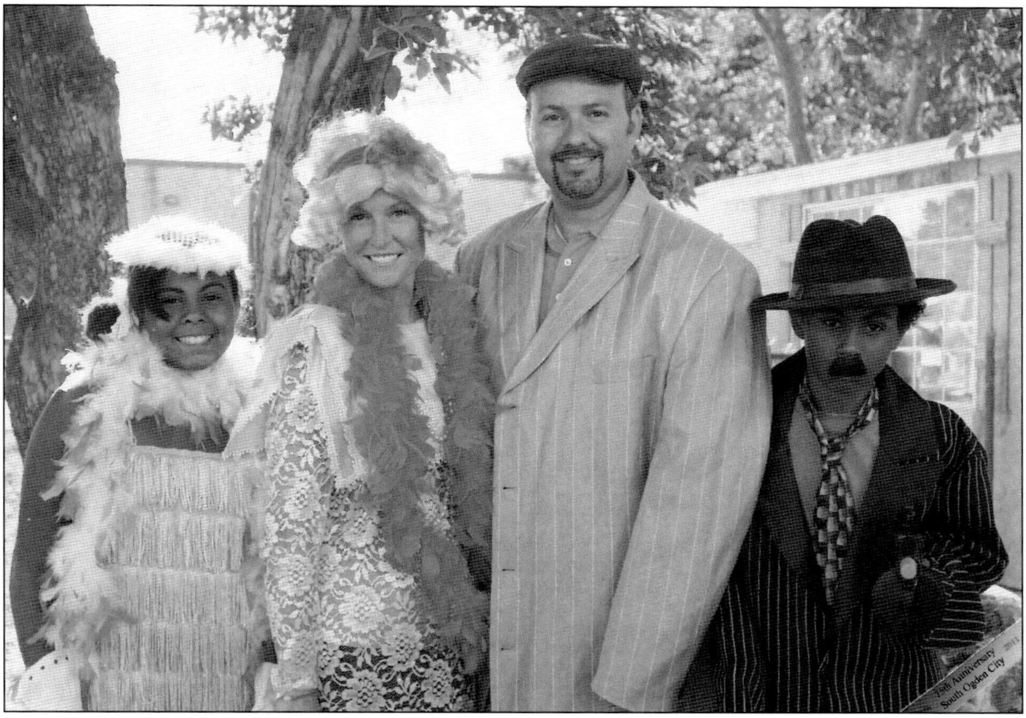

On Wednesday evening June 22, 2011, South Ogden commemorated its 75th anniversary by holding a 1936 Downtown event. Antique shows, restored old home tours, old cars, 5¢ ice cream, and old-time fashions highlighted the night. Photographs like this one were part of the fun options available. Pictured is some of the Benard family, from left to right, Breonca, Monique, Bryan, and Breven. (Courtesy Scott Sumner.)

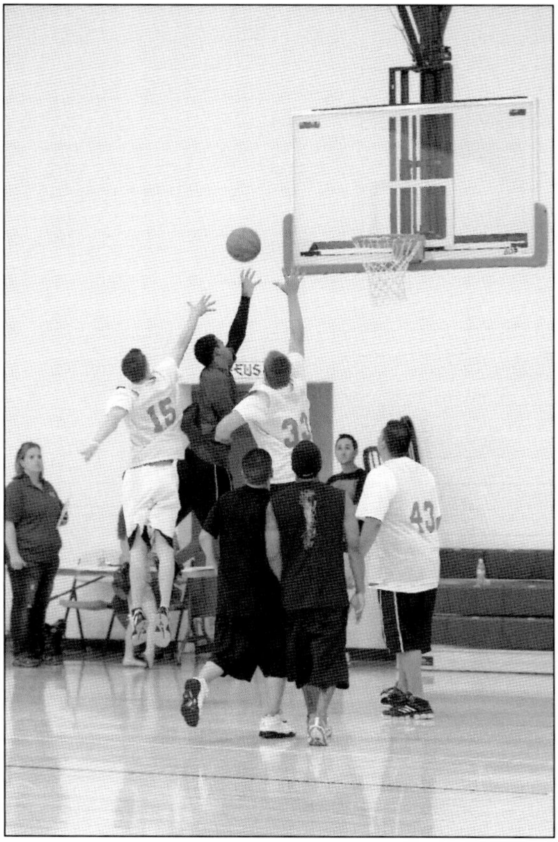

Midweek of South Ogden Days, a three-on-three basketball tournament is held. After being held in 40th Street Park for many years, this 2011 photograph shows the tournament being held in the new South Ogden Junior High gym facilities. Although the view was not as good, having the tournament at the junior high created an increase in courts, allowing more games to be played simultaneously. (Courtesy Scott Sumner.)

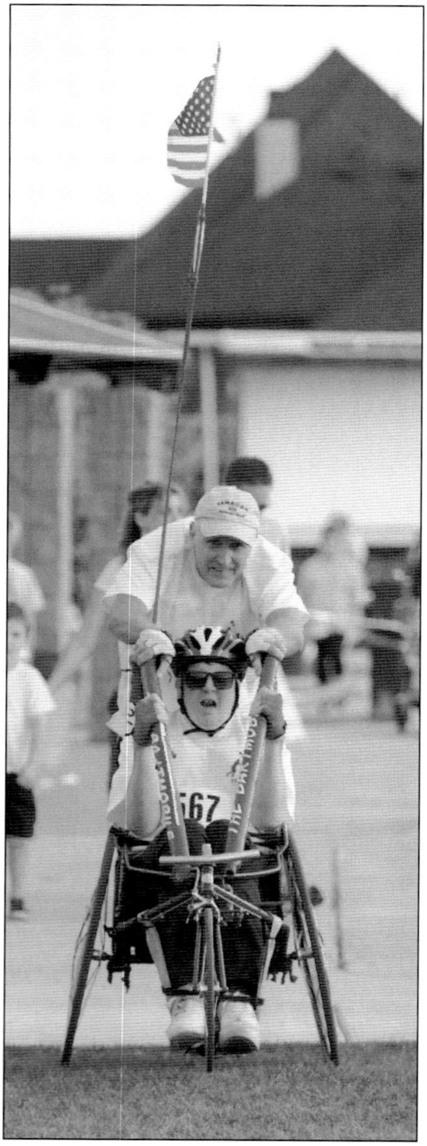

Manuel Cypers pushes Bart Kendrick in a specially designed wheelchair, known as the Bartmobile. The duo has participated in races in the Ogden and Salt Lake area since 2008. They have completed three full marathons, six half marathons, and numerous 5k and 10k races. The members of Team Bart were the grand marshals of the 2010 South Ogden Days Parade. (Courtesy Manuel Cypers.)

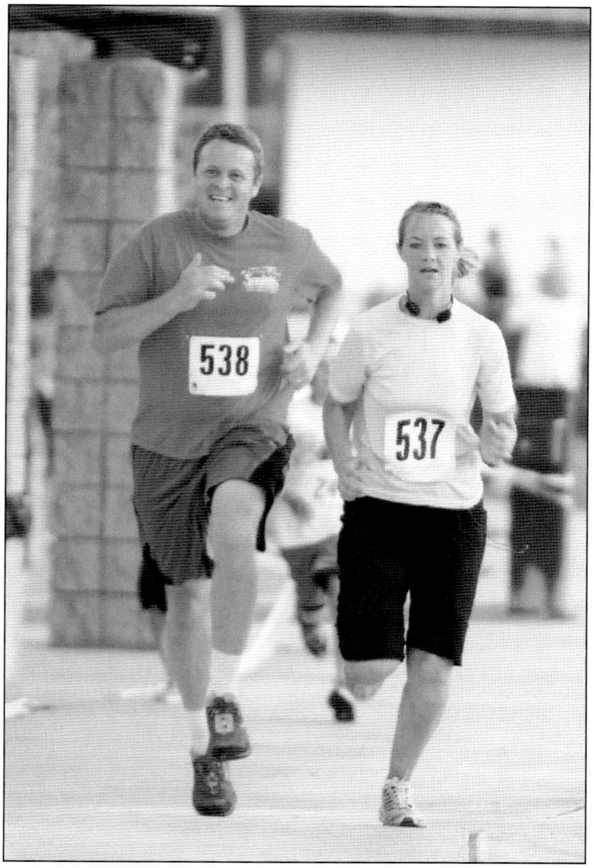

Tyler Degroot (left) and his wife, Laurel, rush to the finish line of the South Ogden Days 5K. The race took place on June 23, 2011, at the Nature Park. (Courtesy Scott Sumner.)

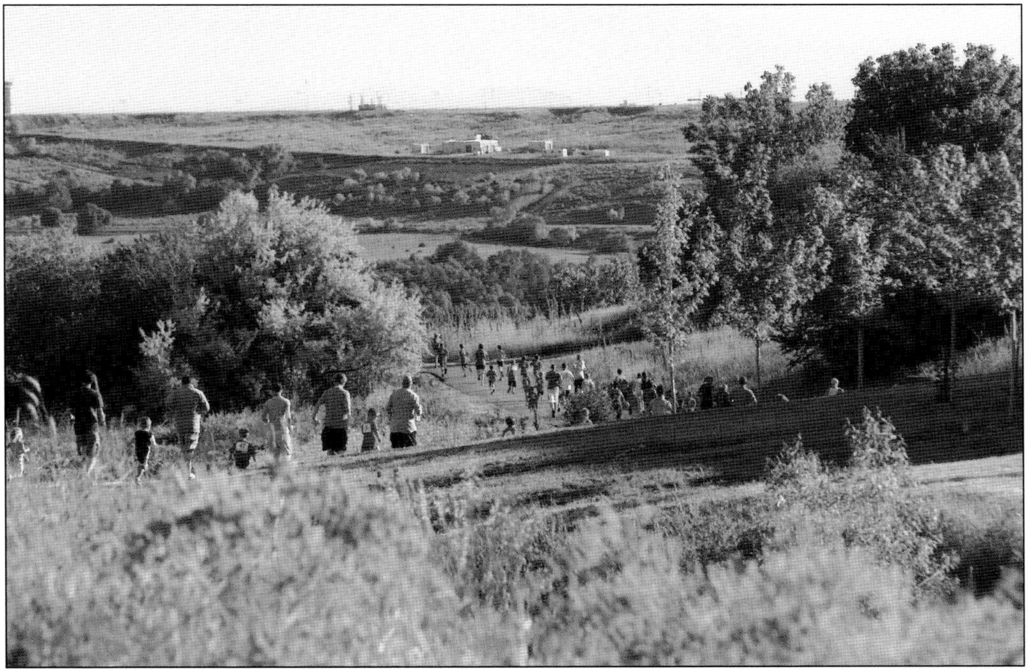

The 2011 Kids K one-mile run was at the South Ogden Nature Park. This view of the park is looking south toward the Weber River Valley; Hill Air Force Base sits on top of the far hill. (Courtesy Scott Sumner.)

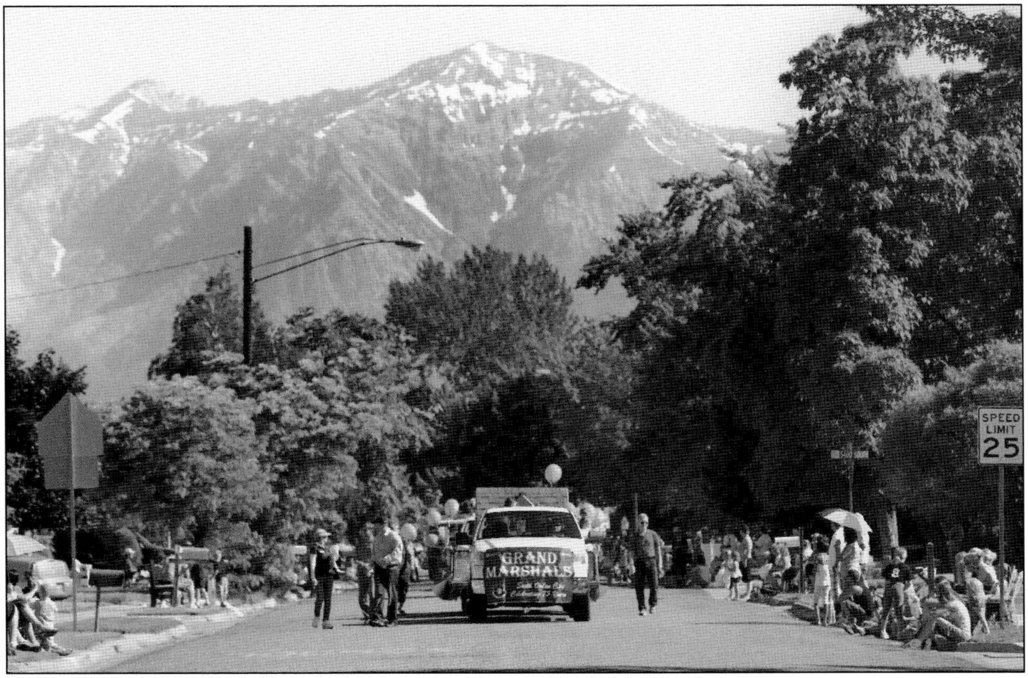

The grand marshals' truck and trailer are pictured during the 2011 South Ogden Days Parade, seen here moving south on 700 East. With 2011 being the 75th anniversary of the city, any residents who had lived in the city for at least 60 years were invited to be grand marshals. (Courtesy Scott Sumner.)

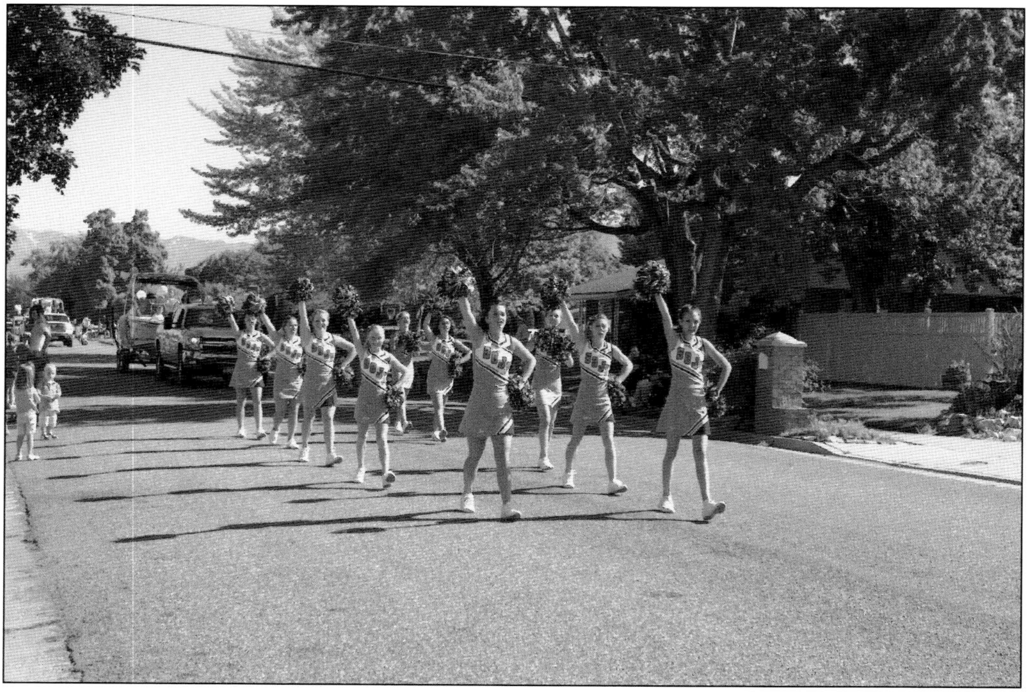

South Ogden Junior High School cheerleaders cheer during the June 25, 2011, South Ogden Days Parade (above). They are, from front to back, (left column) Samantha Greer, Megan Cashmore, Nicole Anderson, Abbie Kier, and Sarah Hayes; (right column) Alexis Hassell, Kennedy Cragun, Melissa Johns, Sierra Sase, and Bentley Ballard. Below, the Sellers family sits on the curb enjoying the June 2011 South Ogden Days Parade. From left to right are Ariana, Braydon, Nathan, Warren, Amy, and Daniel. (Both, courtesy Scott Sumner.)

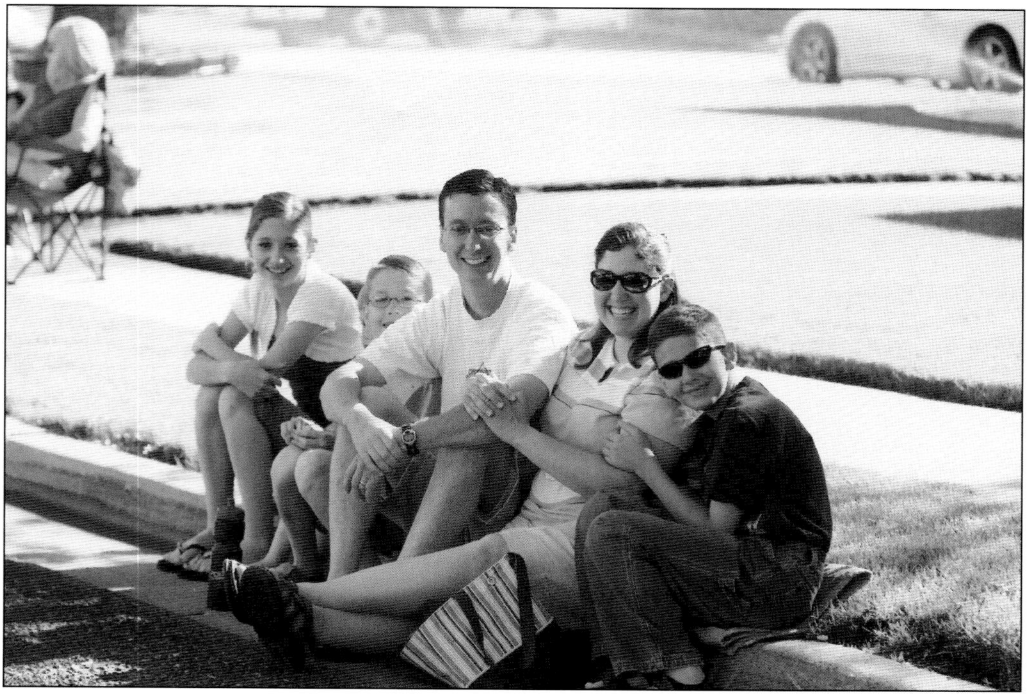

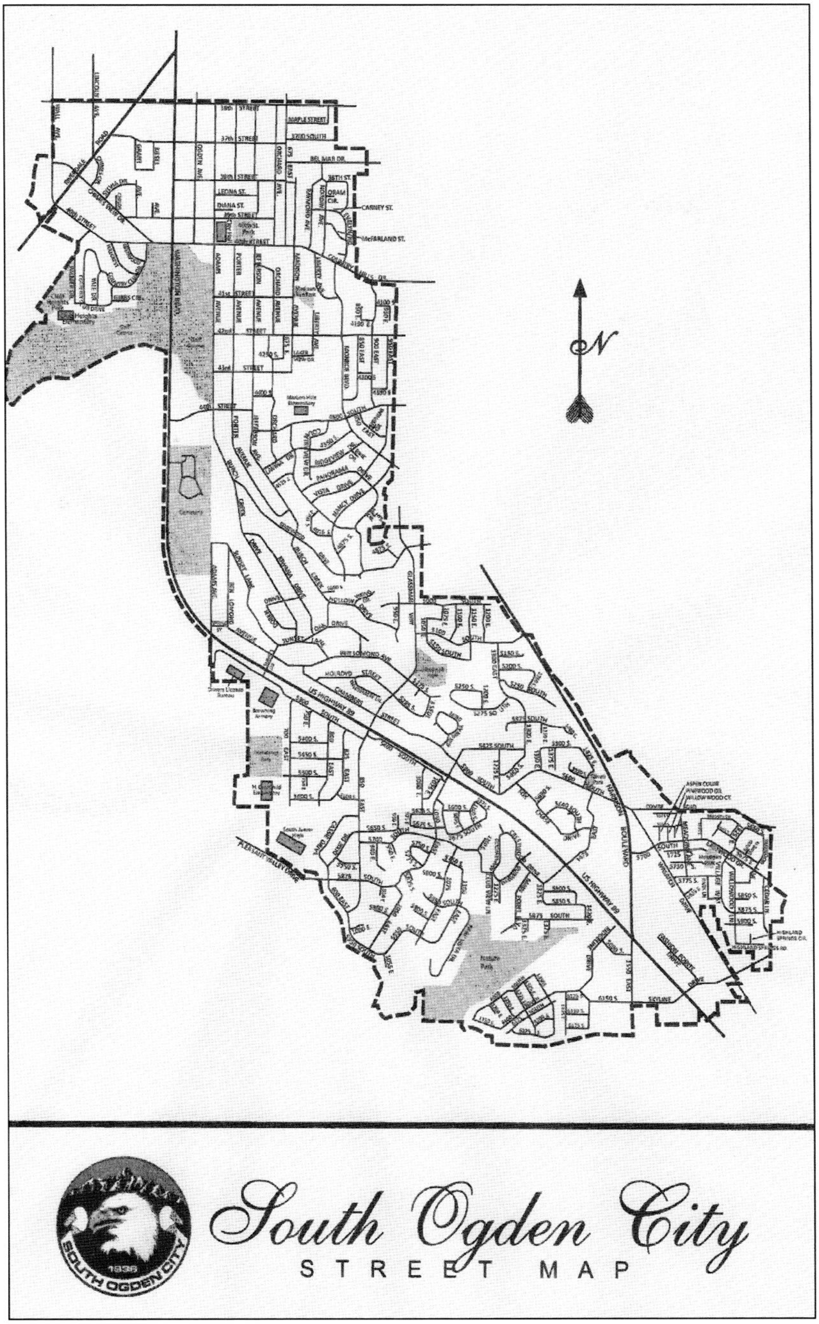

This is a 2011 street map of South Ogden City, Utah. With a 2010 census population of over 16,000, South Ogden is the fourth largest city in Weber County, behind Ogden, Roy, and North Ogden. The city borders Ogden City to the north and east, Washington Terrace on the west, and areas of unincorporated Weber County on the south and east. The jagged border in many places makes it difficult to know what city a person is in; just ask any politician who has gone door-to-door campaigning in the Meadows-Uintah Elementary area. Compare this map to the one on page 26 to see the expansion and growth over the past 50 years. The city has grown in size and population, most of which has been to the south.

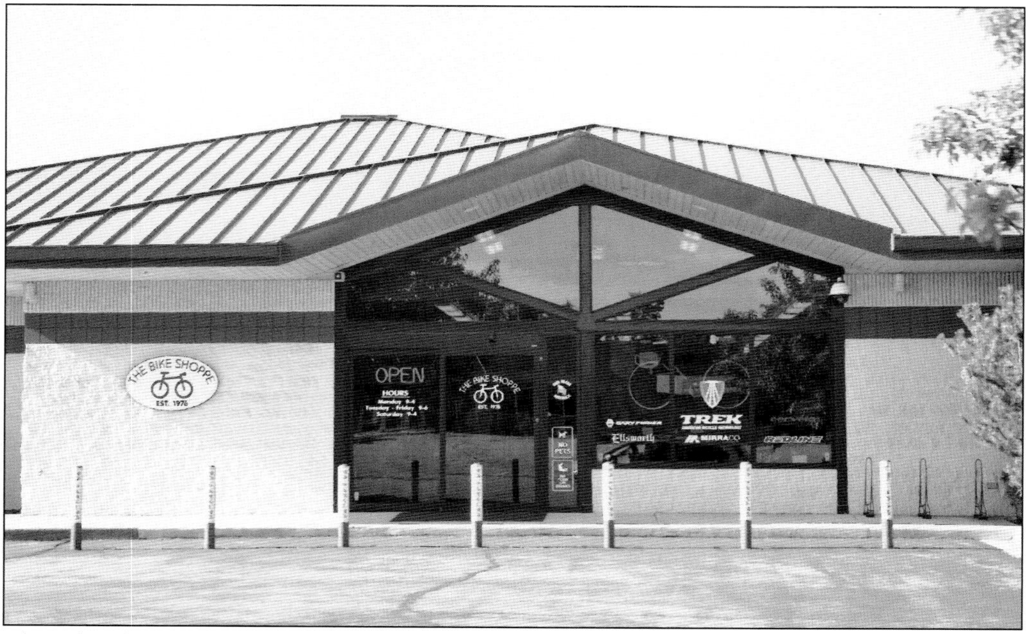

The Bike Shoppe, owned by South Ogden resident Ralph Howard, was established in Ogden in 1976. It moved to its current South Ogden location, at 44th Street and Washington Boulevard, on March 13, 1996. Biking enthusiasts along the Wasatch Front come here, and the Bike Shoppe (TBS) Cycling Club offers weekly riding groups. (Courtesy Nicholas Porter.)

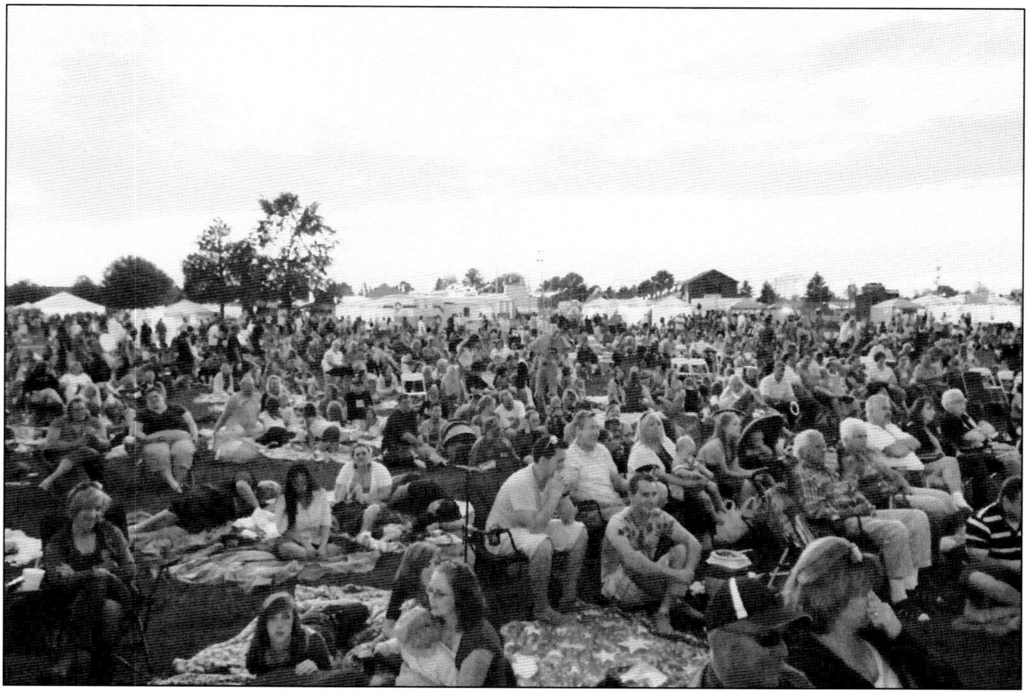

A large crowd gathers in Friendship Park to hear the South Ogden Days concert in June 2011. Over 11,000 people attended the 2011 carnival and concerts over the day-and-a-half period of festivities. For most in the picture, attendance at the events is a family tradition, and they will be in the photographs taken in future years, also. (Courtesy Scott Sumner.)

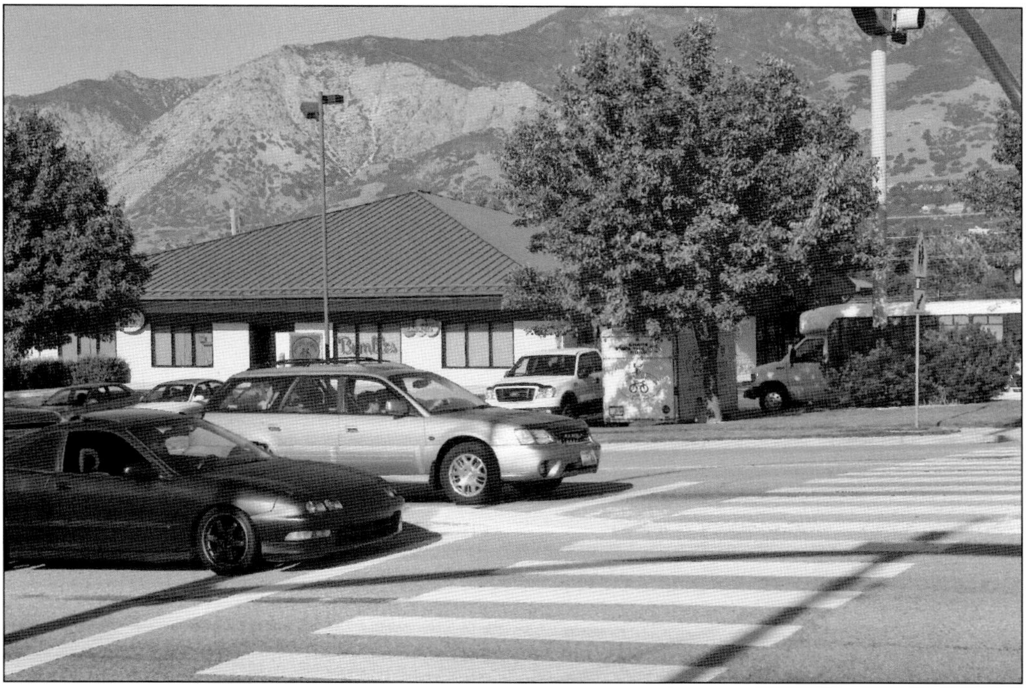

These photographs are of the crosswalk traversing Washington Boulevard (Highway 89) at 4400 South. The process to finally get a safer crossing, with the state adding a crosswalk that stops traffic, has been a long and difficult one. Councilmember Sallee Orr, state representative Dixon Pitcher, and resident Joe Holmes deserve much credit for their persistence in this project. The community has been celebrating for the few months since the completion. It is much safer now for residents, particularly students, to cross over the busy road and get to and from Bonneville High School or wherever else they are headed. (Both, courtesy Nicholas Porter.)

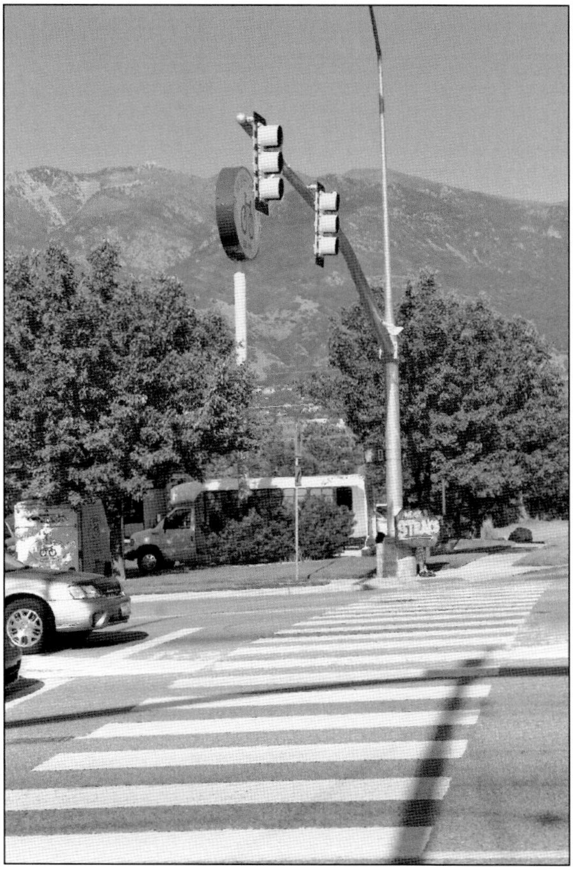

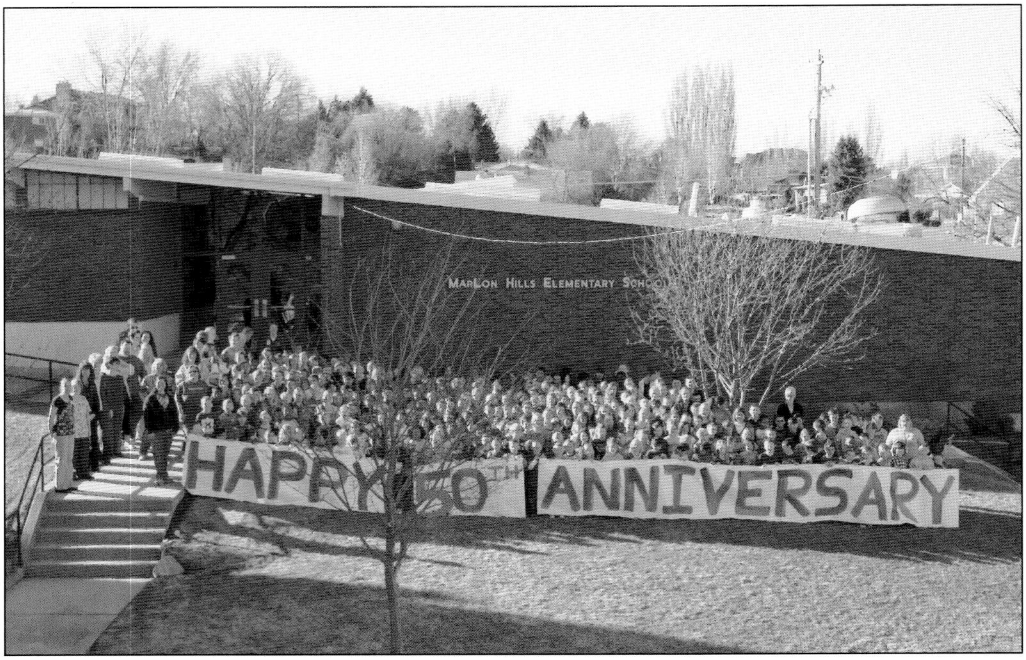

MarLon Hills Elementary students and staff stand in front of their school celebrating the 50th anniversary. An open house was held on April 26, 2011, and many former Mustang students, teachers, staff, and principals returned to take a trip down memory lane. (Courtesy MarLon Hills Elementary.)

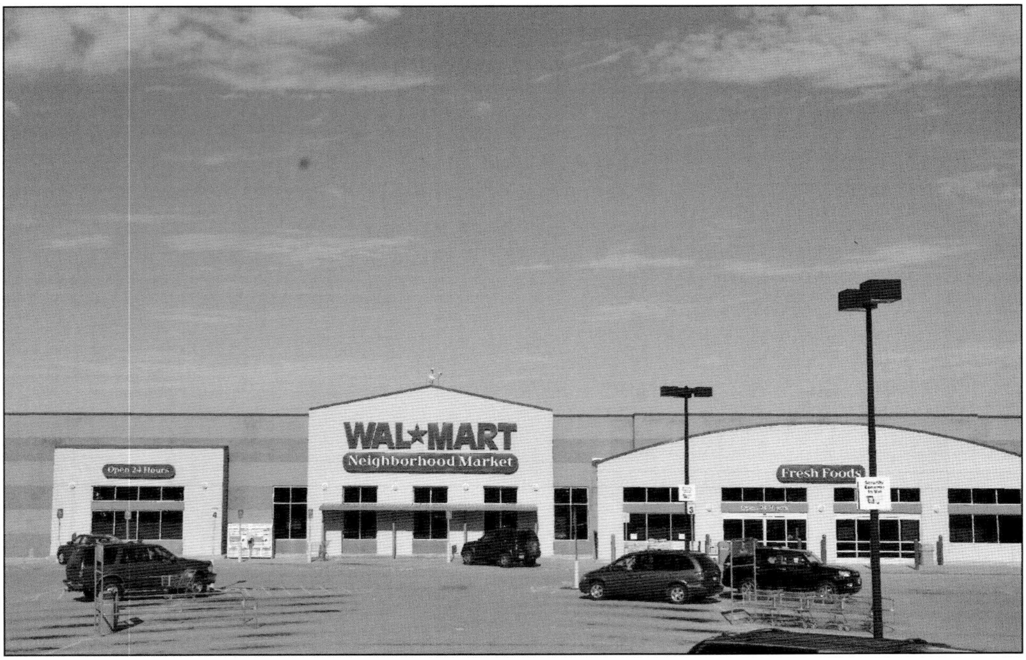

This is a recent photograph of the Wal-Mart Neighborhood Market. The market has been very supportive of local school groups and clubs to raise much needed funds by allowing use of the parking lot for car washes and bake sales. Wal-Mart has also been generous in helping South Ogden City with its celebrations and other city events. (Courtesy Russell Porter.)

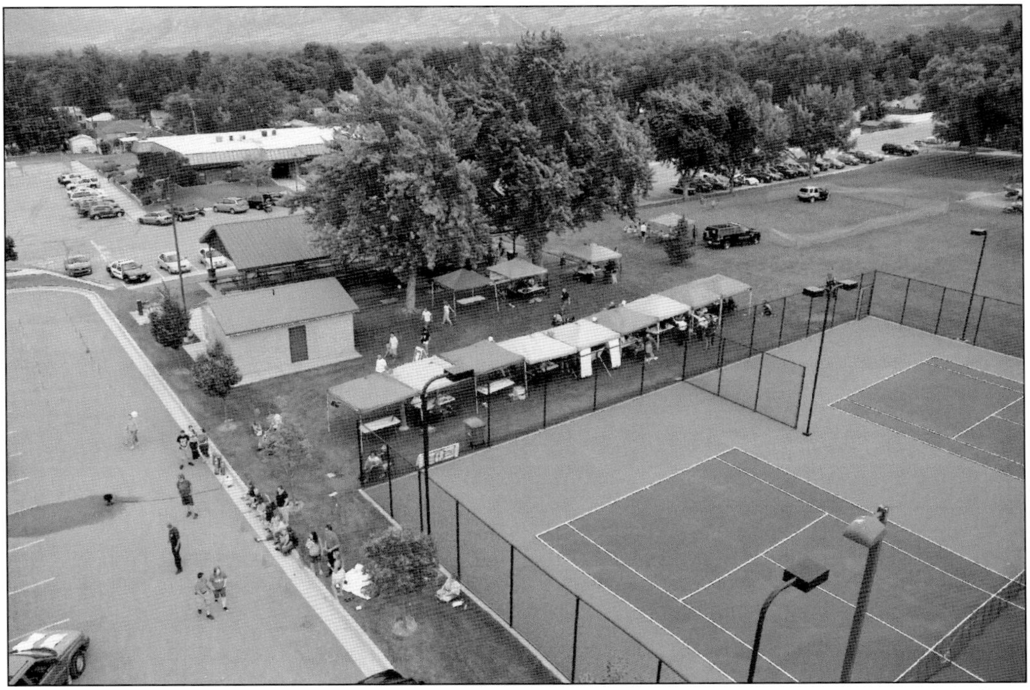

This aerial photograph above shows 40th Street Park during the National Night Out, taken from the bucket at the top of the ladder on engine No. 81, August 3, 2011. Fire and police personnel and their equipment are visible as well as booths and a fenced in area for police K-9 demonstrations. This was South Ogden's third annual time participating in the national event, aimed to educate the public on safety and to encourage citizens to gather with their neighbors and communities and find out what their city has to offer. Below, Logan Lancaster practices putting out a flame with a fire extinguisher. He is assisted by fireman Bill "Stick" Stoddard. (Both, courtesy Sherri Porter.)

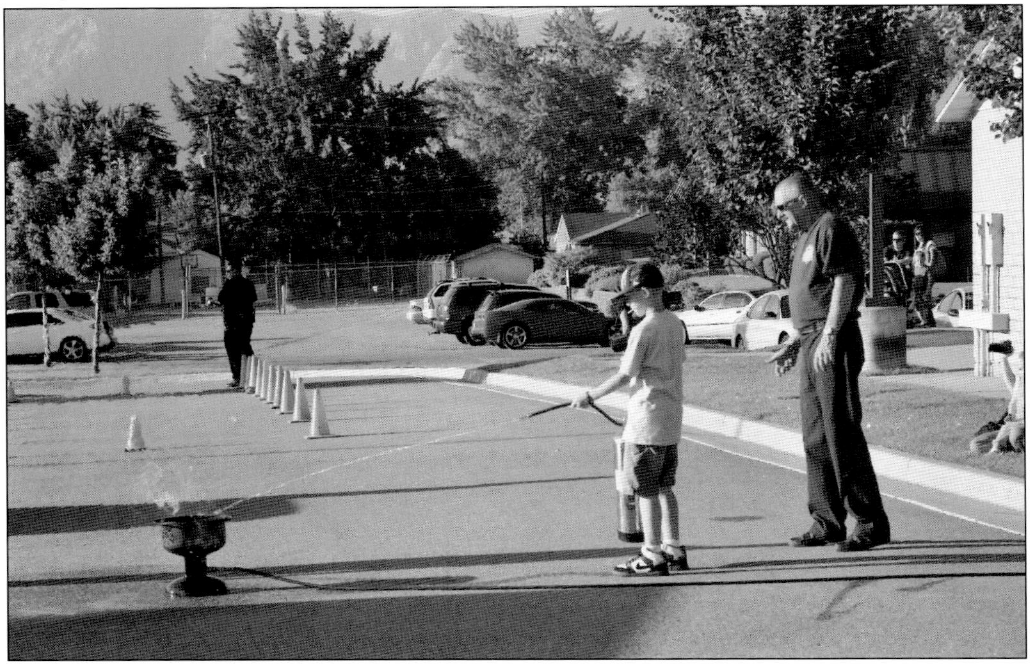

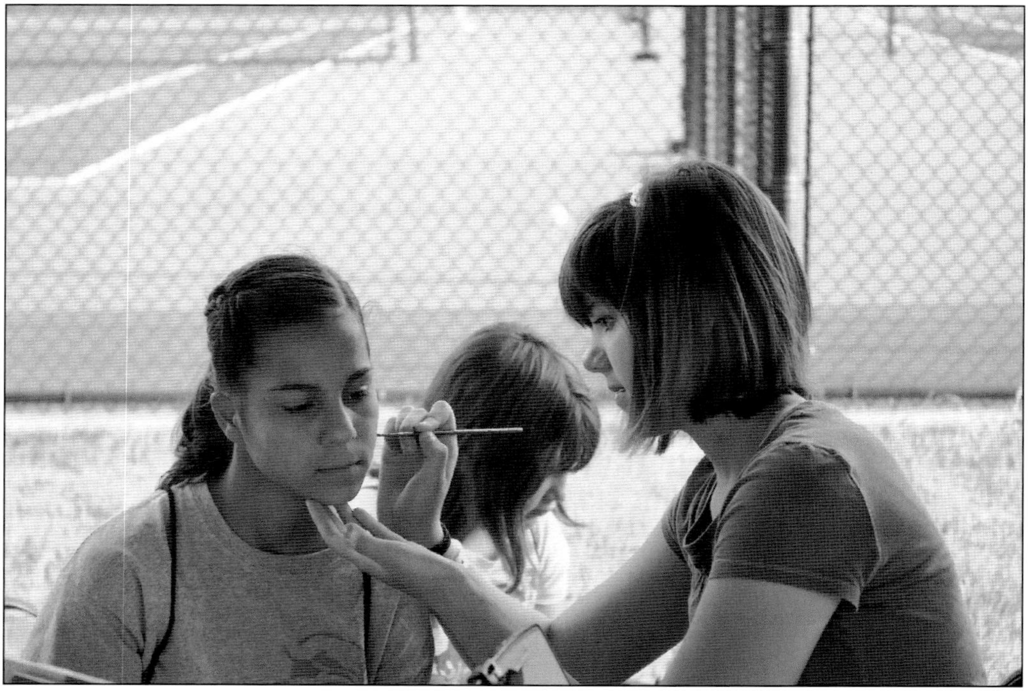

Above, Mia Shaw gets her face painted by Kayla Gonzalez, a member of the South Ogden Youth City Council, at the National Night Out in 40th Street Park. Kara Gonzalez is also is in the photograph. The annual event educates and entertains the community through police, fire, and emergency services displays and activities. Below is a view of the area where spectators get to watch fire crews use the Jaws of Life, the police dogs in action, and motorcycle police officers drive through an obstacle course. (Both, courtesy Sherri Porter.)

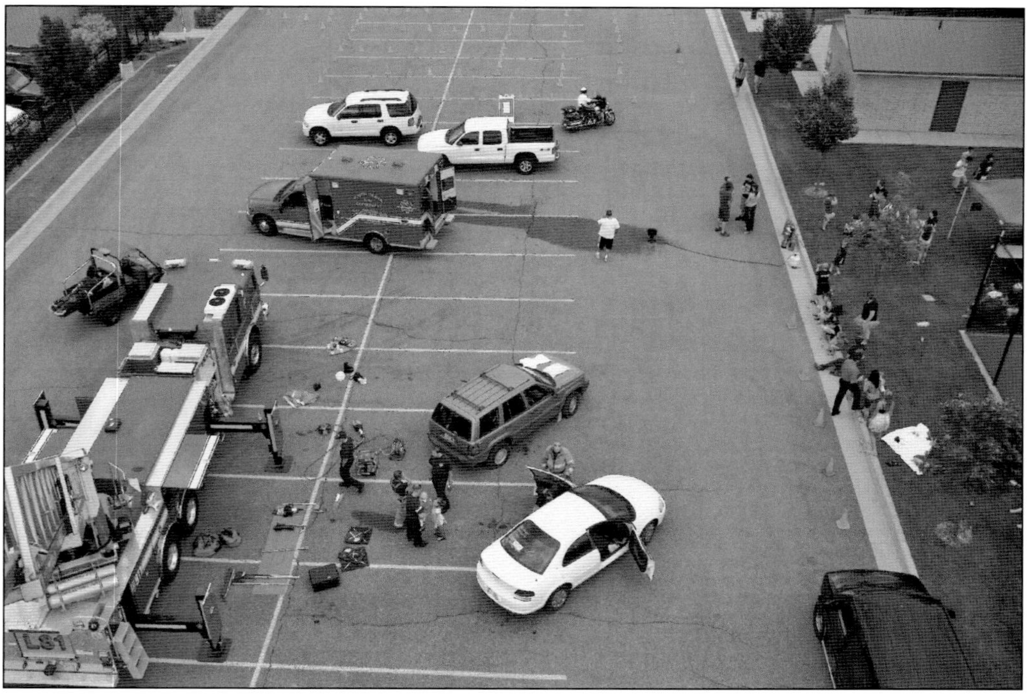

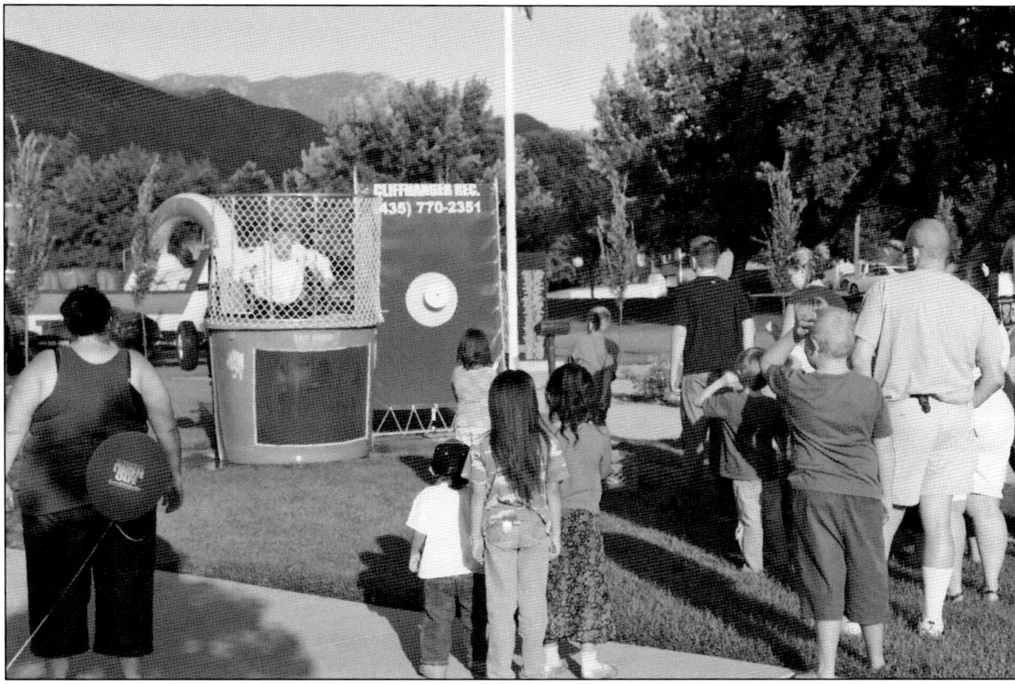

Above, fire battalion chief Rick Rasmussen gets wet in the dunk tank during National Night Out, 2011. Rasmussen was a great sport and drew the biggest crowds of the night. Members of the Youth City Council were also dunked during the evening. Below, from left to right, Morgan Hatch, Tyler Hatch, and Ethan Hatch enjoy the free hot dogs at 40th Street Park in between their visits to the Life Flight helicopter and watching the firefighters repelling from the ladder truck bucket 60 feet up. (Both, courtesy Sherri Porter.)

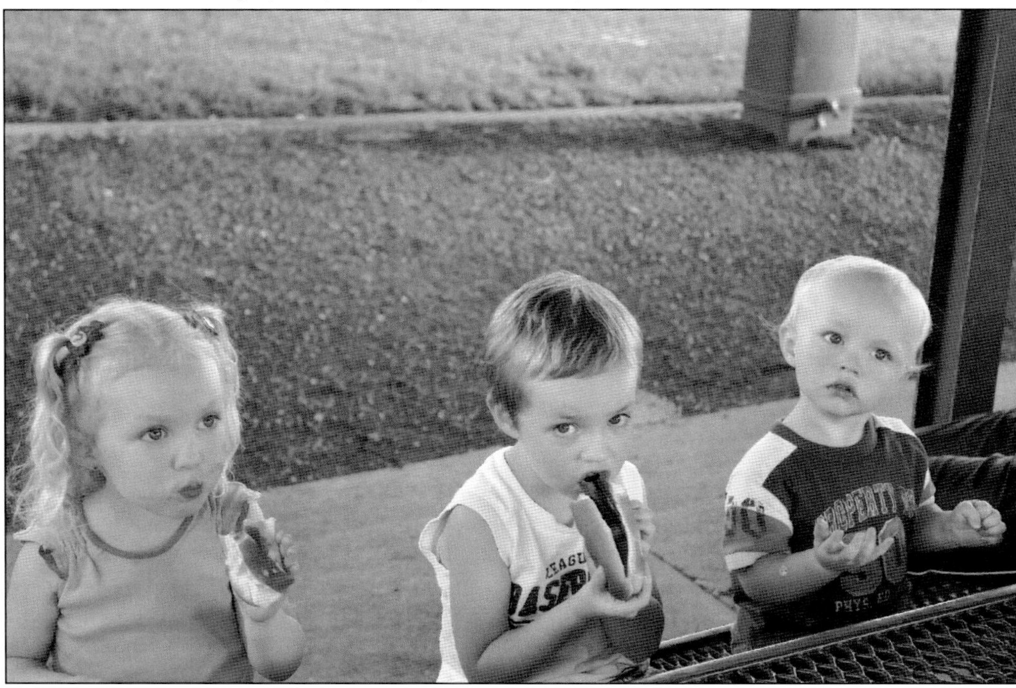

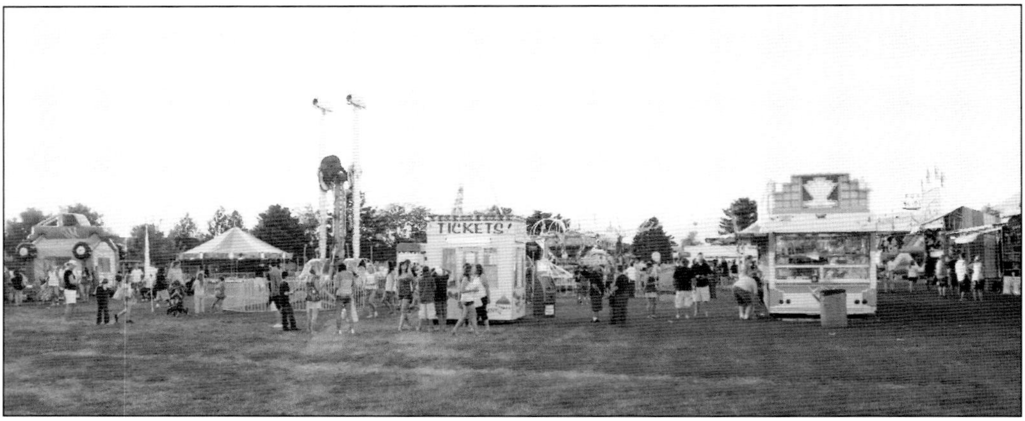

Above, this panoramic photograph shows the carnival attractions at Friendship Park for the 2011 South Ogden Days. Below, an involved crowds views the Macey's and Crown Bedroom stage at the Friday night concert. In 2011, local concerts were held on Friday and Saturday nights; typically, there was only a Saturday night concert by a nationally recognized artist. The concerts have become a popular tradition for residents of all ages. (Both, courtesy Scott Sumner.)

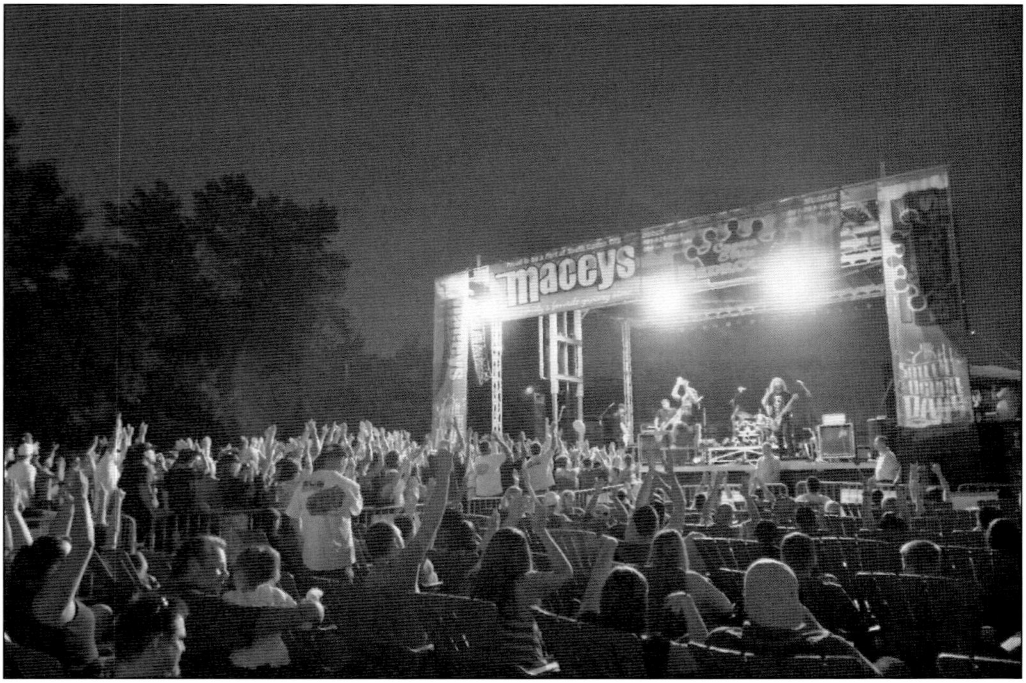

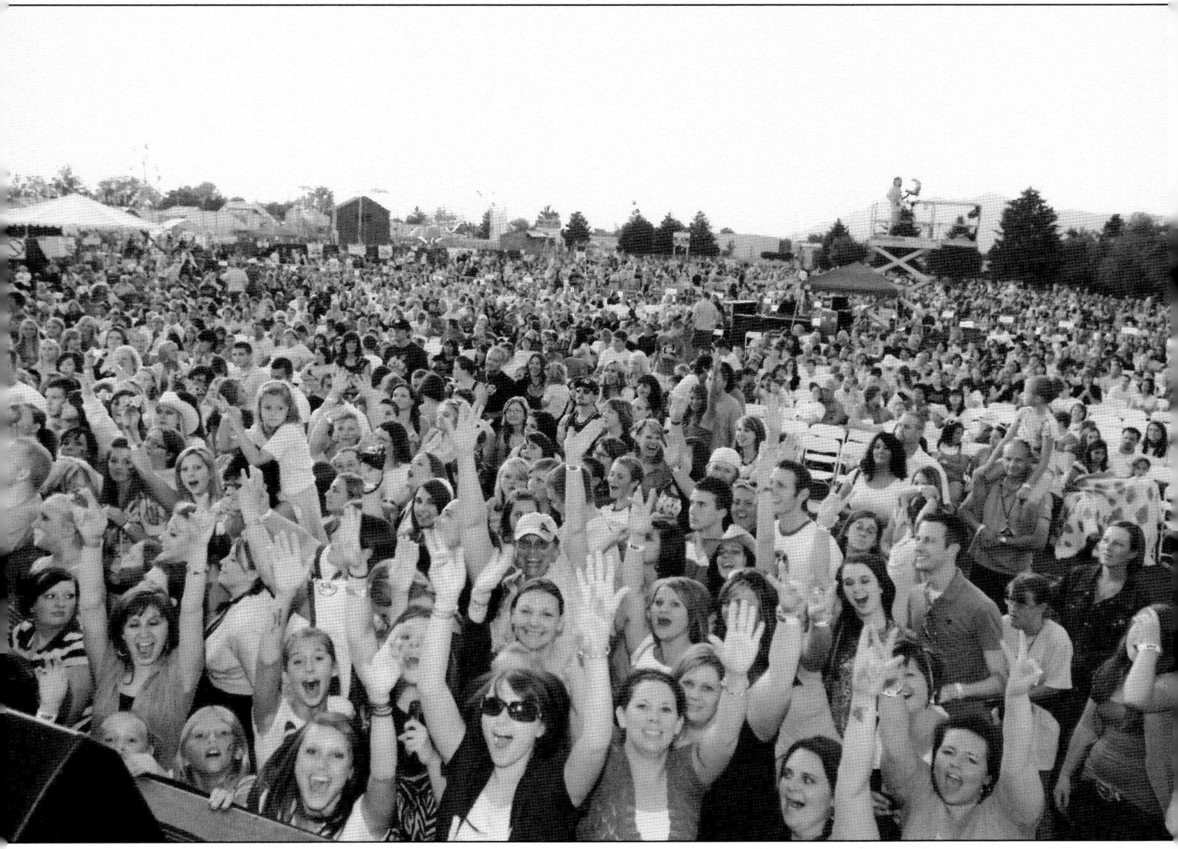

Pictured is the typical crowd at the Saturday night concert ending South Ogden Days. The concert, followed by a fireworks display, is the culminating event of a great week of summer fun in South Ogden City. In the past years, the city has brought in the following entertainers—an impressive list for a small city: Ryan Shupe & the Rubberband, Royal Bliss, Jack Ingram, Josh Gracin, Sammy Kershaw, Joe Diffie, Bryan White, Rockie Lynne, Ty England, Rhett Akins, Chad Brock, Daryl Singletary, Jeff Carson, Blackhawk, Ricky Van Shelton, Doug Stone, Gary Allen, Dan Seals, and the Bellamy Brothers.

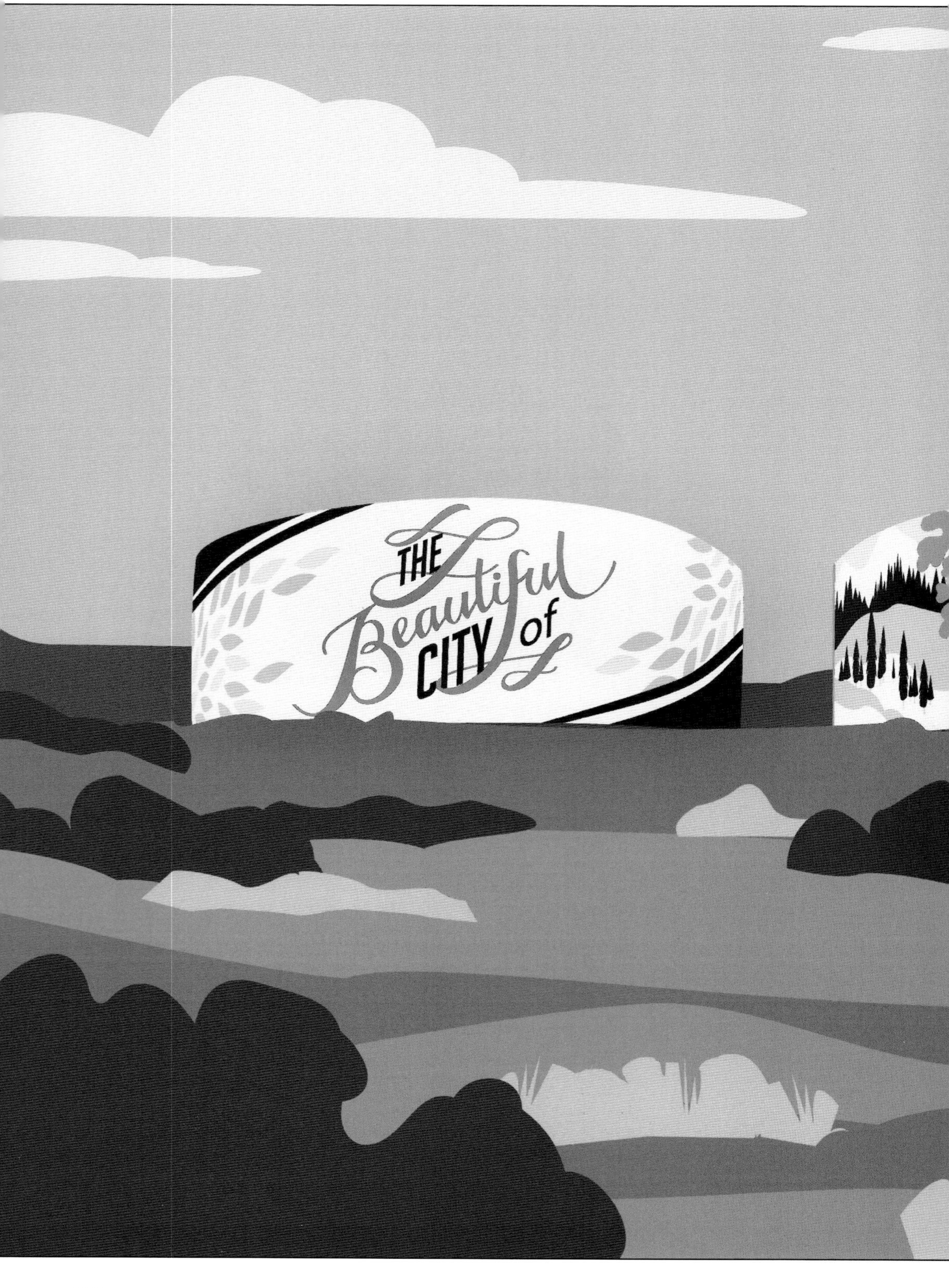
THE Beautiful CITY of

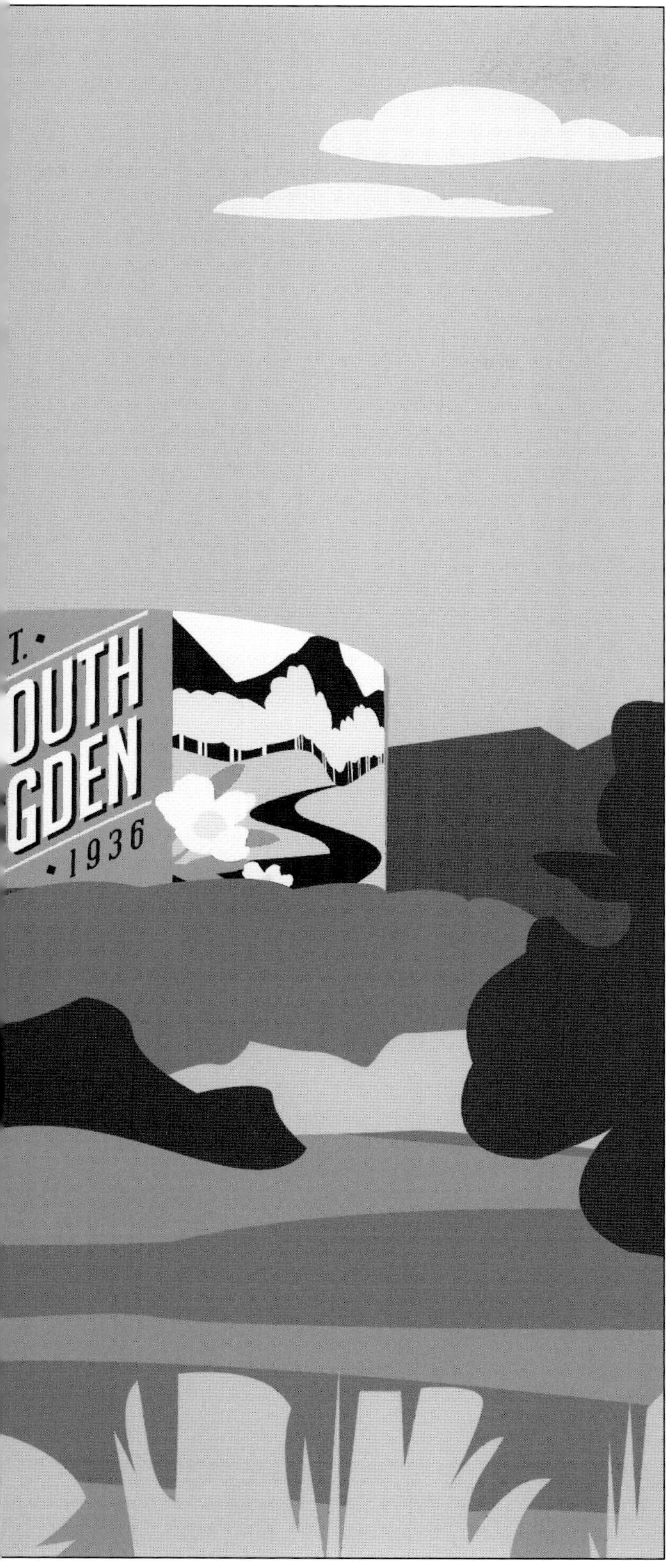

This is an artist's rendition of the future look of the South Ogden water towers. The need for repainting the tanks coincided with the city's 75th anniversary, so special events coordinator Christy McBride proposed making it more artistic and opening it up to local artists to submit ideas. So, South Ogden City, in conjunction with the Weber Arts Council, RAMP, and the Utah Division of Arts and Museums invited artists to submit design concepts to cover the 7,000 square feet of unique canvas. The winning design, as seen on these pages, was submitted by Jill DeHaan. And with the new design, the next 75 years of South Ogden City will begin!

DISCOVER THOUSANDS OF LOCAL HISTORY BOOKS FEATURING MILLIONS OF VINTAGE IMAGES

Arcadia Publishing, the leading local history publisher in the United States, is committed to making history accessible and meaningful through publishing books that celebrate and preserve the heritage of America's people and places.

Find more books like this at
www.arcadiapublishing.com

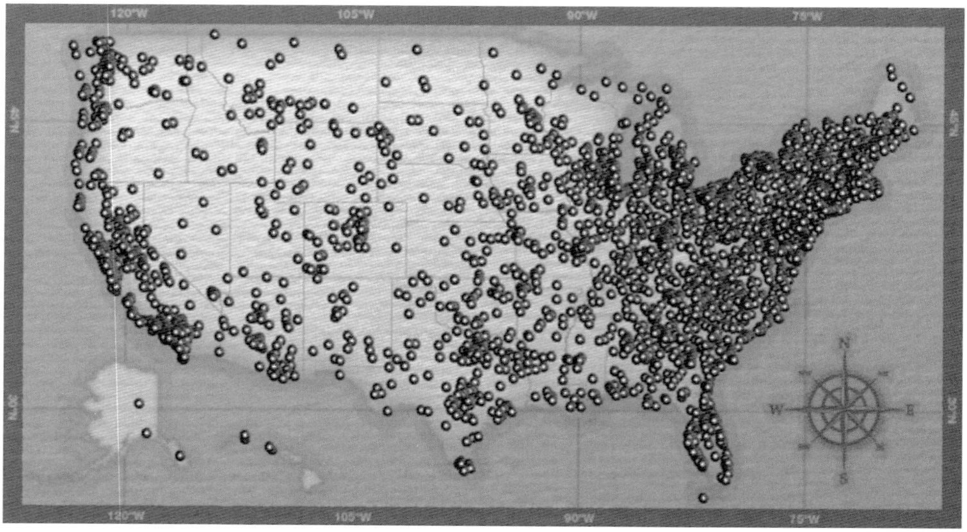

Search for your hometown history, your old stomping grounds, and even your favorite sports team.

Consistent with our mission to preserve history on a local level, this book was printed in South Carolina on American-made paper and manufactured entirely in the United States. Products carrying the accredited Forest Stewardship Council (FSC) label are printed on 100 percent FSC-certified paper.

MADE IN THE USA